Implementing Public Policy

Sage Politics Texts

Series Editor
IAN HOLLIDAY
City University of Hong Kong

SAGE Politics Texts offer authoritative and accessible analyses of core issues in contemporary political science and international relations. Each text combines a comprehensive overview of key debates and concepts with fresh and original insights. By extending acrosss all main areas of the discipline, SAGE Politics Texts constitute a comprehensive body of contemporary analysis. They are ideal for use on advanced courses and in research.

Published titles:

The politics of Central Europe
Attila Ágh

The New Politics of Welfare
Bill Jordan

Rethinking Green Politics
John Barry

Democracy and Democratization
John Nagle and Alison Mahr

International Political Theory
Kimberly Hutchings

Politics and Society in South Africa
Daryl Glaser

Theorizing European Integration
Dimitris N. Chryssochoou

Transforming the European Nation-State
Kjell Goldmann

Local Governance in Western Eruope
Peter John

Implementing Public Policy
Michael Hill and Peter Hupe

Implementing Public Policy:

Governance in Theory and in Practice

Michael J. Hill and Peter Hupe

SAGE Publications
London • Thousand Oaks • New Delhi

First published 2002, Reprinted 2003, (twice).

SAGE Publications Ltd
6 Bonhill Street
London EC2A 4PU

SAGE Publications Inc
2455 Teller Road
Thousand Oaks, California 91320

SAGE Publications India Pvt Ltd
32, M-Block Market
Greater Kailash - I
New Delhi 110 048

British Library Cataloguing in Publication data

A catalogue record for this book is available
from the British Library

ISBN 0 7619 6628 5
ISBN 0 7619 6629 3 (pbk)

Library of Congress Control Number: 2002101995

Typeset by SIVA Math Setters, Chennai, India
Printed and bound in Great Britain by Athenaeum Press, Gateshead

For Betty and Nynke

Summary of Contents

Contents

List of Tables and Figures

Tables

Figures

Preface and Acknowledgements

This book reviews the literature on public policy implementation, relating it to contemporary developments in thinking about governance. It stresses the continuing importance of a focus upon implementation processes. Accordingly it goes on to suggest strategies both for future research on implementation and for the management of implementation processes.

We are very grateful to Ian Holliday for commissioning the book for Sage Politics Texts, and for the support he has given us during our work. We also wish to thank Lucy Robinson of Sage for her support of the venture, and Lauren McAllister and Justin Dyer for all their help with the preparation of the manuscript.

We are particularly grateful to Marianne Vorthoren for her assistance throughout the whole project. She always reacted with good humour to our relentless demands for articles. While we were teaching, doing consultancy and other jobs, she helped to ensure that our work on the book went on. At the last stages of preparation of the manuscript we benefited enormously from Vicky Balsem's typographical and word-processing expertise. Thanks are also due to Jantiene van Elk for her bibliographical support.

We thank all those who provided comments on a draft of the manuscript. In addition to Ian Holliday, these were (in alphabetical order): Bob Hudson, Walter Kickert, Stephen Mitchell, Larry O'Toole, Christopher Pollitt and Arthur Ringeling.

We are grateful to the board of the research group Waardering in en van het openbaar bestuur (The Evaluation of Government) at the Department of Public Administration at Erasmus University, Rotterdam, particularly the chair and treasurer, Arthur Ringeling and Harry Daemen, for their financial support. Similar thanks go to the School of Social Sciences and the Department of Public Administration of Erasmus University, Rotterdam, particularly Wim Derksen, Jan Hakvoort and Percy Lehning, the Dean, for approving Peter Hupe's arrangement to spend his concentrated research time in the second semester of 2000–1 at Goldsmiths College, University of London. Similar thanks go to Nirmala Rao, Head of the Department of Social Policy and Politics at Goldsmiths College, for hospitality for our work, and to the Warden of Goldsmiths, Ben Pimlott, for his approval of our affiliations to the College.

We benefited considerably from the fact that during the later stages of our work there was a sequence of Economic and Social Research Council-supported seminars on implementation. We are accordingly grateful to the organizers, Charlotte Sausman of the Judge Institute of Management Studies at Cambridge University and Jill Schofield of Aston Business School, for inviting us to participate in those events, and to other participants from whom we learnt. We delivered a paper based upon an early version of Chapter 6; its discussant, Sandra Nutley, provided us with a range of helpful comments both at the event and in a subsequent note. Similarly we benefited from presenting a paper developing some of the ideas for Chapter 7 at a seminar at Brighton University. We were particularly grateful for the comments provided by Susan Balloch, the seminar organizer.

Our wives, Betty and Nynke, have both been wise and patient, very committed to what we are doing, while giving us the space to get on with our work. They have been supportive and tolerant when mealtime conversation turned to the book. We therefore dedicate this book to them.

1

Introduction

Introduction

There once was a period of very intense academic debate about the understanding of the phenomenon of implementation. It lasted from about the
time of the publication of Pressman and Wildavsky's influential book
Implementation in 1973 until sometime around the end of the 1980s. In 1997
one of us asked in an article whether implementation was 'yesterday's
issue' (Hill, 1997b). The answer given to that rhetorical question was 'no'.

This book takes a similar stance. In doing so, alongside a discussion of
literature explicitly concerned with implementation will be a recognition of
three facts. The first is that the phenomenon 'implementation' was a matter
of concern and, to some extent, academic study before the word was used.
Secondly it is recognized that implementation was and continues to be a
concern of many writers who do not talk about 'implementation' *per se*, and
indeed may approach it from very different backgrounds to the public
administration specialists who do so. The third fact is that implementation
inevitably takes different shapes and forms in different cultures and institutional settings. This last point is particularly important in an era in which
processes of 'government' have been seen as transformed into 'governance'. The latter means that a wider range of actors may be participating
and that simplistic hierarchical models are being abandoned. Hence linking
implementation with governance is a central element in this book.

This is an exploration of the state of the art of the study of implementation as what we consider to be a sub-discipline of political science and public administration. Our objective in this book is to bring together the major insights presently available from implementation theory and research. We do not present a new theory here, but rather give an overview and make relevant connections. Because of the latter, the exercise can be called 'synthesizing' or 'third-generation', terms used by Goggin et al. (1990). Specifically, however, when we observe inconsistencies, anomalies or conflicts in or between implementation publications, we see it as our primary task to report on these before, eventually, making suggestions to 'solve' them.

Throughout all this literature, examination of implementation – simply 'what happens between policy expectations and (perceived) policy results' (DeLeon, 1999a: 314–5 paraphrasing Ferman, 1990: 39) – has had a dual character. There has been a concern *to explain* 'what happens' and a concern *to affect* 'what happens', with inevitably many of those interested in the first question being interested in the second too. That dual character will be reflected in this book. We will be concerned to look at efforts to explain what happens, and to look at issues about studying and researching implementation, but also at ways in which those who want to affect what happens can be assisted in that task. However, we think it important to be aware of these as separate questions, with good research being assisted if a measure of detachment can be achieved from the preoccupations of those who want to control events and effective control being facilitated by a sensitivity to both the complexity of the task and the nature of the normative issues at stake.

We also recognize that the issues about understanding the process and the issues about controlling the process may be of interest to rather different readers, and that we are taking a risk in trying to write for both kinds of audience at the same time. In the last analysis, however, our approach is surely justified by the fact that if you do not understand, you are very unlikely to be able to control. Nevertheless, we concede that different kinds of people may want to use the book in rather different ways. Hence we will introduce what is to follow by describing the contents of the chapters in a way that takes into account that concern.

Contents

In this chapter we will give attention to some key conceptual issues. In particular that involves asking what we are talking about when we use the word 'implementation' and terms related to it.

Chapter 2 starts from the proposition that just as in the real world there was 'implementation' before this label had been invented (how otherwise could the cathedrals have been built?), there has been 'implementation theory' before and beyond the kind of studies we usually refer to with this term. In Chapter 2 this type of theory, some of it in early political science, some of it in sociological and socio-legal work, is given attention.

Chapter 3 goes on to the examination of the theoretical work that blossomed around and after the publication of Pressman and Wildavsky's *Implementation* (1973), work that can be seen as a kind of dialogue between 'top-down' and 'bottom-up' approaches to theory. Chapter 4 looks at the way theory developed as efforts were made to synthesize these alternative approaches. In Chapters 3 and 4, in a more or less chronological order, the study of implementation is positioned in disciplinary terms and in terms of the various 'schools', approaches, concepts and insights. Together these chapters reflect the body of theoretical knowledge incorporated in implementation studies. Readers who are familiar with the theory, or particularly impatient to see what new things we have to say, may want to skip over these chapters. They will find many references back to specific parts of them in the later chapters.

Chapter 5 positions the development of the sub-discipline in its societal context, exploring the relevance of implementation studies for the practice of public administration. That chapter also considers the implications of the changing nature of governance for the study of implementation.

Chapter 6 examines actual research on implementation, with reference to work carried out in the years immediately preceding the writing of this book. A survey of articles written during the 1990s (see Appendix) was important for the production of this chapter. This chapter, together with the next one, is particularly pertinent for those whose concern is with questions about how implementation should be studied.

In Chapter 7 some methodological and programmatic issues are given attention. Suggestions are offered on how to do implementation research, pitfalls are identified and ways to avoid them are suggested.

Chapter 8 is about the link with practice. It examines what kind of advice, particularly for managers of implementation, can be drawn from the presented insights.

The final chapter summarizes our perspective, making connections between the insights we offer on research and on the practice of implementation.

Some matters of definition

Public policy

Implementation, to us, means just what Webster and Roger say it does: to carry out, accomplish, fulfill, produce, complete. But what is it being implemented? A policy, naturally. There must be something out there prior to implementation; otherwise there would be nothing to move toward in the process of implementation. A verb like 'implement' must have an object like 'policy'. But policies normally contain both goals and the means for achieving them. How, then, do we distinguish between a policy and its implementation?

With these sentences Pressman and Wildavsky (1984: xxi) highlight a question that is of more than linguistic relevance. They continue:

> We can work neither with a definition of policy that excludes any implementation nor one that includes all implementation. There must be a starting point. If no action is begun, implementation cannot take place. There must be also an end point. Implementation cannot succeed or fail without a goal against which to judge it. (p. xxii)

The question at stake here is one of logic. In its most general form the act of 'implementation' presupposes a prior act, particularly the 'cognitive act' of formulating what needs to be done and making a decision on that. But two further groups of questions follow from that basic one. The first is who is the formulator, who is the decision maker and who is the implementer. If they are not integrated as a single actor, there is a need to identify the variety of actors involved. The second group of questions are about whether the formulator or decision maker has more power, or a role that is more legitimized, than the implementer. The former group of questions are empirical ones, while the latter are normative ones. The act of formulation and decision making may take place 'at the bottom'. But even then, it is to be followed by implementation; otherwise the former act remains without consequences. The logical connotation of the original question may be called the *'implementation follows formulation and decision theorem'*.

If implementation in the context of public administration presupposes policy, what is then meant by policy, and particularly by public policy? In academic writings on the latter subject many definitions are provided. Partly, the variety has to do with semantics, partly with diversity in the stress on a specific aspect of the phenomenon as observed in the real world. From the available variety of definitions we will use Hogwood and Gunn's. They identify the following elements in the use of the term 'public policy'. Though policy is to be distinguished from 'decision', it is less readily distinguishable from 'administration'. Policy involves behaviour as well as intentions, and inaction as well as action. Policies have outcomes that may or may not have been foreseen. While policy refers to a purposive course of actions, this does not exclude the possibility that purposes may be defined retrospectively. Policy arises from a process over time, which may involve both intra- and inter-organizational relationships. Public policy involves a key, but not exclusive, role for public agencies. Policy is subjectively defined (Hogwood and Gunn, 1984: 19–23). Hogwood and Gunn summarize this characterization in the following definition: 'Any public policy is subjectively defined by an observer as being such and is usually perceived as comprising a series of patterns of related decisions to which many circumstances and personal, group, and organizational influences have contributed' (pp. 23–4). The subjective aspect in the definition of public policy is underlined by other authors as well. Heclo (1972: 83), for instance, states that what is 'policy' and certainly what is 'the policy' depends on the observer.

For obvious reasons, this subjectivity has not inhibited authors from offering *ex cathedra* a specific definition that can serve as a way to speak of public policy in similar terms. In his textbook, Anderson, for instance, gives the following definition of policy: 'A purposive course of action followed by an actor or set of actors in dealing with a problem or matter of concern.... Public policies are those policies developed by governmental bodies and officials' (1975: 3). Similar definitions can be found in various public policy textbooks. (See, for instance, Kuypers, 1973; Hoogerwerf, 1978; for a variant see Van de Graaf and Hoppe, 1989). In this kind of definition public policy is about means and ends, which have to have a relationship to each other. Where the political functionaries provide the objectives, it is the task of administrators to develop the appropriate instruments. That they are expected to do so in as systematic a way as possible stems from the fact that these administrators are doing their work in public service, dealing with collective problems. Public policy focuses on what Dewey (1927) once described as 'the public and its problems'. Similarly what Lasswell called the 'policy orientation' (Lerner and Lasswell, 1951; Lasswell, 1970) is problem-focused, multi-disciplinary, uses multiple methods and is contextual. In his textbook on public policy Parsons refers to what can be called a 'clinical' attitude as characteristic of the 'policy sciences': 'Knowledge of society could provide a way of making it better' (1995: 20). Parsons decribes the title of Wildavsky's book *Speaking Truth to Power* (1979) as a typical expression of the belief in social science as a form of engineering or medicine. Parsons sees the policy focus as most closely associated with the contributions of four people: Harold Lasswell, Herbert Simon, Charles Lindblom and David Easton. Lindblom's position is special, in the sense that he stresses 'non-rational' aspects of policy that have to do with power, social interaction and the connections between phases and stages.[1]

What is, in general, striking about the definitions of public policy indicated here is the purposive character public policies are expected to have, and the way in which they are expected to be related to (societal) problems. For implementation theory and research this means that contextualization is important: 'implementation' is always connected to specific policies as particular responses to specific problems in society.

The policy cycle

Since Lasswell's seminal publications on public policy it has become quite usual to speak of a 'phase' or 'stage' model of the policy process. When we broaden our scope and look beyond this process in a narrow sense, in fact, we can observe a variety of analytical ways of distinguishing between different 'stages' in the process from thinking to action.

Many writers have set out models of the 'stages' of the policy process (see, for example, Simon, 1945; Lasswell, 1956; Mack, 1971; Rose, 1973; Jenkins, 1978; Hogwood and Gunn, 1984; Dror, 1989). Typically these models embrace processes about how issues get on the agenda, followed by intiation (Jenkins) or 'deciding to decide' (Hogwood and Gunn), then information assembly followed by more precise formulation. After this models include application and implementation. Finally there may be feedback and evaluation, and at the end decisions about 'policy mainte-nance, succession or termination' (Hogwood and Gunn, 1984: 4). Perhaps the most differentiated model is presented by Dror (1989: 163–4). He dis-tinguishes between the major stages of meta-policy making, policy making and post-policy making. Because each of these has sub-stages, there is a total of eighteen (sub-)stages. 'Executing the policy' is the sixteenth stage in the cycle; so a very 'late' one.

Like the means–end definition of public policy, the stages framework is widely used in textbooks on the subject. Criticizing it, Nakamura (1987) speaks of the 'textbook approach', portraying it as unrealistic. It is said to neglect the sometimes blurred distinctions between the 'phases'. In general, it is judged as rationalistic (Nakamura, 1987; D.A. Stone, 1989; Lindblom and Woodhouse, 1993; see Jenkins-Smith, 1991, for perhaps the most elabo-rate criticism; and Van Gunsteren, 1976, for a general critique of rationalist thinking in public affairs). Though we understand the nature of these com-ments, we see a continuing role for the stagist framework. It is useful both analytically and heuristically for both the study and practice of the policy process. With Parsons, we do have an additional requisite, however:

> [T]he idea of 'stages' must be expanded to include a wider contextualization of different frameworks and methods or approaches. There can be no one definition of policy analysis (Wildavsky, 1979: 15), and no one theory or model can capture or explain the complexity involved in what Easton once termed the 'web of decisions' (Easton, 1953: 130) which comprise public policy. (Parsons, 1995: xvii)

The strength of the stages framework, as stressed by Parsons (pp. 80–1), is that it provides a systematic approach to capture the multiplicity of reality. Each 'stage' relates to a specific part of the context in which public policy is being made, while within that partial context various variables and approaches can be seen as appropriate. It is from this perspective that in Chapter 8 we will develop a framework adapted from the stagist one.

Implementation

What can be called 'public policy', and thus has to be implemented, is the product of what has happened in the earlier stages of the policy process.

Nevertheless, the content of that policy, and its impact on those affected, may be substantially modified, elaborated or even negated during the implementation stage, as Anderson points out. '[P]olicy is made as it is being administered and administered as it is being made' (1975: 79). Yet implementation is something separated from policy formation. Only very seldom are decisions self-executing, implying that there is no separate implementation stage. If generally there is such a stage, then there is also a good case for the analysis of that part of the policy process. 'Much that occurs at this stage may seem at first glance to be tedious or mundane, yet its consequences for the substance of policy may be quite profound' (Anderson, 1975: 78–9).

One of the most influential definitions of implementation is that formulated by Mazmanian and Sabatier:

> Implementation is the carrying out of a basic policy decision, usually incorporated in a statute but which can also take the form of important executive orders or court decisions. Ideally, that decision identifies the problem(s) to be addressed, stipulates the objective(s) to be pursued, and in a variety of ways, 'structures' the implementation process. The process normally runs through a number of stages beginning with passage of the basic statute, followed by the policy outputs (decisions) of the implementing agencies, the compliance of target groups with those decisions, the actual impacts – both intended and unintended – of those outputs, the perceived impacts of agency decisions, and finally, important revisions (or attempted revisions) in the basic statute. (1983: 20–1)

Similarly Pressman and Wildavsky say in their preface to their first edition (1973): 'Let us agree to talk about policy as a hypothesis containing initial conditions and predicted consequences. If X is done at time t1, then Y will result at time t2' (1984: xxii). Thus defined, implementation is a complicated process, or rather sub-process. Therefore much can go wrong. 'The longer the chain of causality, the more numerous the reciprocal relationships among the links and the more complex implementation becomes' (p. xxiv). Nevertheless, it is inevitable that this chain is usually long.

Seen 'from the bottom', the perspective on implementation is fundamentally different. (The alternative perspectives of the top-down and bottom-up theorists will be explored further in Chapter 3.) For those at the end of Pressman and Wildavsky's implementation 'chain' there is not so much concern about 'the transmission of policy into a series of consequential actions', but a policy–action relationship. The latter rather 'needs to be regarded as a process of interaction and negotiation, taking place over time, between those seeking to put policy into effect and those upon whom action depends' (Barrett and Fudge, 1981a: 4). Many implementation scholars in one way or another refer to what Barrett and Fudge call the 'policy–action continuum'. For Dunsire, policy implementation is seen as pragmatization (1978a: 178). John speaks of 'the post-legislative stages of decision making' (1998: 27), while he elsewhere calls implementation 'the stage in the policy process concerned with turning policy intentions into action' (p. 204). O'Toole identifies the central question in implementation research as: 'What happens between the establishment of policy and its impact in the world of action?' (2000a: 273). Elsewhere he defines policy implementation as 'what develops between the establishment of an apparent intention on the part of government to do something, or stop doing something, and the ultimate impact in the world of action' (p. 266). Earlier, and even more concisely, he remarked that policy implementation 'refers to the connection between the expression of governmental intention and actual results' (1995: 43). Boiling down all kinds of elaborate definitions, DeLeon calls the study of implementation 'little more than a comparison of the expected versus the achieved' (1999a: 330). We noted in the introduction to this chapter Ferman's particularly concise definition. It is one we will keep very much in mind in this book.

Implementation and policy formation

The process emphasis, ultimately expressed in the continuum between policy and action, implies that in the implementation stage policy *making* continues. This empirical observation is contrary to the emphasis in the theory of bureaucracy developed from the classic theoretical contributions of Max Weber and Woodrow Wilson. In that theory, discussed further in Chapter 2, administration starts where politics – read here 'policy' – ends. The possibility that there could be interaction between the different phases, as well as between functionaries playing different roles like the ones of decision maker and implementer, was neglected for a long while. It was the fact that the 'black box' of implementation was not opened in much political science influenced by this view that made Hargrove (1975) speak of the 'missing link'.

What is needed is a way of combining the analytical benefits offered by the 'stages' model with a recognition of the interaction between the stages. We consider that this is best achieved by talking of policy *formation* (rather than making). This is then distinguishable, in most cases, from an implementation process within which policy will continue to be shaped. If the term 'policy making' stands for the policy process as a whole, then both implementation and policy formation refer to respectively 'late' and 'early' sub-processes in that process. While some authors focus on policy design (Ingraham, 1987; Weimer, 1993) and others on the societal and 'bureau-political' struggle around it (Lindblom, 1965; Allison, 1971), this combined character of thought and action is crucial. Though Allison (1971), in his analysis of the Cuban missile crisis, was one of the first to point at the synchronic relevance of these different views on policy formation, he did not synthesize them. Nevertheless, the interplay between 'intellectual cogitation' and 'social interaction' particularly in the sub-process of policy formation, and expressed in the combination of, respectively, formulation and decision making, can to a certain degree explain the often ambiguous character of policy that has to be implemented. Therefore this interplay is crucial for the study of implementation. (For a systematic elaboration of this mixed character of policy formation – though in Dutch – see Kuypers, 1980; see also Van de Graaf and Hoppe, 1989.)

Outputs and outcomes

One of the most influential models of the relationship between politics and administration is Easton's 'political system' (1953). 'Inputs' go into that system and the things that come out are called 'outputs' and 'outcomes'. Implementation can be seen as a part of the 'throughput' taking place within the 'system'. Sometimes, in both the practice and the study of implementation, the distinction between inputs, outputs and outcomes is overlooked. Given, for instance, concern about lack of crime prevention the political opposition in parliament may call for more 'police on the street'. The idea is then that a larger number of personnel – in operational service – will automatically lead to a decline in crime. All kinds of intervening, but perhaps less manipulable, variables are often forgotten. In fact, policy inputs ('more police') here are taken automatically to produce policy impacts or outcomes (less crime) (Mazmanian and Sabatier, 1983: 22). Also in 'output' analysis the issues of defining and operationalizing the various categories at stake are sometimes muddled. This is the case, for instance, when the researcher merely looks at indices like expenditures. It is argued here that these should be regarded as 'input' rather than 'output' variables. (For an advance of this argument, see Hill and Bramley, 1986; for the use of this argument in the analysis of welfare state performance, see also Mitchell, 1991.)

Besides, it can be observed that outputs and outcomes are sometimes confused.[2] A great deal of implementation literature is about the extent to which policy makers successfully grappled with the question whether their policies were properly designed to address the problems they were alleged to address. Not surprisingly it does this in terms of whether wars on poverty, crime, and so on, actually dealt with those problems. Lane and Ersson argue: 'Thus, outcome analysis in evaluation research came to include all kinds of results that were relevant to the understanding of policies, including outcomes that had no link whatsoever with a policy but affected the evaluation of whether a policy had succeeded or not' (2000: 62). They emphasize the need for a clear distinction between outputs and outcomes, saying of the latter: 'Outcomes are the things that are actually achieved, whatever the objectives of policy may have been. Outcomes are real results, whether intended or unintended, at the same time as outcomes are not government action' (p. 63).

For implementation research, dependent variables may be outputs or outcomes, after the implementation process, but where they are the latter it is particularly important to identify influences that are quite independent of that process.

Making judgements about implementation

Speaking of outputs and outcomes implicitly or explicitly means making judgements. Comparing what is achieved with what was expected (DeLeon, 1999a) can often lead to the observation of an 'implementation gap' (Dunsire, 1978a). An alternative is to use a term like 'implementation failure'. In daily practice such qualifications are easily used. Similarly in the study of implementation a qualification in terms of 'success' or, more often, 'failure' is commonly given. And indeed, sometimes, as in the case of a specific serious accident or disaster, the use of the label 'policy fiasco' seems justifiable (Bovens and 't Hart, 1996). What has to be kept in mind, then, is that the judgement given in such a case, however analytically supported it may be, is in the end – and should be – a normative one. The question here is: Does the researcher or analyst consider this normative judgement as separated from or as integrated in the empirical analysis? Parsons applies Morgan's metaphorical models of organization (1986, 1993) to explore the value of adopting alternative perspectives on implementation failure. He shows that using a different metaphor means looking at and labelling the causes and consequences of implementation failure in a different way. Implementation failure can be seen, for instance, as a result of a poor chain of command and of problems with structures and roles (machine metaphor); as a result of difficult 'human relations' or 'the environment' (organism metaphor); as a result of poor information flows or 'learning' problems (brain metaphor); as a result of labour/management conflict (domination metaphor); as a result of the 'culture' of an organization (culture metaphor); as a result of subconscious forces, group-think, ego defences or repressed sexual instincts (psychic metaphor); as a result of a 'self-referencing' system (autopoietic metaphor); or as a result of power in and around the implementation process (power metaphor) (Parsons, 1995: 489). Important here is that no one metaphor *a priori* provides a better picture. Actually, what one portrays as empirical reality depends upon what kind of metaphor is used.

This interpretative view involves integrating values, though in sets varying according to the metaphor, into the way of looking at the world. When doing so the researcher is always right, or in any case as long as he or she chooses the metaphor fitted to the context at hand. A systematic and controlled confrontation between 'theory' and 'empirical reality' is thus avoided. There is no check on the provisional character of knowledge. Because values are completely integrated into the way of looking at reality, any attempt to interpret the findings is irrelevant. There is no sense in discussing from a normative standpoint what the conclusions of an analysis could be, because these form an integral part of such an analysis. In fact, at stake here is a classic epistemological issue that divides the 'positivists' in their various variants from the 'interpretivists'. We see the value of metaphorical 'explanations', of the kind presented by Morgan and Parsons, as contributions to public discourse. But as criteria for the development of a field like implementation studies, we think a broader academic engagement is required, aiming at the accumulation of knowledge. Our stance is that, both on different occasions and in several parts of the empirical cycle, we see functions for interpretative contributions, mainly of a heuristic and evaluative ('making sense of') kind. As far as the development of empirical studies is concerned, we consider that such contributions have uses. However, these are particularly functional in the 'early' parts of the empirical cycle, concerning problem definition and the formulation of working hypotheses; as well as in the 'later' parts of that cycle, focusing on the interpretation of findings, the drawing of conclusions and the formulation of advice. Of course, values are always involved. Nevertheless, concepts need to be defined and operationalized in a neutral fashion, so that then there can be an orientation towards testing in one way or another.[3] In the 'middle part' of the empirical cycle we therefore plead for a systematic, and if possible comparative, approach to empirical reality; for conceptual parsimony; and for aiming at the testing of propositions, in a quantitative, qualitative or combined way. In a fully fledged research design the goal will be explaining variance. In any case, our perspective implies a need to make research decisions explicit and to justify epistemological stances when doing implementation research.

Implementation and evaluation

Talking of an 'implementation failure' or 'implementation deficit' means giving a normative qualification as a result of a comparison between what is observed and what is expected, where the latter is defined in terms of the values either of the observer or of one or more of the actors involved in the process. In that sense, an evaluation is then provided. Nevertheless, the distinction between implementation and evaluation as two successive 'stages' in the policy process is analytically relevant enough to maintain. The definitions of evaluation given in the literature vary in broadness. In a monograph on the subject, Fischer defines policy evaluation as 'the activity of applied social science typically referred to as "policy analysis" or "policy science"' (1995: 2). He refers to Dunn, who speaks of policy analysis as an applied endeavour 'which uses multiple methods of inquiry and argument to produce and transform policy-relevant information that may be utilized in political settings to resolve policy problems'

(1981: 35). Classic texts are Patton (1978), Rossi and Freeman (1979) and Palumbo (1987), or, for a 'naturalistic' approach, Guba and Lincoln (1987).

In the 1984 edition of *Implementation* Wildavsky dedicated a chapter to the meaning of evaluation for implementation, written in 1983 with Angela Browne. Referring to Jan-Erik Lane (1983), this additional chapter wants to connect the study of implementation with the newer interest in evaluation. Wildavsky and Browne observe this relationship as follows:

> The evaluator collects and analyzes data to provide information about pro-gram results. The implementer consumes this information, using it to check on past decisions and to guide future actions. Implementation is ... about learning from evaluation. It is in their production and consumption of infor-mation (that is, learning) that implementers and evaluators engage in complementary relationships. (1984: 204)

Lane asks: 'Is implementation analysis the same as evaluation analysis? The concept of implementation as evolution amounts to a strong denial of any identity between the two, because if objectives and outcomes contin-uously interact, how could the outcomes be evaluated in terms of a fixed set of objectives?' Browne and Wildavsky conclude that the conceptual distinction between evaluation and implementation is important to main-tain, however much the two overlap in practice. They state: 'Evaluators are able to tell us a lot about what happened – which objectives, whose objectives, were achieved – and a little about why – the causal connec-tions' (p. 203).

Parsons makes the implementation/evaluation distinction by indicat-ing that evaluation examines 'how public policy and the people who deliver it may be appraised, audited, valued and controlled', while the study of implementation is about 'how policy is put into action and prac-tice' (1995: 461). The conceptualization used in this book can be summa-rized as shown in Table 1.1.

TABLE 1.1 *Implementation and evaluation research*

	Object	**Research act**
Implementation	Process/behaviour	Description
	Outputs	Explanation
	Outcomes	Theory building and testing
	Causal connections	Analytical judgements
Evaluation	Outcomes–values links	Value judgements

Implementation research

Theory and research on public policy implementation concern 'the development of systematic knowledge regarding what emerges, or is induced, as actors deal with a policy problem' (O'Toole, 2000a: 266).

Almost thirty years ago, Pressman and Wildavksy were amazed that there was so little that deserved the heading 'implementation research'. Some years later they described the situation quite differently:

> The study of implementation is becoming a growth industry: tens, perhaps hundreds, of studies are underway now. Yet researchers are visibly uneasy. It is not so much that they expect to discover all the right answers; they are not even sure they are asking the right questions. ... But this uneasiness is not surprising, for the attempt to study implementation raises the most basic question about the relation between thought and action: How can ideas manifest themselves in a world of behavior? (1984: 163)

Implementation research has grown to what can be seen as a sub-discipline, developed particularly within the disciplines of political science and public administration. In the past thirty years the field has flourished, but disappointment has been expressed about the low degree of theoretical coherence and the lack of cumulative effect from the research undertaken (O'Toole, 1986). Some authors are very dismissive: 'While the concept of implementation remains useful as a conceptual tool to understand the failure and success of policy, the project of creating implementation analysis as a separate field of study has largely failed' (John, 1998: 30). In Chapter 5 we look at the development of the field, exploring reasons for such a negative judgement – a judgement that we can understand, but do not adhere to. Why we are more positive on both the state and the future of the field has to do with the recent emergence of the phenomenon and concept of 'governance'.

Governance

Somewhere in the 1990s, the times of 'governance' or 'new governance' were seen as having arrived (Pierre and Peters, 2000). This term refers to the way in which collective impacts are produced in a social system. Several authors have given definitions of the concept of governance already, others focus on a specific sort of governance, while some authors distinguish different models of governance.[4]

Lynn et al. define governance as 'regimes of laws, administrative rules, judicial rulings, and practices that constrain, prescribe, and enable governmental activity' (1999: 2–3). In Rhodes' view governance 'refers to self-organizing, inter-organizational networks' (1997: 15), while for Wamsley governance 'connotes the use of authority in providing systemic steering and direction' (1990a: 25), and stands for 'choosing, prioritizing, directing and steering' (1990b: 114). In E.B. McGregor's definition the term 'governance' refers to 'the application of power and authority in a way that commits relevant political actors to managerial decisions' (1993: 182). Stoker (1991) speaks of an 'authority, exchange and governance paradigm'.

Referring to Clarence Stone (1989), he calls governance 'creating the "capacity to act", bringing together the resources required to accomplish the collective ends of society' (1991: 51).

Kooiman (1999) gives a classification of the various ways in which the term 'governance' has been used in the literature thus far. He adds some categories to the list Rhodes (1997) made earlier. Kooiman distinguishes ten different meanings of the term: (1) governance as the minimal state; (2) corporate governance; (3) governance as new public management; (4) 'good governance'; (5) governance as socio-cybernetic governance; (6) governance as self-organizing networks; (7) governance as 'Steuerung' (German) or 'sturing' (Dutch); (8) governance as international order; (9) 'governing the economy' or economic sectors; and, finally, (10) governance and governmentability. In the anthology of six definitions Kooiman next selects, he gives as his own one: 'solving problems and creating opportunities, and the structural and processual conditions aimed at doing so' (1999: 69).

By adding an adjective, several authors particularly focus on a specific *sort* of governance. Kooiman, for instance, speaks of 'modern governance' (1993), 'social-political governance' (1999; see also Lawson, 2000, with 'socio-political governance') and 'self-governance' (Kooiman and Van Vliet, 2000). The latter uses the concept of 'communicative governance', too (Van Vliet, 1993). In the view of Pierre and Peters the term 'governance' in Europe refers to 'new governance': ideas of the involvement of society in the process of governing. By contrast, in the USA the term 'retains much of its original steering conception' (2000: 7). Rhodes (1997) and Saward (1997) also use the term 'new governance'. Toonen (1990) speaks of 'co-governance'; Greca (2000) of 'institutional co-governance'; Huxham (2000) of 'collaborative governance'; Hupe and Meijs (2000) of 'hybrid governance'. Earlier, Kickert (1997) spoke of 'public governance' and Rhodes (1992) of 'local governance'.

Besides, some authors give a broad definition, which they then differentiate into a number of *models of governance*. Under that heading Pierre and Peters (2000), for instance, distinguish between three scenarios: 'reasserting control'; 'letting other regimes rule'; and 'communitarianism, deliberation, and direct democracy'.

Implementation research and governance

Among these many definitions of governance circulating, the one formulated by Milward and Provan in our view shows an appropriate balance between comprehensiveness and specificity; and is therefore used in this book:

> Governance ... is concerned with creating the conditions for ordered rules and collective action, often including agents in the private and nonprofit sectors,

as well as within the public sector. The essence of governance is its focus on governing mechanisms – grants, contracts, agreements – that do not rest solely on the authority and sanctions of government. (1999: 3)

The conceptualization of governance is designed 'to incorporate a more complete understanding of the multiple levels of action and kinds of variables that can be expected to influence performance' (O'Toole, 2000a: 276). Governance has consequences for the way the object of implementation research is defined. Implementation research can be brought under the heading of governance research, but in doing so it has to be broadened. Then new connections, with other fields and sub-fields in the social sciences, also need to be brought into the picture. In some of them, like public management, converging movements can be observed. Lynn and his colleagues, for instance, practise such 'governance research' (see Lynn et al., 1999, 2000). In broad outline their project constitutes an effort to synthesize influences on policy performance of several sorts and from several levels. As both a participant in that project and an implementation researcher, O'Toole is positive on the consequences of the former for the latter, because the project referred to is 'taking account of the standard concerns of implementation researchers and integrating these with other kinds of related analyses' (2000a: 278). In his view, 'implementation per se has moved to the background, in favour of attention to concerted action across institutional boundaries on behalf of public purpose' (p. 278).

Multiple loci, layers and levels

The broadened heading for implementation research has several consequences. First, with the distinction between government and governance, the difference between structures and processes, between institutions and activities, and between locus and focus has become important. The latter distinction refers to the separate character of the *what* and the *how* of scholarly attention.[5] In the diversity of political-societal relations within a (national) political-administrative system a variety of *loci* can be observed. For instance, looking at what civil servants in public bureaucracies 'at the street level' are doing, Lipsky (1980) leaves aside what takes place in the Washington departments. Hanf and Scharpf (1978), on the contrary, gave attention to the external relations between both public and private organizations. It is obvious, therefore, that not all implementation researchers focus at the same locus, while exactly that variety needs to be incorporated in the analysis of implementation and governance.

Second, explicit attention is given to the layered character of the political-administrative system. Instead of the antagonistic top–bottom distinction, the various institutional relations get attention, both vertical and horizontal ones. For the loci of the formal, legitimate political-administrative institutions, including representative organs with a certain territorial competence, we would like to reserve the term *layers*. In a federal system, for example, these layers involve the federation, the states, the counties and municipalities. In a 'decentralized unitary state' like the Netherlands, apart from the 'functional' waterboards there are three territorial administrative layers: the *rijk*, the provinces, and the municipalities, each with a certain degree of autonomy. A specific public policy may be both formed and implemented at one and the same political-administrative layer. Many policies, however, while following their policy intentions–policy outputs trajectory, encounter a variety of such layers. While at each of the layers there are official competences and there is legitimate politics at work, it depends on the legal framework of the specific public policy whether just implementation or, in fact, 'policy co-formation' is required.

Third, the act of management is taken seriously; more or less a new feature in implementation research. The term then refers to 'the set of conscious efforts to concert actors and resources to carry out established collective purposes' (O'Toole, 2000b: 21). Here we are talking about the realm of action. Our supposition is that in all of the loci in political-societal relations action of a varied character takes place. Action may involve designing institutions as well as managing implementation. Research of such different activities means specifying *levels of analysis*. Consequentially, the acknowledgement of this multiplicity implies a contextual approach, both in research and in practice.

Multiplicity demands contextualization

The broadening of the perspective on implementation to a multi-disciplinary, multi-level and multi-focus exercise looking at a multiplicity of actors, loci and layers clearly should be welcomed. Hence, questions of implementation can be reframed in terms of 'performance via governance in the delivery of policy results' (O'Toole, 2000a: 281). Nevertheless, some things remain the same: 'Explaining – and ultimately improving – the way policy intention influences policy action is the research agenda, by whatever name' (O'Toole, 2000a: 283).

Interestingly, however, in his introduction written with Majone to the 1979 edition of *Implementation*, Wildavsky made an observation that can be seen as entirely relevant to this new perspective:

> If implementation is everywhere, as one of the authors suggested in another connection, is it ipso facto nowhere? ... No doubt this is why students of implementation complain that the subject is so slippery; it does depend on what one is trying to explain, from what point of view, at what point in its history. (1984: 164)

It means, perhaps even more than before, that contextualization is needed. The consequences for the agenda of implementation research and for the practice of managing implementation are explored further in Chapters 7 and 8.

Notes

1 See Parsons (1995: 27) for a list of the key texts on the study of public policy.
2 In an appendix to his book on politics, values and public policy Fischer (1980) points at some early examples of comparative research aiming at establishing causal linkages between dependent and independent variables of policy models. He mentions Rae and Taylor (1971), and, for a critical review of the literature, Jacob and Lipsky (1968). He also refers to Hammond and Adelman (1978) for an illustration of the integration of social scientific data about policy variables and normative judgements about the variables elicited from the political environment. As a 'post-positivist', Fischer is critical of the extent to which what he calls 'the scientific approach' – formal modelling – can contribute to integrating empirical and normative judgements.
3 Compare Popper's statement (1959) on the preliminary character of all scientific knowledge.
4 For a relatively early use of the term, see Wittrock (1983).
5 Though we cannot trace anymore where and when, it was Robert Golembiewski who introduced this distinction to us.

2

Positioning Implementation Studies

Introduction

It has become conventional to see implementation studies as emergent in the 1970s. Hargrove then (1975) wrote of the 'missing link' in the study of the policy process while Pressman and Wildavsky's influential *Implementation* was published in 1973. The reaction of one of us to Pressman and Wildavsky's claim that they could find next to no literature on implementation was to draft a short paper for his colleagues headed by a quotation from Molière's *Le Bourgeois Gentilhomme*: 'Gracious me! I have been talking prose for the last forty years and have never known it.' While not at that stage being able to claim forty years experience of academic work, earlier work had involved trying to reinforce longstanding concerns in public administration with ideas from organization theory in the implementation part of the policy process (Hill, 1972). Obviously, implementation was a central concern, though that word was seldom used. Pressman and Wildavsky's bibliography, ostensibly demonstrating the absence of an implementation literature, did not contain such classic American works as Blau's *The Dynamics of Bureaucracy* (1955), Kaufman's

The Forest Ranger (1960) and, above all, Selznick's *TVA and the Grass Roots* (1949).

Van Meter and Van Horn, in another of the seminal contributions to the modern implementation literature, were similarly critical of Pressman and Wildavsky's omissions:

> While we share Pressman and Wildavsky's concern that far too little attention has been paid to the question of policy implementation, their criticism of the literature is unnecessarily harsh and shortsighted. Our argument is put simply: there is a rich heritage from the social sciences which is often overlooked by those purporting to discuss the policy implementation process. This literature includes theoretical and empirical work in several disciplines, including sociology, public administration, social psychology and political science. While most of these studies do not examine specifically the policy implementation process, close inspection reveals that it takes little imagination to comprehend their relevance. (1975: 452–3)

Hargrove, obviously stung by such comments, argued in a later paper:

> It could be argued that I misstate the problem. In fact, there is plenty of theory around to be applied to cases. One could cite organization theory in general or, more specifically, the rich literature of public administration. However, very little of this work deals with the contemporary problems of policy implementation which preoccupy political scientists and analysts. (1983: 280)

He went on to claim that the new implementation theory addresses problems not faced in the older public administration literature.

Of course we could leave it there and launch immediately into a discussion of the implementation literature that has developed since the 1970s. That was a time when academic work in the social sciences was exploding, and when there were all sorts of efforts to apply social scientific ideas to the policy process. However, we think it worthwhile briefly to look back in time. We consider that to do so helps us to develop a clear view about the literature on implementation, and particularly on the difficulties that have been encountered in advancing the 'implementation perspective'. This is what we will do first in this chapter. The discussion will develop into an examination of literature that, even after the so-called 'discovery' of implementation as an issue, explores questions pertinent to that subject without using the term 'implementation' or making explicit connections with implementation theory. Within that literature concerns are expressed that are very central to controversy within implementation theory: about the rule of law, accountability and the roles of civil servants within the policy process. Then we look at institutional theory in political science and sociology, which has concerns that overlap with those of analysts of implementation research. This section is followed by some observations on postmodern perspectives, which develop the viewpoint of those institutional theorists who question the feasibility of systematic generalization about the policy process. Overall this mixture of topics offers an account of a range of work that in one way or another 'talks' about implementation without explicitly using the term or developing the analytical approach to that topic that we will be exploring in the rest of the book.

Concerns about implementation: historical origins

Clearly some of the earliest human activities must have involved the setting of objectives. It is pointless to speculate to what extent achievements identifiable today arose out of purposive activity, just as it is difficult to make assumptions about the relationship between actions and preceding objectives when we observe the behaviour of others. Where analysis does become possible is where (a) individuals secured actions from others and (b) left information that enables us to infer that they were setting goals for these actions. The evidence we have of the earliest collective actions comes from the relics that have survived. We can observe some extraordinary achievements – stone circles, pyramids, palaces, and so on – that must have been products of collective action, and in many cases there is evidence that this action was on behalf of some dominant individual or group.

There is nothing in the basic definition of implementation that ties it, as the modern literature does, to the idea of *public* policy. That fact suggests that the study or analysis of implementation should be seen as a part of the study of organizational behaviour or of management. That chimes in with a very modern view that the management of public policy should be regarded as no different from the management of any other activity (see Dunsire, 1995, and Gray and Jenkins, 1995, for discussions of this view). There is obviously something to be said for seeing the study of public policy implementation as being simply the study of the management of organized behaviour. We must therefore consider what might make public policy implementation different.

Again it is helpful to explore this issue in historical terms, confronting the question: Under what circumstances may we identify some implementation activities that were different from simple private efforts to manage collective endeavours? What then seems to be the case is that there were, from very early times, some sustained activities over a long period or a broad geographical area that were led by people who sought to exercise some overall system of government. At this stage, little progress can be made with any analysis of implementation without grappling with the two topics very central to political science – authority and the state. The evidence we have of the earliest 'states', 'kingdoms' or 'empires' consists of the relics they left behind. Where there are no written records these are the remains of constructions, as has already been noted. With these we know only of the implementation successes of these very early political systems (though we may perhaps infer failure too from the fact that many remarkable achievements were ultimately left to decay). Later, written records are available, of varying but increasing sophistication, which enable us to identify accounts of organizational achievements. A significant amount of Greek and Roman literature is about the implementation problems confronting those who sought to organize societies and engage in war.

Much of this early material tends to be read as concerned with explaining the 'power' of rulers or the effectiveness of quasi-democratic systems. We cannot easily make interpretations about the relationships between objective setting and the carrying out of those objectives. Systems of rule can be perceived to have been set up, to have survived for a period and then to have been modified or undermined. Wars were conducted with inevitably varying degrees of success. Cities came and went, trading systems operated with mixed achievements. Perhaps the most interesting phenomena were those that must have required sustained co-ordination over long periods of time. Systems for the control of water – to prevent flooding, provide irrigation, and so on – have attracted particular attention. These have been seen as explaining 'empires' (Wittfogel, 1963), but the questions about how they were achieved are equally interesting. Similarly the extension of power systems across great tracts of territory, where it could take months to send a punitive expedition against rebels, has long attracted the interest of scholars. (Above all, the rise and fall of the Roman Empire involved a complex sequence of 'implementation problems'.)

It is not our intention here to offer an elaborate historical analysis of implementation. We have already noted that what we see of the activities of the distant past depends very much upon what has survived. It should also be noted that those who have left us records of these activities were largely those in dominant roles, or closely allied to such people. Much less easily recognizable are the many implementation successes that depended upon bottom-up forms of collective action. The history of 'empires' tends to be very much the history of those who controlled them.

The study of power in these early states has of course generated a literature that seeks to explain the puzzles about how control was exercised. We know quite a lot about the various ways in which naked power was exercised, a topic that we could translate into the language of implementation studies in terms of bloody reprisals for implementation failure. We can trace a variety of complex devices – the use of spies, eunuchs, foreigners, and so on – to try to ensure the loyalty of subordinates over whom it was very difficult to exercise direct supervision. There is much evidence of the use of approaches to power that depended upon a feudal system of some kind in which a sort of hierarchy of opportunities for gain was operated. These can perhaps be seen as power systems that allowed for implementation deficit. So long as the ruler got the taxes and the military support when it was needed, other control over local events could be traded down the hierarchy. Tax farmers, for example, profited if they could collect a surplus over what their ruler required, and were punished if they achieved a deficit. The criterion for implementation success was simple.

There has also been an enormous interest in the extent to which it was possible to legitimize rule. Here of course we are in the realm of the literature about Max Weber's systems of authority (1947). It is appropriate to be in Weber's 'company' as we jump forward from speculation about very early systems of power. If we look at implementation in terms of Weber's three types of authority, we can dismiss one type – charismatic authority – as essentially involving no concept of separation between goal setting and sustained independent action and as being ephemeral in nature unless 'routinized', transforming it into one of the other types. On the other hand we cannot so readily move on from the concept of traditional authority. After all there have been long periods – in European history from the early Middle Ages until even the nineteenth century, almost throughout recorded Chinese history and in much of the history of the Islamic world – in which extensive policy implementation occurred. That was legitimated largely in terms of adherence to goals set by religious leaders or absolute rulers (or both in concert). During this long period of traditional authority the modern notion of the state began to emerge with some very explicit assertions of rights to rule – over territories much more explicitly defined – and thus clearer expectations of implementation success.

Over a period between about the fourteenth and the twentieth centuries legitimizing ideologies within states gradually took on three new characteristics. One of these involved assertions of *the idea of the nation state* – seeing collective action as legitimized by notions of shared racial, cultural or linguistic characteristics. This is not particularly pertinent to the study of implementation, except inasmuch as it provided a context for the other two developments. These were the emergence of the idea of the *rule of law* and the *development of democracy*. These ideas need careful consideration for the implications they have for the way we think about implementation. They are in various respects connected, but can be analysed separately as they raise rather different themes for this discussion.

The rule of law

The issues about the rule of law are important for the study of implementation because implicit in that concept is the notion that citizens should be able to predict the impact of the actions of the state upon themselves and secure redress when affected by illegitimate actions. Wade (1982) suggests that the 'rule of law' has four aspects:

- 'Its primary meaning is that everything must be done according to the law', which when applied to the powers of government means that 'every act which affects the legal rights, duties or liberties of any person must be shown to have a strictly legal pedigree. The affected person may always resort to the courts of law, and if the legal pedigree is not found to be perfectly in order the court will invalidate the act, which he can then safely disregard' (p. 22).
- 'The secondary meaning of the rule of law ... is that government should be conducted within a framework of recognized rules and principles which restrict discretionary power' (p. 22).
- Disputes about the law should be settled by a judiciary that is independent of government (p. 23).
- The 'law should be even-handed between government and citizen' (p. 24).

The particular way those principles are enunciated by Wade may have characteristics that are peculiar to the Anglo-Saxon countries, but the general thrust of the principles is accepted wherever it is claimed that governments operate within the 'rule of law'. For the purposes of this discussion it is what Wade calls the primary meaning that is important, for what it implies is that there should be some connection between policy implementation and the statutes that authorize it. This provides one of the foundations of the concerns of the top-down approach to implementation, which will be given much further consideration later in this book.

The importance of the 'rule of law' as a basis for legitimate rule is explored in Weber's third type of authority: 'rational legal'. Weber argues (in a text originally put together in the early years of the twentieth century): 'Today the most usual basis of legitimacy is the belief in legality, the readiness to conform with rules which are formally correct and have been imposed by accepted procedure' (1947: 131). He goes on to distinguish order derived from voluntary agreement from one that is imposed – but calls this distinction 'only relative'. The first of the ideas that he sees as central to the 'effectiveness' of legal authority is

> That any given legal norm may be established by agreement or by imposition, on grounds of expediency or rational values or both, with a claim to obedience at least on the part of the members of the corporate group. This is, however, usually extended to include all persons within the sphere of authority or of power in question – which in the case of territorial bodies is the territorial area – who stand in certain social relationships or carry out forms of social action which in the order governing the corporate group have been declared to be relevant. (p. 329)

In that rather convoluted argument, of course, lies the concept of the state. The second idea is that 'every body of law consists essentially in a consistent system of abstract rules which have been intentionally established' (p. 330).

The remaining ideas go on to emphasize other aspects of the system by which this body of rules is established, in which we see glimpses of Weber's emphasis on the importance of bureaucracy. There is no suggestion that democracy is essential for the rational legal order. On the contrary, elsewhere, Weber says of France: 'Without this juristic rationalism, the rise of the absolute state is just as little imaginable as is the Revolution' (Gerth and Mills, 1947: 94). In Weber's approach to the concept of the 'rational legal order' there are two notions that need separating. One of these is the idea that obedience is to an identifiable body of rules. This is clearly very like the key principle embodied in the idea of the rule of law. In this sense the 'rationality' is embodied in the structure of the rules, wherever they come from. The other is that Weber is concerned to stress the importance for their legitimacy of the way the rules are made – even though he does not invoke the idea of democracy – in terms of the extent to which they are the product of the work of a body of officials working in a systematic and impersonal way. In short the idea of the rational legal order and the idea of bureaucracy are closely linked together. This is the controversial aspect of Weber's work. Whilst a body of rules could be created in a variety of different ways, and could even be developed and renegotiated through 'bottom-up' processes, the bureaucratic model is essentially hierarchical and by implication the rules are dominated by principles dictated from the top of that hierarchy, and are conservative and very stable.

The arguments about Weber's ideal-typical model of bureaucracy are not our concern here, but it is important to recognize the extent to which one of the roots of the concern about implementation as a controlled and predictable process comes from a widespread belief in the need for this. Weber was not so much prescribing (though that is a matter of dispute) as identifying bureaucracy as taken for granted in the organization of government in the early twentieth century.

In the examination of Weber's 'rational legal' and 'bureaucratic' ideal-types by sociologists in the mid-twentieth century, questions were raised about the limits to control through bureaucratic models. That examination closely paralleled discussions in management theory about the case for formal organization along what are often called Fordist lines, based upon the very strict organization of motor assembly lines influenced by the management theory of F.W. Taylor (1911).

With the development of the social sciences in the 1940s and 1950s, two developments in organization theory – one stimulated by the work of Max Weber, the other by work that questions the formal management model (see particularly Mayo, 1933) – began to come together. Sociologists, using Weber's work (or their understanding of it) as their starting point, set out to show the importance of patterns of informal relationships alongside the formal ones. Social psychologists, on the other hand, sought to explore the conflict between human needs and the apparent requirements of formal organizations. Drawing on this work, administrative theorists sought to update the old formal prescriptive models with more flexible propositions based upon this new understanding of organizational life (D. McGregor, 1960; Argyris, 1964; Herzberg, 1966).

There are two related issues emergent from this literature – whether the formal prescription of behaviour from the top is feasible, and whether it is desirable. We will see in later chapters the various ways in which these emerge in discussions of implementation. In the context of the 'rule of law', under discussion here, an interesting related debate has emerged about administrative discretion. The issues here are about the extent to which the behaviour of public officials can and/or should be precisely prescribed by laws, or conversely about the extent to which officials need to use their discretion to interpret and under some circumstances modify the impact of the law. In Britain the roots of that debate seem to lie in concerns about delegated legislation, that is, basic framework laws that can be amplified by subsequent regulations. A particular target of critics of this legislation has been what have been nicknamed 'Henry VIII clauses', after the arbitrary rule of that monarch, which give very wide scope to ministers to amplify original legislation. In many respects the arguments about delegated legislation relate to the law-making process, and thus to issues about the relationship between legislature and executive. Hence, they are not so much about the absence of the rule of law as about the capacity for a government to make law without going through rigorous parliamentary procedures. However, they have been seen, by legal philosophers like Dicey (1905), as symptomatic of the development of collectivism, giving government powers that cannot easily be controlled by citizens through legal processes. In that sense the issues about what we may call discretionary policy making become linked with wider issues about discretion in the implementation process, when the amplification of a law occurs a long way away from the legislative process, perhaps by a low-level official.

The more modern attack on discretion by legal theorists has largely been led by an American, K.C. Davis. According to Davis: 'A public officer has discretion wherever the effective limits on his power leave him free to make a choice among possible courses of action and inaction' (1969: 4). Davis argues that rule structures within which discretion is exercised should be drawn as tightly as possible: 'Our governmental and legal systems are saturated with excessive discretionary power which needs to be confined, structured and checked' (p. 27). Later in the same book he asserts that 'we have to open our eyes to the reality that justice to individual parties is administered more outside courts than in them, and we have to penetrate the unpleasant areas of discretionary determinations by police and prosecutors and other administrators, where huge concentrations of injustice invite drastic reforms' (p. 215).

Other legal theorists (Jowell, 1973; Dworkin, 1977; Galligan, 1986; Baldwin, 1995) have explored the variety of ways in which Davis's aspiration is difficult to achieve, given the need for public officials to deal with situations that are inherently difficult to regulate precisely in advance. Dworkin (1977) distinguishes between strong discretion, where the decision maker creates the standards, and weak discretion, where standards set by a prior authority have to be interpreted. Galligan (1986) is similarly concerned to analyse discretion in this way, identifying that decision makers have to apply standards to the interpretation of facts. These distinctions may seem very academic, but they are important in administrative law for distinctions between decisions that are within an official's powers and ones that are not.

This debate, largely carried out between lawyers, is important for the study of implementation in highlighting the issues that emerge, in relation to complex policies, about control over implementation processes. These are issues that have been recognized as particularly evident once government becomes active in trying to regulate economic activities and provide welfare benefits and services. In these circumstances laws have to deal with complex situations and with contingencies that are hard to anticipate in advance.

These issues have also been given attention by sociologists of law, in ways that are particularly relevant for a scholarly theme important for the study of implementation, that of 'street-level bureaucracy' (see Mashaw, 1983). This topic is explored further later in this book, with particular reference to the work of Michael Lipsky (see Chapter 3, pp. 51–3). Kagan (1978) distinguishes between styles of rule application. In his study *Regulatory Justice*, looking at rule application in regulatory agencies, he makes a distinction between the emphasis on adherence to rules and the emphasis on the realization of organizational ends. On the basis of these dimensions he distinguishes between the judicial mode, legalism, unauthorized discretion and retreatism as modes of rule application. The first one he calls 'the preferred pattern of rule application in American regulatory agencies' (Kagan, 1978: 91). On the basis of Kagan's work other sociologists of law have made elaborations of and adaptations to his distinction. Knegt (1986) speaks of three styles of rule application: a bureaucratic style, a 'political' style and a pragmatic style (see also Aalders, 1987; Van Montfort, 1991).

Some analysts of public administration (Ringeling, 1978; Van der Veen, 1990) distinguish between various sources of what they call 'policy discretion', such as the character of the rules and regulations involved; the structure (labour division) of the implementing organization; the way in which democratic control is exercised; and work circumstances in the narrow sense, particularly interaction with clients.

There has been a tendency for each category of street-level bureaucracy to have its own kinds of studies concentrating on that specific (semi-)profession. In studies of the police, for instance, J.Q. Wilson (1968) was one of the first to discover patterns in the way police officers use their discretion. He speaks of the watchman style, the legalistic style and the service style. Van der Torre (1999: 19) argues that 'police styles' are connected with regulations or policy programmes that have to be implemented. He defines a 'police style' as 'the range of values, norms and view of a group of police officers that forms the basis of the patterns in their behaviour'. He distinguishes between 'pragmatists', 'pessimists', 'law enforcers' and 'social workers'.

Conceptual contributions like the ones presented here have enriched the scholarly theme of street-level bureaucracy and therefore implementation studies. They elaborated the insight that public servants working on the street level have a relative autonomy, while on that level a specific 'logic of implementation' can be observed. Street-level bureaucrats see themselves as decision makers, whose decisions are based on normative choices, rather than as functionaries responding to rules, procedures or policies (Maynard-Moody and Musheno, 2000). Enhancing street-level discretion may, under certain conditions, be more functional for the implementation of those policies than curbing it (for an example see Maynard-Moody et al., 1990).

As a specific category of public servants, street-level bureaucrats have a lot in common, as Lipsky has indicated (pp. 51–3). Nevertheless considerable attention has been given in the sociological literature and elsewhere to the relevance of expertise. While there is a general sense in which any 'agent' with a delegated task carried out in conditions that his or her superior cannot totally comprehend or control is an 'expert', much of the debate concerns those highly expert functionaries who are often described as 'professionals'. This is an issue that has secured much modern attention. A widespread popular view on this subject is embodied in a widely quoted aphorism written by Bernard Shaw in his play *The Doctor's Dilemma* in 1911: 'All professions are conspiracies against the laity.' In a pure market system that 'conspiracy' is a problem that the laity have to confront alone, but states have seldom been prepared to leave them on their own in this respect. However, the new dimension introduced by the active state is the use of professionals in the implementation of public policy. In an influential book published in 1970, an American, Eliot Freidson, attacked the medical profession, elaborating Shaw's argument, and alleging that publicly provided health services particularly enhance the power of doctors by placing them in a monopoly situation. We do not subscribe to this simplistic statement of the issues. There has been a vast literature exploring them further (for an overview see Moran and Wood, 1993). However the 'conspiracy' view of professionalism does highlight a general question that has to be addressed in the study of implementation: Does the involvement of professional decision making in policy implementation processes undermine the prospects for top-down control over the process?

The discussion of discretion and the related issues about professions started from a lawyers' concern about control over implementation processes. Inasmuch as lawyers recognize limits to the use of top-down control, their remedy is that discretionary activities should be carefully hedged within a framework of rules and that there should be scope for adjudicative procedures that enable discretion to be challenged in a court or a tribunal. The sociological contribution here adds, in particular, scepticism about the feasibility of this. However, there is something else lying in the background of this whole discussion, that is, the extent to which the best way to ensure the rule of law lies in the maintenance of a democratic political system. When this is introduced into the discussion two key questions emerge. First: To what extent does the real problem of unregulated discretion lie in the fact that public officials may be carrying out actions not authorized by their elected 'superiors'? And second: To what extent may such control (given the discussion above about complexity) need to be exercised by more complex democratic mechanisms than simply top-down control by the legislature? This leads us to the next section.

The implications of the idea of democracy

Without democracy – except inasmuch as there are concerns about the predictability of implementation as embodied in the concerns about the rule of law discussed in the previous section – issues about control over public policy implementation are much the same as those that concern the owners and managers of private organizations. While the latter may not want to avoid having their goals modified or subverted by their staff, they face no problems of accountability extending beyond their own ranks. There are of course some examples of private organizations with quasi-public faces – with obligations to shareholders or members. Some of the remarks below about democratic accountability will also apply to them.

The simplest ideas of democracy involved direct participation of citizens in the running of their communities or organizations – as allegedly practised in ancient Greek cities and to some extent in more recent times in the smaller Swiss cantons and some of the New England towns. Implicit in the idea of direct democracy is the absence of a split between policy formation and implementation. But in practice even the members of the most participative small organizations soon find that there are circumstances in which they have to delegate tasks. Nevertheless we may follow the broad drift of the concerns of democratic theorists that beyond a certain very limited size self-governing communities have to develop indirect approaches to representation, and argue that this issue also applies to control over implementation.

We therefore have to see the concerns of the political philosophers with the nature of representative government as very crucial for the setting of the modern implementation agenda. Page (1985) offers an analysis of this issue in his discussion of what has already been identified above as a closely related issue: the relationship between bureaucracy and democracy. He suggests that three ways of democratizing bureaucracy have been identified:

- The 'representative bureaucracy' view that 'a system is more democratic when the socio-economic and ethnic backgrounds of top government officials resemble those of the nation as a whole' (pp. 163–4). This is a view that has been explored in influential studies of the social composition of the civil service (see Kingsley, 1944; Aberbach et al., 1981).
- The 'pluralistic approach', with 'democracy in public decision-making ... guaranteed by the absence of centralized political authority'. Officials have to take part in 'bargaining and negotiation, partisan mutual adjustment with a variety of groups' (Page, p. 164). (This is a view central to pluralist theory – see Truman, 1958; Dahl, 1961; Bentley, 1967 – and to the more complacent view of 'incrementalism' as stated in the early work of Lindblom, 1959, 1965, and Braybrooke and Lindblom, 1963.)
- The 'institutional' view, in which 'democratic "control" exists to the extent that representative institutions participate in policy-making' (Page, p. 164). This perspective focuses attention upon the mechanisms that link politicians with the administration. It has perhaps been the dominant perspective in British studies of public administration (see, for example, Hennessy, 1989) and is found as a central concern of a variety of American studies that explore the influence of the President and Congress (see, for example, Cater, 1964; Cronin, 1980; Nathan, 1983).

It will be evident from various words in the extract from Page that his concern is with activities involving the 'top' of bureaucracy and 'policy formation'. He is reviewing a considerable literature that has been concerned with the extent to which public officials may be seen as a 'power elite' who may undermine democratic control over policy formation. But we can usefully take our lead from his taxonomy inasmuch as the issues about implementation are closely related to these. The third of Page's categories is what may be seen as the dominant or taken-for-granted view, until the careful examination of implementation in the modern age, that the top policy formers (even if they include senior civil servants) *should* 'control' the implementation process. However, we do find – in various forms and varying in importance from country to country – echoes of the other two categories in models of control over policy implementation. The first is seen in models of implementation in which there is a high concern about grass-roots participation, and in a curious way pre-democratic models of local implementation often embodied a version of this ideal. This can be seen, for instance, in the role given to appointed magistrates in English local administration. The second model, which is particularly important in American discussions of democracy, has also had an impact upon the way implementation processes are conceptualized in the United States.

It is generally correct to say that large-scale government and democracy have evolved side by side. However, there have been differences between countries in the rates of growth of these two phenomena, and of course in the actual forms either large-scale governmental organization or democracy has taken. Two nations in the Western world are often contrasted in these respects: Germany, where complex governmental institutions were developed before democracy; and the United States, where democracy developed at a time when government activities were still very limited in scale. Other nations may be seen as somewhere between these two extremes.

There is a sense therefore in which, while a key German preoccupation has been how to inject democratic control into the management of government, the American concern has been how to develop efficient government despite democracy. That contrast, at least as viewed from the American side, is brought out very clearly in Woodrow Wilson's famous essay that attempts to draw a distinction between politics and administration (1887). Wilson saw the need to reform American administration; he belonged to a school of political theorists and activists who saw political interference in the minutiae of administration as a source of inefficiency and corruption. He argued:

> The field of administration is a field of business. It is removed from the hurry and strife of politics; it at most points stands apart even from the debatable ground of constitutional study. It is a part of political life only as the methods of the counting-house are part of the life of society; only as machinery is part of the manufactured product. (Reprinted in Woll, 1966: 28)

Yet he ended that paragraph:

> But it is, at the same time, raised very far above the dull level of mere technical detail by the fact that through its greater principles it is directly connected with the lasting maxims of political wisdom, the permanent truths of political progress.

Hence Wilson is trying to find an ideal path between his admiration of the efficiency of Prussian administration and his hostility to the political environment in which that was developed:

> ... Prussia's particular system of administration would quite suffocate us. It is better to be untrained and free than to be servile and systematic. Still there is no denying that it would be better yet to be free in spirit and proficient in practice. (p. 26)

Some years after Wilson's essay, Max Weber, in his writings on German politics (see particularly his 'Politics as a Vocation' in Gerth and Mills, 1947: 77–128), addressed some of the same issues. He saw the need to stimulate a lively 'politics' in Germany to give a sense of a democratic direction to an administration that would otherwise just go its own way. On the other hand he regarded German bureaucrats as impersonal and objective servants of the state and was fearful of demagoguery and of the emergence of a class of politicians who would be, like their American counterparts, living *off* politics rather than *for* politics.

Wilson was an early example of an important group of writers on American politics engaged in a quest for greater rationality in government (see, *inter alia*, Dewey, 1927, 1935; Simon, 1945). His idea that there should be a clear split between politics and administration is echoed in much modern work that is concerned about the subversion of the goals of top-level decision makers – the President, Congress, the executive, the federal government, and so on – in the implementation process. He was both identifying an important problem regarding administrative accountability and recognizing that the United States faced a set of institutional arrangements that made political problem solving very difficult. It took another ninety or so years after Wilson had struggled with this issue for American political scientists to lay the foundations of implementation studies. Between the 1880s and the 1970s in many walks of life – most of all in the organization of production – a rational model of implementation had come to be seen as essential to national achievement. This influence upon the development of implementation studies is explored further in Chapter 5.

There is a strange contradiction within American politics that despite a set of institutional arrangements that very often render them impotent, politicians stress their capacity to do anything they want and express their commitment to rational problem solving both in statements about what they will do and in their appointments of a multitude of rationally oriented experts (note here the enormous importance of think tanks, policy research, and so on, see Heinemann et al., 1990).

Woodrow Wilson's rationalism has attracted a great deal of criticism.[1] The alternative view on his politics/administration dichotomy is that this is a distinction that bears little relation to the reality of political and administrative behaviour. When this view is advanced with particular reference to the United States, two approaches to the original determination of the political and institutional structure of that society are invoked. One of these is what is described as the Madisonian insistence on the division of powers:

> Fearful of the oppressive potential of centralized power, the Founding Fathers devised a political system to prevent factions from overrunning minorities that makes such collective action nearly impossible. The separation of powers, the federalist structure of government, and the different constituencies of elected officials served to institutionalize a system of checks and balances designed to guard against the worst abuses of power. While this system has been fairly successful in stymieing serious threats to democratic rule, it has also been the source of institutional incapacity. (Ferman, 1990: 40)

The other approach is associated with another significant figure in the early history of the United States, Andrew Jackson. He was President between 1829 and 1837 and is seen as a key figure in the development of the spoils system, under which there are very considerable opportunities for a successful politician to introduce his or her supporters into a wide range of public offices. While this system has been much curbed since the mid-nineteenth century, through the efforts of people who shared Woodrow Wilson's disapproval of it, it remains as a way in which politics may be infused into administration.

What is important about Woodrow Wilson's perspective, shared with many other 'progressives' in the United States (Waldo, 1948), is the way his ideal division influenced thinking about the management of government, and thus about implementation, in the United States and elsewhere. The main burden of his critics is that his aspirations were unrealistic, in the face of deeply embedded institutional arrangements. His response to that comment might be to agree that the difficulties in achieving administrative reform would be considerable, but to argue that is not a reason not to try. In that sense he, and those many who have followed his lead, asserts the desirability of top-down politically inspired domination.

A very different line of criticism, then, is to suggest that there are different approaches to accountability that may be either more practical or superior (or both). These involve, to go back to the other approaches identified by Page, either pluralism (Madisonian democracy) or representative bureaucracy (Jacksonian democracy). Again, Wilson would doubtless argue that these were democratic mechanisms designed for an age when the activities of government were simpler. Hence those who adopt versions of these approaches need to advance ways of dealing with the problem of accountability that take into account organizational complexity. In many ways the dominant view until very recently has been to accept the case for top-down – organizational – accountability. Alternatives have only begun to emerge with an increased awareness of organizational inefficiency. This is a theme to which we will return in Chapter 8.

Institutional theory

The issues explored at the end of the previous section raise questions about the extent to which implementation processes need to be placed in their constitutional and institutional contexts. This is a theme by no means neglected by mainstream implementation theorists, whose work will be examined in the next two chapters. (That is particularly true of some of the more recent contributors to the literature, whose work will be considered in Chapter 4.) However, a body of theory about the impact of institutions upon the policy process developed during the last decades of the twentieth century can be seen as having a distinct impact upon thinking about implementation.

That body of theory has manifestations within other disciplines as well as political science. In economics an institutional perspective developed that challenged the relatively context-free way in which classical economics analysed market relationships, pointing out the importance of seeing these exchanges within structures with their own rules and expected practices (Coase, 1937; Williamson, 1975). But it was within sociology that a concern developed about the impact of institutions that is particularly pertinent for the study of implementation. In some respects institutional analysis is fundamental for the discipline of sociology, raising questions about the extent to which human actions are structurally determined. It is then given an emphasis that is particularly important for organizational activities, and thus clearly important for the analysis of implementation.

A distinction is made, in much of this sociological work, between 'organizations' and 'institutions'. A key influence here is the work of Selznick, who argues:

> The term 'organization' ... suggests a certain bareness, a lean no-nonsense system of consciously coordinated activities. It refers to an expendable tool, a rational instrument engineered to do a job. An 'institution', on the other hand, is more nearly a natural product of social needs and pressures – a responsive adaptive organism. (1957: 5)

This distinction emphasizes the social world within which organizations have been created, drawing attention both to the impact of the external environment and to the way people bring needs and affiliations into organizations that shape the informal social systems that develop there. Selznick explains this perspective very clearly in his classic study of one of Franklin Roosevelt's important policy initiatives, *TVA and the Grass Roots* (1949):

> All formal organizations are moulded by forces tangential to their rationally ordered structures and stated goals. Every formal organization – trade union, political party, army, corporation etcetera. – attempts to mobilize human and technical resources as means for the achievement of its ends. However, the individuals within the system tend to resist being treated as means. They interact as wholes, bringing to bear their own special problems and purposes; moreover the organization is embedded in an institutional matrix and is therefore subject to pressure upon it from its environment, to which some general adjustment must be made. As a result, the organization may be significantly viewed as an adaptive social structure, facing problems which arise simply because it exists as an organization in an institutional environment, independently of the special (economic, military, political) goals which called it into being. (p. 251)

Whilst later sociologists have seen Selznick's approach as too deterministic, the general thrust of his argument remains pertinent. Later work has emphasized the need to see institutions as 'cultural rules' (Meyer and

Rowan, 1977) and to identify the way in which 'structural isomorphism' occurs so that organizations working in similar 'fields' tend to develop similar characteristics (DiMaggio and Powell, 1983). W.R. Scott has played a key role in developing institutional theory in a systematic way, writing about three 'pillars' of institutions:

- regulative, resting upon 'expedience' inasmuch as people recognize the coercive power of rule systems
- normative, resting upon social obligations
- cognitive, depending upon taken-for-granted cultural assumptions. (1995: 35)

This sociological work attacks the issues about policy implementation from a rather different direction to that of the political scientists. It is concerned with questions not about how public policy develops but about how organizations work, including, therefore (as, for example, in the case of the Tennessee Valley Authority), what happens within organizations with responsibilities for the implementation of public policy. Not surprisingly, therefore, this work has something to say about why organizations may be unreceptive to efforts to change their practices and why they may not collaborate very well with each other (see Aldrich, 1976; Benson, 1982). Similarly, individuals whom we will find very important for the study of implementation, namely street-level bureaucrats (see the discussion of the work of Michael Lipsky, Chapter 3, pp. 51–3), have also been the focus of attention among organizational sociologists exploring issues about compliance within organizations (see particularly key contributions by Gouldner, 1954; Merton, 1957; Etzioni, 1961).

Within political science, institutions tend often to be taken for granted (as organizations). That is evident in the traditional emphasis upon the prerogatives of those who formulate policy and in the concerns about the 'rule of law'. In the period when behaviourist approaches to political analysis were dominant there was some tendency to lose sight of the importance of institutional structures. But then a group of theorists emerged who combined the older concern about structures with a recognition, influenced by the institutional school in sociology, that questions had to be raised about how institutions work in practice. Of particular importance here is the work of James March and Johan Olsen (1984, 1989, 1996). March and Olsen explain their view of the importance of the institutional approach as follows:

Political democracy depends not only on economic and social conditions but also on the design of political institutions. The bureaucratic agency, the legislative committee, and the appellate court are arenas for contending social forces, but they are also collections of standard operating procedures and structures that define and defend interests. They are political actors in their own right. (1984: 738)

Similar points are made by others of the institutionalist school of thought (see, for example, Hall, 1986). Such observations suggest that an examination of a policy process – and accordingly of an implementation process – needs to be seen as occurring in organized contexts where there are established norms, values, relationships, power structures and 'standard operating procedures'. Those structures may be handled in systematic work on implementation as independent variables, influencing outputs and outcomes of implementation as dependent variables. However, much of the work in the institutionalist tradition is also concerned to look at how those structures were formed and to elucidate the extent to which they impose explicit constraints and the circumstances in which they are subject to change. The revision or reinterpretation of the rules ('meta-policy making') is important. In that sense there is here a set of issues about the implementation of meta-policy – about the issues entailed in changing structures and about the implications of structural changes for substantive policy changes (see Dror, 1986; Hupe, 1990).

There are also issues (particularly examined in the institutionalist work of Skocpol, 1995) about the extent to which a policy change at one point in time creates institutions that may serve as a barrier to change at a later point. As March and Olsen say: 'Programs adopted as a simple political compromise by a legislature become endowed with separate meaning and force by having an agency established to deal with them' (1984: 739 – drawing here upon Skocpol and Finegold, 1982).

But the focus here should not simply be upon the institutions of government. Rothstein suggests, from a study of the development of Swedish labour market policy that examines the way trades union interests were built into the policy process, that '[i]n some, albeit probably rare, historical cases, people actually create the very institutional circumstances under which their own as well as others' future behavior will take place' (1992: 52). Similarly, analyses of health policy have been concerned to look at the way decisions about the structuring of health services put doctors in a position in which their future collaboration would be important for the implementation of new policies (Alford, 1975; Ham, 1992).

Clearly this institutional approach to the study of the policy process involves interpretation. It does not suggest that outcomes can be easily 'read off' from constitutional or institutional contexts. Immergut sets this out in a games analogy as follows: 'Institutions do not allow one to predict policy outcomes. But by establishing the rules of the game, they enable one to predict the ways in which policy conflicts will be played out' (1992: 63). What is significant about that sort of remark is the suggestion that institutional analysis may lay so strong an emphasis upon specific configurations of institutional situations and actors that all it can offer is an account of past events, from which little generalization is possible. This is the direction some of the things March and Olsen had to say about the institutional approach seem to be leading:

[T]he new institutionalism is probably better viewed as a search for alternative ideas that simplify the subtleties of empirical wisdom in a theoretically
useful way.

The institutionalism we have considered is neither a theory nor a coherent
critique of one. It is simply an argument that the organization of political life
makes a difference. (1984: 747)

Going even further down this problematical path, March and Olsen
have given us, from their earlier work with Cohen, a memorable expression to typify an extreme version of the institutional approach: 'the
garbage can model'. They say, in a later reference to their own idea,
almost as if distancing themselves from it:

In the form most commonly discussed in the literature, the garbage-can
model assumes that problems, solutions, decision-makers, and choice opportunities are independent, exogenous streams flowing through a system
(Cohen, March and Olsen, 1972). They come together in a manner determined
by their arrival times. Thus, solutions are linked to problems primarily by
their simultaneity, relatively few problems are solved, and choices are made
for the most part either before any problems are connected to them (oversight) or after the problems have abandoned one choice to associate themselves with another (flight). (March and Olsen, 1984: 746; see also March and
Olsen, 1989)

Such a perspective suggests a policy process in which policy formation cannot be distinguished from implementation (a theme that will
certainly be explored further in later chapters). But what it also suggests
is that the policy process is merely a flow of reactions to events and the
reactions of other actors. Kingdon (1984) has picked up this theme in
comparing the policy process to chance events in the early history of
evolution, with policy ideas floating around as in 'primeval soup'. In
going down that road any attempt to generalize is likely to be left
behind. Researchers on the policy process are being required to take a
position like a purist atheoretical historian, determined to let the facts
speak for themselves without any principles to help organize attention
or lessons to draw from the study. Accounts of events will be stories –
told as accurately as is feasible (though that feasibility itself is a topic of
some dispute amongst historiographers and other social science
methodologists). It will offer a strong emphasis upon unique situations,
dealing with the inspiration of key figures or with chance reactions to
events.

Clearly the extreme position described in the last few paragraphs is not
typical of the institutional school, but much institutional analysis of the
policy process has pushed it in an intuitive and interpretative direction.
There are others who are prepared to take that position further; their
perspective is examined in the next section.

Postmodernist theory

'Postmodernism' has become a term frequently employed. Though more often it is linked with architecture or literature, the term is even used in relation to public administration. The distinction between 'postmodern' and 'postmodernist' is important. With the first term reference is made to contemporary phenomena, like the widespread use of electronic communication in a 'global village', the rise of multi-national conglomerates in the mass media industry, or the birth of so-called 'bourgeois bohemians' as a new cultural elite (Brooks, 2000). While some of *what* we observe is very 'up to date' and therefore can be called 'postmodern', the qualification 'postmodernist' refers to a certain, particularly artistic, *way* of approaching reality. An example of the latter is presenting a regular *pissoir* as a work of art and exhibiting it as such in a museum, as Marcel Duchamp did. Characteristic of this way of looking is especially a casual breaking away from the norms and conventions seen as standard hitherto. A cultivation of eclecticism as 'anything goes' deliberately replaces the distinction between what is seen as 'done' and 'not done'; between 'high' and 'low' culture.

How, then, are both these terms used in public administration? First, the term 'postmodern' is applied with an eye on what is contemporary. Clegg (1990), for instance, gives his book on modern organizations the subtitle 'organization studies in the postmodern world'. Zuurmond (1994), describing the ways in which new information technology transforms working procedures in municipal social services departments, speaks of the rise of an 'infocracy'. On the other hand Lash (1988), for instance, speaks of 'postmodernism as a regime of signification', and Frissen (1999) calls his book on politics, governance and technology 'a postmodern narrative on the virtual state'. In fact, given the substance of this narrative, it could rather have been called 'postmodernist'.

Essentially two dimensions are relevant here: a scientific and a normative, or political, orientation. One can look at postmodern phenomena while having a more positivist epistemological stance, in whatever variant, or a more interpretative/hermeneutic one, also with possible variants (see Chapter 1, pp. 10–11). This scientific stance is independent of the answer to the question of whether or not one actively propagates forms of direct, participative democracy.

A variety of scholarly attention to postmodernity can be observed. In Zuurmond's study of 'infocracy' mentioned above and, for instance, in the study by Pröpper and Steenbeek (1999) of citizens' participation in Dutch policy processes, the analysis is systematic, giving these studies a standard descriptive-analytical character. Both Zuurmond and Pröpper and Steenbeek focus on contemporary phenomena in public administration, using a more or less positivist approach.

In her article on 'the listening bureaucrat' Stivers states: 'The experience of listening involves openness, respect for difference, and reflexivity' (1994: 364). These notions seem to refer directly to the kind of thought and concepts developed by French postmodernist philosophers like Baudrillard (1973, 1981) and Lyotard (1979). It is interesting that Stivers uses the notions as part of a plea for greater participation between public servants and citizens in political-administrative processes: 'Thus public officials can be good listeners (they can be responsive) by encouraging citizens' responsibility to listen to one another and solve disputes' (p. 368). In their *Postmodern Public Administration* Fox and Miller (1995) have a similar message. This also goes for some of the contributions to *Telling Tales*, which has as a subject 'work done by evaluators at the crossroads of evaluation and narrative' (Abma, 1999: 6). Bevir and Rhodes (2000) show that the use of a 'narrativist' method or approach is not necessarily connected with making an explicit plea for more democratic participation 'from the bottom'.

An author like Yanow (1993, 1996) is interested in a critical exposure of the values and language of administrators. Van Twist (1994) also focuses onthat language, while he approaches the study of public administration as an art; more specifically, an art of telling convincing stories. Between what happens in the material world, and on the level of words, language and stories, there are connections, but for analysts of public administration it all comes down to aiming at 'verbal renewal'. In contrast to Yanow's, Van Twist's perspective on public administration, generally supportive of the status quo, seems that of a consultant.

Although authors like Zuurmond, Pröpper and Steenbeek, Van Twist, Yanow and Stivers have their attention for *The Postmodern Condition* in common, they differ as far as the nature of their specific attention is concerned. This is shown in Table 2.1.

TABLE 2.1 *Scholarly attention to the 'postmodern condition'*

	Epistemological stance	
Stance on democracy	Positivist	Interpretative
Neutral	'Infocracy'	'Verbal renewal'
Deliberative	'Interactive policy	'The listening
democracy	making'	bureaucrat'

In their attention to contemporary phenomena in public administration, the contributions in the left column may be called 'postmodern'. As far as the interpretativist contributions referred to in the right column entail a change in the way in which public administration is usually approached and studied, they can be called 'postmodernist'. This change particularly concerns the view that systematic testing of ideas is irrelevant. The differentiation made is important, because interpretativism and postmodernism cannot be equated. Aiming at 'telling stories', postmodernist scholars generally are interpretativists. On the contrary, however, not all interpretativist scholars are postmodernists. Different from the latter, mainstream interpretativists remain adherent to the standard norms of social science, particularly as far as methodology is concerned (for example, Roe, 1994).

The kind of contributions presented have functions for our subject matter. First, they direct scholarly interest to phenomena that are highly contemporary and therefore justify attention. Second, although most of these studies are not highlighting the nuts and bolts of implementation in the narrow sense, they broaden the conceptual perspective on public policy making in general.

Conclusions

The discussion at the beginning of this chapter suggested that there have been concerns to secure successful implementation ever since people sought to co-opt the efforts of others to undertake complex tasks. But to acknowledge that is simply to say that the analysis of implementation is the analysis of human organization under another name. There are merits in taking that view, and in not seeking to construct a separate intellectual activity alongside organizational sociology. It certainly reminds us of the need to recognize the many ways in which implementation is studied without that word being used. This has led this chapter in two different directions. One of these involved the examination of two themes that provide very important contexts for the study of public policy implementation: concerns that activities of governments should be in conformity with the rule of law and ideas about democratic control over those activities. The other direction was to stress how the exploration of aspects of human organization – particularly in the literature on institutions – has led to work that throws light upon implementation processes carried out by scholars – many of them sociologists – uninterested in and indeed sometimes unaware of the implementation literature. Issues about implementation were the subject of extensive debate and scholarly activity long before anyone wrote about 'implementation studies' *per se*. There is a literature that both precedes and parallels the modern work on implementation.

Issues about the rule of law and about democracy have, however, been particularly significant preoccupations in modern discourse about government and politics. But of course that discourse has to be put in context with other issues about 'modernity', particularly the concerns about the size, scope and complexity of human activities in modern societies and about the aspirations of the state to influence and control those activities. In that sense we must also site the roots of the contemporary concerns about implementation in the extent to which public policies are being developed that are very often difficult to translate into action.[2]

In observing government efforts, we can observe the growth of complex activities on which governments have been reluctant to be extravagant and which have been the subject of substantial resistance by powerful groups. This is particularly true of social policy, the area (outside of defence policy) where twentieth-century growth was most significant. In other words: what characterizes public policy development is a level of complexity never attempted before. Where implementation deficit would have been tolerated in low-level activities, which the central state was happy to delegate to local implementers and leave them to go their own ways most of the time, it could not do so where it had made central commitments or even political mandates to achieve new social goals (compare poor law administration with modern social security, health care and social care programmes).

In Chapter 5 we will explore further the way in which concerns of the kind outlined above contributed to the development of implementation studies. It will then be shown how new models of governance – developed after the 1970s – have reshaped the agenda.

Notes

1   It is perhaps not irrelevant that he became an American President and the dominant figure in the post-First World War settlement in Europe, which gave rise to a set of institutional divisions along alleged national 'self-determination' lines that people are still fighting about.

2   That statement is as true of war as of peace, and it must be noted in passing that there is a literature about the art and science of war that stands quite apart from the literature about public administration. What characterizes war is an enormous extravagance in the use of people and materials so that implementation inefficiencies are compensated by the amount of effort going in ('overkill' – often in the literal sense). It is also probably often the case that the high level of goal consensus means that levels of efforts to frustrate policy implementation are much lower (except of course those of the enemy).

3

Implementation Theory:

The Top-down/Bottom-up Debate

CONTENTS

The discovery of the 'missing link'

The previous chapter challenged the view that implementation studies started in the 1970s when Erwin Hargrove (1975) wrote of the 'missing link' in the study of the policy process and Jeffrey Pressman and Aaron Wildavsky wrote a highly influential book with the main title of *Implementation* (1973). Nevertheless it is clear that a distinct approach to the study of implementation did emerge at that time. Efforts to develop government interventions to address social problems of various kinds were rapidly increasing, and there was awareness that these interventions were often ineffective. This was a period in which there was a substantial growth in studies that were concerned to evaluate policy (see Rist, 1995). In the course of this activity it became recognized that it might be problematical, in evaluation studies, to treat the administrative process between 'policy formation' and 'policy outcomes' as a 'black box' irrelevant to the latter (as in policy analysis models such as that developed by Easton, 1965).

The often quoted sub-title of Pressman and Wildavsky's book expresses this new concern perfectly: 'How Great Expectations in

Washington are Dashed in Oakland; or Why It's Amazing that Federal Programs Work At All, This Being a Saga of the Economic Development Administration as told by Two Sympathetic Observers who Seek to Build Morals on a Foundation of Ruined Hopes.' There is an expression here of the translation of the frustration felt by many Americans about the failures, or limited successes, of the War on Poverty and Great Society programmes of the late sixties into a concern to look at the implementation process as well as, or even perhaps, rather than, the initial policy process.

The assumption made by the new students of implementation that their subject had been neglected can be challenged. This was the central argument in the previous chapter. To some extent it was merely the case that political scientists began to use a new concept 'implementation' in policy analysis and administrative studies. Nevertheless it is perhaps true that until the end of the 1960s there had been a tendency to take it for granted that political mandates were clear and that administrators would do what their political bosses demanded of them. In formal statements of constitutional law, implementers, like civil servants, have often been entirely ignored. Furthermore the neglect of the examination of administrative processes can be partly attributed to the difficulties involved in looking into the 'black box', after parliamentary processes, particularly in a secretive administrative culture like the British one. We will also find at least one implementation theorist (Hjern, see pp. 53–5) who suggests that implementation studies should be seen as distinctly different from studies of public administration (though in doing so he consigns to the 'public administration' category many of those whose work will be discussed here).

In this chapter and the next one we will look at the implementation literature that has emerged since the early 1970s, by highlighting the contributions of some of the key scholars. This analysis would become tediously repetitive if we were to try to do justice to the work of everyone who had something to say on this subject. Though the choice of whose work to highlight is necessarily, to a certain extent, an arbitrary one, here it is influenced by our view of who had something rather different to say as the debate between implementation scholars emerged. We have left out some figures who undoubtedly made important contributions during the development of the debate (notably Williams, 1971, 1980; Derthick, 1972; Hargrove, 1975, 1983; Berman, 1978; Dunsire, 1978a, 1978b). In emphasizing what we see as the main contributions, we will try to ensure that other significant but rather similar efforts are at least referenced.

In providing this account of the literature we have inevitably been influenced by our views of what are the key issues when implementation is studied now and by some of the concerns we want to explore in the rest of the book. In presenting the various key contributions we will highlight the way they approach what we see as the main problems regarding the study of implementation. These particularly concern the issues about the relationship between policy formation and its implementation, which were discussed in Chapter 1 (see pp. 8–9). This took the form of a lively debate, in the early years of implementation studies, that has been described as one between the 'top-down' and the 'bottom-up' perspectives. This chapter will highlight the work of the major exponents of these two positions. Then the next chapter will look at the contributions of scholars who have sought to synthesize the two perspectives or to move away from that debate. We present these two chapters as brief accounts of key authors, in broadly chronological order. While we highlight key issues in their arguments and point out ways in which they differ from each other, we do not aim to provide a critical commentary. Clearly those very familiar with the literature, or eager to move on to our more substantive recommendations, may want to skip these chapters. However, it seems to us that it is appropriate to give readers a general map of the literature at this stage.

While the top-down/bottom-up debate was heavily influenced by the question of how to separate implementation from policy formation, that was only part of a wider problem about how to identify the features of a very complex process, occurring across time and space, and involving multiple actors. It will be seen that writers on implementation vary in the way they respond to that complexity. In the social sciences methodological questions about how to handle complexity have preoccupied many theorists. We have no intention of trying to review the various approaches to those questions here, but simply need to recognize that similar alternative approaches occur in the implementation literature. We find that some writers have been eager to reduce the number of variables to be given attention to a limited number seen as critical, whilst others have built models that try to take into account all identifiable variables. The difficulties with either of these approaches have influenced an alternative view that systematization and generalization are impossible and that the only approach possible is to provide an accurate account of specific implementation processes.

Clearly the last group of scholars offer a reminder that those who seek to try to develop a general theory of implementation are in a sense, if we look for synonyms for 'implementation', trying to develop a theory of 'doing' or 'a theory of action'. This is so even if we are unwilling to go in the atheoretical 'postmodern' direction to which these authors are pointing us. For that reason there is a need to ask whether there are certain limiting conditions within which specific approaches to the study of implementation will be applicable. We have in mind here two considerations of this kind, which we will find many of the implementation theorists struggling with:

- variations between policy issues, or types of policy issues; and
- variations between institutional contexts, which may include questions about the extent to which generalizations apply outside specific political systems or national contexts.

The classical top-down writers

Jeffrey Pressman and Aaron Wildavsky: the founding fathers

As indicated above, the American scholars Jeffrey Pressman and Aaron Wildavsky (1984; 1st edn 1973) tend to be celebrated as the 'founding fathers' of implementation studies (see, for example, Goggin et al., 1990; Parsons, 1995; Ryan, 1995a). Notwithstanding some backing away from that perspective by Wildavsky in a second edition produced after Pressman's death (see the comment below), the overall approach of their book places them quite explicitly with the other authors whom we will typify here as 'top-down' in approach. Their book's subtitle, quoted above, surely indicates that.

As we showed in Chapter 1, for Pressman and Wildavsky, implementation is clearly defined in terms of a relationship to policy as laid down in official documents. They say, 'A verb like "implement" must have an object like "policy"', and go on: 'policies normally contain both goals and the means for achieving them' (Preface to the first edition, reprinted in the third edition, 1984: xxi). Much of the analysis in their book, a study of a federally mandated programme of economic development in Oakland, California, is concerned with the extent to which successful implementation depends upon linkages between different organizations and departments at the local level. They argue that if action depends upon a number of links in an implementation chain, then the degree of co-operation between agencies required to make those links has to be very close to a hundred per cent if a situation is not to occur in which a number of small deficits cumulatively create a large shortfall. They thus introduce the idea of 'implementation deficit' and suggest that implementation may be analysed mathematically in this way.

This particular formulation has been seen as responsible for a pessimistic tone in much implementation literature, since it suggests that purposive action will be very difficult to achieve wherever there are multiple actors. Bowen (1982) points out that such a formulation disregards the extent to which the interactions between these actors occur in contexts in which they rarely concern simply 'one-off' affairs; rather, these interactions are repeated and accompanied by others. Hence it is perhaps more appropriate to use game theory rather than probability theory to analyse them. In which case it can be seen that collaboration becomes much more likely and that recommendations can be made about ways to strengthen that possibility.

Pressman and Wildavsky's original work takes very much a 'rational model' approach: policy sets goals; implementation research is concerned with considering what then makes the achievement of those goals difficult. However, by the second edition (as indicated above), Wildavsky had begun to have doubts about that model. It is of more than biographical interest to note that Wildavsky's new collaborator, with whom he wrote a new last chapter called 'Implementation as Evolution', was an Italian, Giandomenico Majone. It seems reasonable to assume that experience of the contrast between rigid law making and flexible implementation in the Italian administrative system would lead to scepticism about the 'rational model'. The title of that new chapter indicates its alternative view, seeing the relationship between policy formation and implementation as an interactive process. The chapters added in the 1983 edition reflect Wildavsky's further elaboration of that alternative view. As we showed in our Introduction, in those chapters implementation is approached in terms of learning, adaptation and exploration.

Donald Van Meter and Carl Van Horn: system building

The contribution to the literature by the American scholars Donald Van Meter and Carl Van Horn consists in moving forward from the more general approach of Pressman and Wildavsky to offer a model for the analysis of the implementation process (1975). They refer to Pressman and Wildavsky's work alongside a variety of other empirical studies (particularly Kaufman, 1960; Bailey and Mosher, 1968; Derthick, 1970, 1972; Berke et al., 1972). But they argue that '[w]hile these studies have been highly informative, their contributions have been limited by the absence of a theoretical perspective' (Van Meter and Van Horn, 1975: 451).

In developing their theoretical framework Van Meter and Van Horn describe themselves as having been 'guided by three bodies of literature' (1975: 453):

- organization theory, and particularly work on organizational change – here they recognize the importance of the concerns about organizational control in sociological work influenced by Max Weber, including Crozier's classic French study of bureaucratic resistance to change (1964) and Etzioni's analysis of forms of compliance (1961);
- studies of the impact of public policy and particularly of the impact of judicial decisions, such as Dolbeare and Hammond's study of the factors that influenced responses to US Supreme Court rulings on school prayers (1971); and
- some studies of inter-governmental relations, in particular the work of Derthick (1970, 1972) and, of course, Pressman and Wildavsky.

Van Meter and Van Horn's presentation of their theoretical perspective starts with a consideration of the need to classify policies in terms that will throw light upon implementation difficulties. Their approach is comparatively simple. They suggest that there is a need to take into account the amount of change required and the level of consensus. Hence they hypothesize that 'implementation will be most successful where only marginal change is required and goal consensus is high' (1975: 461). They present this, however, in terms of an interrelationship, suggesting, for example, that high consensus may make high change possible, as in a wartime situation. We will see that a number of subsequent theorists have tried to get beyond these very basic propositions about the characteristics of policy, though with only limited success.

Van Meter and Van Horn go on to suggest a model in which six variables are linked dynamically to the production of an outcome 'performance'. The model is set out in Figure 3.1 below. They clearly see implementation as a process that starts from an initial policy decision: '[p]olicy implementation encompasses those actions by public and private individuals (or groups) that are directed at the achievement of objectives set forth in prior policy decisions (p. 447). That process is presented as going through a series of stages, with the arrows in Figure 3.1 pointing forward or sideways and not back to the policy. Accordingly Van Meter and Van Horn argue that 'it is vital that the study of implementation be conducted longitudinally; relationships identified at one point in time must not be extended causally to other time periods' (p. 474). Hence theirs is clearly a 'top-down' approach. Nevertheless, when they stress concerns about consensus and compliance they recognize the importance for these of participation in the policy formation by 'subordinates' (p. 459). The contrast here with some of the bottom-up approaches that we will look at later is that this is participation at a prior policy-formation stage.

The six variables (surely they are in fact clusters of variables) identified in Figure 3.1 are:

- policy standards and objectives, which 'elaborate on the overall goals of the policy decision ... to provide concrete and more specific standards for assessing performance' (p. 464);
- the resources and incentives made available;
- the quality of inter-organizational relationships (we find in their discussion of this, as in so much of the American literature on implementation, an extensive discussion of aspects of federalism);
- the characteristics of the implementation agencies, including issues like organizational control but also, going back surely to inter-organizational issues, 'the agency's formal and informal linkages with the "policy-making" or "policy-enforcing" body ' (p. 471);
- the economic, social and political environment; and
- the 'disposition' or 'response' of the implementers, involving three elements: 'their cognition (comprehension, understanding) of the policy, the direction of their response to it (acceptance, neutrality, rejection) and the intensity of that response' (p. 472).

Van Meter and Van Horn's comparatively straightforward model provided a valuable starting point for a number of studies of implementation processes. Their model aims to direct the attention of those who study

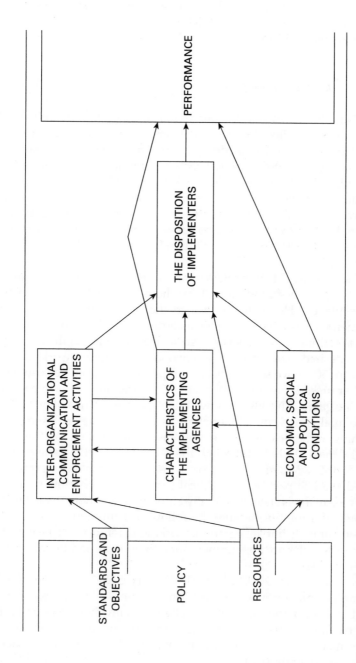

Figure 3.1 A model of the policy-implementation process
Source: Van Meter and Van Horn, 1975: 463

implementation rather than provide prescriptions for policy makers. Two theorists we will examine below, Sabatier and Mazmanian, have much in common with them, but tend to frame their top-down perspective in rather more prescriptive terms. First, however, we look briefly at another writer who was very much concerned to prescribe.

Eugene Bardach: fixing the game

In 1977 another American, Eugene Bardach, wrote an influential book on implementation called *The Implementation Game*, reviewing early contributions to the literature and adding case-study material of his own. In this book we see a top-down perspective embracing recognition of the inevitability of interference with pre-set goals. Hence Bardach provided both ideas that were to influence the top-down writers, who devoted extensive attention to measures to try to protect those goals (people who are discussed in the next two sub-sections), and ammunition for the bottom-up theorists, who were to argue for a rather different approach to goal setting.

Bardach suggests that implementation processes need to be perceived as involving 'games', and he outlines the wide variety of the games that may be played. Hence his advice to the 'top' consists of two sets of recommendations. One of these concerns the need for great care in the 'scenario writing' process, so as to structure the games in the right way to achieve desired outcomes. In Hogwood and Gunn's work, discussed below (pp. 50–1), we see a typical example of advice on scenario writing. The other prescription from Bardach is that attention needs to be given to 'fixing the game'. This involves two related usages in the notion of 'fixing', in colloquial American: as mending (as in 'I had the car fixed') and as something rather close to cheating (as in the notion of 'Mr Fixer'). Crucially these are linked through the celebration, in the early part of the book, of the work of a Californian politician, Frank Lanterman, who devoted the last part of his political career to the promotion of mental health reform in his state. Essentially Lanterman was not satisfied to be the promoter of a reform measure; he followed it through with day-to-day involvement in its implementation, working to remove practical obstacles to change, to influence appointments and to promote additional legislation where necessary.

Hence, we see in Bardach's work the very clear exposition of a view that implementation is a 'political' process, and that 'successful' implementation from a 'top-down' perspective must involve a very full 'follow-through'. In this sense he is critical of the 'wounded' rationalism voiced in Pressman and Wildavsky's apparent anguish about the capacity of Oakland to frustrate Washington.

In a much later work, *Getting Agencies to Work Together* (1998), Bardach returns to the perspective on implementation he developed earlier. Here we see a strong emphasis on the informal, with street-level workers being seen as 'craftsmen', often with a commitment to their work, who must be brought together when collaboration is required, not so much by formal devices as by the encouragement of a shared approach to problem solving.

Paul Sabatier and Daniel Mazmanian: process modelling

The next contribution from the top-down perspective comes from two more American scholars, Paul Sabatier and Daniel Mazmanian. Sabatier has been allowed a 'double dip' in these two chapters, first as a theorist offering a strictly 'top-down' approach in his early work with Daniel Mazmanian (Sabatier and Mazmanian, 1979, 1980; Mazmanian and Sabatier, 1981, 1983) and then backing off from that position a little, at least in methodological terms. Much of this account of their position is based upon Sabatier's own characterization of it in a later work (1986). The starting point for Sabatier and Mazmanian is, as for Van Meter and Van Horn, the expectation of analysing the implementation of a 'top'-level policy decision and then asking:

1. To what extent were the actions of implementing officials and target groups consistent with ... that policy decision?
2. To what extent were the objectives attained over time, i.e. to what extent were the impacts consistent with the objectives?
3. What were the principal factors affecting policy outputs and impacts, both those relevant to the official policy as well as other politically significant ones?
4. How was the policy reformulated over time on the basis of experience? (Sabatier, 1986: 22)

We see here a very clear distinction being made between policy formation and policy implementation, but at the same time a recognition of a feedback process. The phenomena identified in the fourth question would presumably be the starting point for a new implementation study.

The factors impacting upon the implementation process are then seen as falling under three headings:

- factors affecting the 'tractability of the problem';
- 'nonstatutory variables affecting implementation'; and
- the 'ability of the statute to structure implementation' (Sabatier and Mazmanian, 1980: 544).

While it is the last group of factors that are crucial for Sabatier and Mazmanian's advice to those seeking to control the implementation process, it is important to recognize that their approach does not fail to recognize the factors in the other two lists that are likely to make successful implementation difficult. The problem is that it is the interactions between these (which includes variables likely to determine political support) and the efforts to 'structure implementation' that may be crucial for the implementation process.

We see here then both a methodology – involving identifying factors that will cause difficulties and factors that may be controlled – and recommendations to the 'top' about the steps to be taken to try to control implementation. They have a great deal in common with the list produced by the next theorists we will consider.

Brian Hogwood and Lewis Gunn: recommendations for policy makers

The approach to implementation of two British writers Brian Hogwood and Lewis Gunn derives to a large extent from a lecture to civil servants that Gunn published (1978). The pragmatic approach of that work is also reflected in the title of their book in which we see these ideas developed: *Policy Analysis for the Real World* (1984). Hogwood and Gunn defend their 'top- down' view (in a discussion of the alternative perspective of two other British writers to be discussed below, Susan Barrett and Colin Fudge [1981c], on the ground that those who make policy are democratically elected.

It has already been noted that Hogwood and Gunn, like Sabatier and Mazmanian, offer propositions that can be read as recommendations to policy makers. These are that policy makers should ensure:

- that circumstances external to the implementing agency do not impose crippling constraints;
- that adequate time and sufficient resources are made available to the programme;
- that not only are there no constraints in terms of overall resources but also that, at each stage in the implementation process, the required combination of resources is actually available;
- that the policy to be implemented is based upon a valid theory of cause and effect;
- that the relationship between cause and effect is direct and that there are few, if any, intervening links;
- that there is a single implementing agency that need not depend upon other agencies for success, or, if other agencies must be involved, that the dependency relationships are minimal in number and importance;
- that there is complete understanding of, and agreement upon, the objectives to be achieved, and that these conditions persist throughout the implementation process;
- that in moving towards agreed objectives it is possible to specify, in complete detail and perfect sequence, the tasks to be performed by each participant;

- that there is perfect communication among, and co-ordination of, the various elements involved in the programme; and
- that those in authority can demand and obtain perfect obedience (a précis of Hogwood and Gunn, 1984: 199–206).

Just as Sabatier and Mazmanian avoid the charge of naïvety about such an activity by their recognition of factors that are hard to control, Hogwood and Gunn site their propositions in the context of an argument about the unattainability of 'perfect implementation'. The list above sets out the conditions necessary for the realization of that. The concept of 'perfect implementation' derives from the work of Christopher Hood (1976). He suggests:

> One way of analysing implementation problems is to begin by thinking about what 'perfect administration' would be like, comparable to the way in which economists employ the model of perfect competition. Perfect administration could be defined as a condition in which 'external' elements of resource availability and political acceptability combine with 'administration' to produce perfect policy implementation. (p. 6)

Hood goes on to develop an argument about the 'limits of administration' (his book title) that focuses not so much on the political processes that occur within the administrative system as on the inherent limits to control in complex systems. This is similarly the concern of a two-volume contribution to the subject by another British writer, Andrew Dunsire (1978a, 1978b). This approach involves the use of an abstract model of the problems to be faced by persons attempting top-down control over the administrative system. It obviously offers a way to help researchers to identify characteristics of real implementation processes. Like the economic concept from which it is derived, it postulates a model against which to measure reality. Hence, while it, like perfect competition, seems to be a purely analytical concept, in practice it carries the normative connotation that there is an ideal to which we should try to make the real world correspond.

The bottom-up challenge

Michael Lipsky: street-level bureaucracy

Michael Lipsky's analysis of the behaviour of front-line staff in policy delivery agencies, whom he calls 'street-level bureaucrats', has had an important influence upon implementation studies. We present him here as in many respects the founding father of the 'bottom-up' perspective. He first presented his ideas in an article in 1971, interestingly even before his American compatriots Pressman and Wildavsky published their book. Lipsky's influential book, however, was not published until 1980.

Lipsky is widely misrepresented simply as the writer who demonstrates how difficult it is to control the activities of street-level bureaucrats. If that was actually what he had to say, he could merely be seen as someone reinforcing the top-down control-oriented perspective, albeit – along the lines of Sabatier and Mazmanian's 'factors affecting the tractability of the problem' or Hogwood and Gunn's limits to 'perfect implementation' – stressing the difficulties. In those terms he is co-opted in support of the political Right's argument for market solutions to distribution problems, to circumvent the capacity of suppliers to control public monopoly services.

But in fact what Lipsky had to say was rather different, indeed much more subtle. Certainly he argues that 'the decisions of street-level bureaucrats, the routines they establish, and the devices they invent to cope with uncertainties and work pressures, effectively become the public policies they carry out' (1980: xii). But he goes on to say that this process of street-level policy making does not involve the advancement of the ideals many bring to personal service work to the extent that might be hoped; rather, that the process induces practices that enable officials to cope with the pressures they face:

> [p]eople often enter public employment with at least some commitment to service. Yet the very nature of this work prevents them from coming close to the ideal conception of their jobs. Large classes or huge caseloads and inadequate resources combine with the uncertainties of method and the unpredictability of clients to defeat their aspirations as service workers. (p. xii)

Lipsky argues that, therefore, to cope with the pressures upon them, street-level bureaucrats develop methods of processing people in a relatively routine and stereotyped way. They adjust their work habits to reflect lower expectations of themselves and their clients. They

> often spend their work lives in a corrupted world of service. They believe themselves to be doing the best they can under adverse circumstances and they develop techniques to salvage service and decision-making values within the limits imposed upon them by the structure of work. They develop conceptions of their work and of their clients that narrow the gap between their personal and work limitations and the service ideal. (p. xii)

Thus Lipsky handles one of the paradoxes of street-level work. Such workers see themselves as cogs in a system, as oppressed by the bureaucracy within which they work. Yet they often seem to have a great deal of discretionary freedom and autonomy. He speaks of the street-level bureaucrat's role as an 'alienated' one (p. 76), stressing such classic features of alienation as that work is only on 'segments of the product', that there is no control over outcomes, or over 'raw materials' (clients' circumstances),

and that there is no control over the pace of work. Lipsky also emphasizes that street-level bureaucrats face uncertainty about just what personal resources are necessary for their jobs. They find that work situations and outcomes are unpredictable, and they face great pressures of inadequate time in relation to limitless needs. On the whole, control from the top to combat the alleged failures of street-level staff involves the intensification of these pressures.

There is a sense, therefore, in which Lipsky is providing a variant on the Marxist dictum: 'Man makes his own history, even though he does not do so under conditions of his own choosing.' Street-level bureaucrats make choices about the use of scarce resources under pressure; contemporary fiscal pressure upon human services makes it much easier for their managers to emphasize control than to try to put into practice service ideals. In a sense he makes 'heroes' of street-level bureaucrats, because while they are caught in situations that are fundamentally tragic – in the original sense – they still try to make the best of it.

Why regard Lipsky as a key figure for the development of the 'bottom-up' perspective on implementation studies? First, his emphasis on the crucial nature of the street-level bureaucrat role is used by others as a justification for methodological strategies that focus upon that work, rather than upon the policy input. Later we will see this point being developed by Richard Elmore. But, second, and more importantly, he is suggesting that the preoccupation of the top-down perspective with 'how great expectations in Washington are dashed in Oakland' is really beside the point. This is because, for him, the implementation of policy is really about street-level workers with high service ideals exercising discretion under intolerable pressures. Therefore attempts to control them hierarchically simply increase their tendency to stereotype and disregard the needs of their clients. This means that different approaches are needed to secure the accountability of implementers, approaches that feed in the expectations of people at the local level (including above all the citizens whom the policies in question affect). This is an issue that Lipsky addresses in his last chapter. We will see later that it is one that others have tried to address. It is this shift of normative concern away from questions about how those at the top can exert their wills that above all characterizes the 'bottom-up' approach to implementation.

Benny Hjern: implementation structures

Benny Hjern is a Swedish scholar who developed his approach to the study of implementation whilst working on studies of European employment and training programmes at a research institute in Berlin. Whilst we have singled out Hjern here, it is important to recognize that his ideas were developed in close collaboration with others, particularly David Porter, Kenneth Hanf and Chris Hull. Crucial for the development of

Hjern's methodology was the fact that the policies he and his colleagues were studying depended upon interactions between several different organizations. It should be noted that this issue was central to Pressman and Wildavsky's pioneering work, too. We will find it also as a theme in much of the work of those, discussed in the next chapter, who aimed to synthesize the top-down and bottom-up approaches. Note, for example, the work of Elmore and also of Scharpf. The latter was an influence upon Hjern's thinking; the difference between them being that Hjern took Scharpf's emphasis upon the importance of networks in a distinctively 'bottom-up' direction. It is also relevant that at the time Hjern developed his theoretical approach sociological studies of organizations were beginning to come to grips with the fact that the emphasis on formal boundaries of organizations might misleadingly structure the way people actually construct working relationships without necessarily respecting those boundaries (Aldrich, 1976; Benson, 1977).

Hence Hjern and his colleagues saw activities as within 'implementation structures' formed from 'within pools of organizations' and 'formed through processes of consensual self-selection' (Hjern and Porter, 1981: 220). They used a methodology that, whilst starting from an identified pool of relevant organizations, 'snowballed' to collect a sample of respondents who were working together. In this way they constructed empirically the networks within which field-level decision-making actors carried out their activities without predetermining assumptions about the structures within which these occurred.

But Hjern must not simply be seen as a theorist arguing for a bottom-up methodology. In an article reviewing Mazmanian and Sabatier (1981) he argued: 'The aim of the exercise for Mazmanian and Sabatier is to help federal and state politicians to better control public administration. This is not perforce to ensure effective implementation' (1982: 304). Is Hjern suggesting here that there is a definition of 'effective' implementation that can be independent of any issue about control, or is he just challenging the top-down approach to the latter? He goes on to argue that traditional implementation work of that kind is trapped 'in the public administration notion of stable and sequential relationships between politics and administration'. Hjern and Hull argue that this work involves 'policy output analysis' (1982: 107) and that the effective study of implementation must be 'organization-theory inclined' in a way that does not privilege any specific actor or set of actors.

This is more than an argument about methodology. Hjern and Hull go on to argue that:

> Once we are clear about who participates how and with what effect in policy processes, then we can begin to think about how politics and administration could and should be (re-)combined in the policy process. In this sense implementation research continues political science's long tradition of constitutional analysis – and as empirical constitutionalism can hopefully fructify that tradition. (p. 114)

Here Hjern and Hull suggest that implementation research can tackle the issues raised by Lipsky when he, at the end of his book, raised questions about new mechanisms of accountability linking street-level bureaucrats and the public. Unfortunately they left the issue there, promising some new work dealing with the philosophical issues about public accountability that has not yet materialized. It leaves as the core of their contribution the challenging of the ' "single-authority, top-down" approach to political organization' (p. 107).

Susan Barrett and Colin Fudge: policy and action

Susan Barrett and Colin Fudge, two British scholars who entered into the debate in the early 1980s, strongly commend Hjern's 'implementation structure' approach. In their discussion they, like Hjern and his associates, draw upon developments in organization theory that involved challenging hierarchical perspectives on the way organizations work. They particularly emphasize the notion that much action depends upon compromises between people in various parts of single organizations, or related organizations. One organization theorist whose work they find particularly pertinent is Anselm Strauss. Barrett and Fudge make use of his notion of 'negotiated order'. Quoting Strauss that 'wherever there are social orders, there are not only negotiated orders but also coerced orders, manipulated orders and the like' (1978: 262), they go on to pose the following questions:

> First, why, in what circumstances, and with what assumptions are the various modes of action utilized? Second, is there a relationship between the utilization of the different modes and the differential power relations between the interacting parties? If there is, what is the nature of that relationship? And third, are there connections between the different modes of action? (Barrett and Fudge, 1981b: 264)

This emphasis upon 'action' in Barrett and Fudge's work is related – as the title of their edited book *Policy and Action* suggests – to policy, with the two seen as linked 'dynamically'. Hence 'policy cannot be regarded as a constant. It is mediated by actors who may be operating with different assumptive worlds from those formulating the policy, and, inevitably, it undergoes interpretation and modification and, in some cases, subversion' (1981b: 251). Elsewhere they indicate, as have others (see Hill, 1997a: 8–9), that policy is a problematic concept, offering the interesting suggestion that one way of looking at policy is as 'property'. Different actors may make different claims as to its true features.

This analysis brings Barrett and Fudge to a distinct position on the normative assumptions embedded in the traditional 'top-down' literature. They argue that there is a tendency in the top-down implementation literature to depoliticize the policy–action relationship. Their alternative view emphasizes the continuing political processes occurring throughout implementation. In effect this suggests that it is very difficult to separate implementation from policy formation.

Barrett and Fudge argue that, as, for example, for Pressman and Wildavsky in their original formulation, 'if implementation is defined as putting policy into effect then *compromise* by the policy-makers would be seen as policy failure' (1981b: 258). They then offer a formulation like that provided by Hjern (see pp. 53–5 above) namely, that 'if implementation is seen as "getting something done", then performance rather than conformance is the main objective and compromise a means of achieving it' (p. 258).

We have here then a clear rejection of the normative assumption embedded in the top-down approach. Such a perspective poses problems for methodology. In fact Barrett and Fudge do not address methodological issues, except inasmuch as they endorse Hjern's network analysis approach. However, if it is not possible to separate policy formation from implementation, there is a difficulty in setting the limits for an implementation study. And even more seriously: How can effectiveness be assessed in 'getting something done' or a compromise be judged as achieving something as opposed to throwing away an objective, without reference to at least someone's policy goals?

In some respects Barrett and Fudge must therefore be seen as making a case against the study of implementation *per se,* or as the first of the theorists who reject, in more or less postmodernist terms, the case for more than individual qualitative case-study analysis. In a later section (p. 64) we will find the issues highlighted in the last paragraph featuring as part of Sabatier's argument against the stronger forms of the 'bottom-up' perspective.

Conclusions

As mentioned in the introduction to this chapter, the debate between the top-down and bottom-up perspectives moved on to efforts to synthesize the approaches, picking out key ideas from each. The methodological elements in the debate were not, in themselves, particularly contentious. The same was true of those elements in the debate that concerned the most realistic way to perceive implementation processes. Writers began to argue that mixed approaches might be used or that the right approach might depend upon the issue. The normative debate could not so easily be resolved, embodying as it did alternative stances on democratic accountability; here synthesis depended upon recognizing the legitimacy of complex formulations of this topic. These issues are explored through the examination of writers whom we loosely describe in the next chapter as 'the synthesizers'. All of them, apart from Elmore and Scharpf, made their main contributions later than the scholars considered in this chapter.

4

Implementation Theory:

The Synthesizers

Introduction

The subject of this chapter is the variety of contributions to the implementation theory debate that followed on the initial arguments between the top-down and bottom-up perspectives. Central is the work of a range of scholars who developed approaches building on those original theories, while largely synthesizing them. The chapter will not be subdivided, like the previous one, into 'schools of thought'. Rather it presents the work of these scholars in date order (determined by the dates of their most widely recognized contributions). It will then end with a concluding section, which sums up the arguments in this and the previous chapter.

Key Contributions

Richard Elmore: innovative methodology

Because of his emphasis upon the use of a bottom-up methodology, American scholar Richard Elmore can be seen as a crucial contributor to the bottom-up perspective. Despite the fact that he was a very early contributor to implementation studies, at the same time, however, he must be seen as the first of the synthesizers because of his plea for the use of mixed methods. In his 'Organizational Models of Social Program Implementation' (1978) Elmore takes a cue from an influential decision-making, or policy formation, study of the Cuban missile crisis (Allison, 1971). He suggests that, in the study of complicated events, it can be valuable to triangulate accounts, using different theoretical models, to try to achieve a satisfactory explanation of what happened. He thus contrasts 'implementation as systems management', 'implementation as bureaucratic process', 'implementation as organization development' and 'implementation as conflict and bargaining'.

Elmore stands out amongst the early writers on implementation for his concern to emphasize the issues about how to study implementation rather than to offer rules about how to control implementation. In doing so he picks up from Lipsky's work the need to understand what is happening from the bottom end of a policy system. He takes that much further in his later work on backward mapping, which he developed when undertaking a study of youth employment programmes at the local level in the United States. Elmore defines 'backward mapping' as

> 'backward reasoning' from the individual and organizational choices that are the hub of the problem to which policy is addressed, to the rules, procedures and structures that have the closest proximity to those choices, to the policy instruments available to affect those things, and hence to feasible policy objectives. (1981: 1; see also Elmore, 1980)

Focusing on individual actions as a starting point enables them to be seen as responses to problems or issues in the form of choices between alternatives. It is interesting to note, however, that the 'backward-mapping' approach has been seen by others not only as a methodology for analysis but also as something to be recommended for policy development in practice (Fiorino, 1997). One of Elmore's justifications for the 'backward-mapping' approach derives from a recognition that in many policy areas in the United States implementation actors are forced to make choices between programmes that conflict or interact with each other. It is argued that, by comparison with a top-down methodology, this approach is relatively free of predetermining assumptions. It is less likely to imply assumptions about cause and effect, about hierarchical or any other structural relations between actors and agencies, or about what should be going on between them. In a later essay Elmore (1985) gives a prescriptive twist to his emphasis upon mapping, suggesting that there may be situations in which policy is best left fluid to be formulated more precisely through implementing activities at the street level.

Fritz Scharpf: pioneering network analysis

The concept of networks is used in bottom-up theory (see particularly the work of Hjern) and is very important for many of the attempts to synthesize the different approaches. By the early 1980s, this idea had become very important both for political science and for organizational sociology. While it is in some respects invidious to single out any particular theorist, there is nevertheless one figure who seems particularly important for the introduction of these ideas into the study of implementation. Therefore, following the pattern of attaching significant developments to the identities of specific people, we will interpose a discussion of these important concepts by way of a consideration of the work of an influential German scholar, Fritz Scharpf. It was an essay of his, published as far back as 1978, that particularly emphasized that 'it is unlikely, if not impossible, that public policy of any significance could result from the choice process of any single unified actor. Policy formulation and policy implementation are inevitably the result of interactions among a plurality of separate actors with separate interests, goals and strategies' (1978: 347). Now, while this was in the concluding essay in a book on inter-organizational policy studies, it should be clear from much that has been said in the previous chapter that concerns about how different organizations relate to each other are very central to implementation studies.

The initial remarks in Scharpf's essay are addressed to another issue that is also very salient for implementation studies. He writes of the problems entailed by the divergence of two theoretical perspectives:

> Under the first ('prescriptive') perspective, policy making appears as a purposive activity which calls for evaluation of its results in the light of its goals. In terms of the second ('positive') perspective, policy making is an empirical process which calls for an explanation in terms of its causes and conditions. (p. 346)

We may substitute 'implementation' for 'making' in that quotation. Scharpf goes on to stress the extent to which the prescriptive perspective tends to work with a notion of unitary goals developed by individuals or consensual groups. By contrast the evidence collected from the positive perspective challenges that, while stressing interactions, along the lines set out in the first quote from Scharpf. He goes on to suggest that though, of course, in scientific studies regard to prescriptive concerns is not central, 'public policy making is still the only vehicle available to modern societies for the conscious, purposive solution of their problems' (p. 349). Purpose does matter to the actors involved in the policy process. Hence 'scientific studies' in this field cannot disregard it.

Scharpf's solution to this divergence is to develop an approach to the study of policy formation and implementation processes in which issues about co-ordination and collaboration are given central attention, through the identification of the need for specific types of co-ordination and the examination of the empirical factors 'facilitating or impeding' this. This entails a focus upon the nature of the networks that may be formed, and upon the resource dependencies and exchanges that facilitate the process.

It is not suggested that Scharpf was the originator of the use of network concepts for the explication of policy processes. He was merely pulling together in his 1978 essay some crucial ideas, a number of which had been around for a while in both political science and sociology (see Knoke, 1990; M.J. Smith, 1993; or Klijn, 1997, for reviews of the literature). Martin Smith thus argues that

> [t]he notion of policy networks is a way of coming to terms with the tradi-
> tionally stark state/civil society dichotomy.... State actors are also actors in
> civil society, they live in society and have constant contact with groups which
> represent societal interests. Therefore the interests of state actors develop
> along with the interests of the group actors and the degree of autonomy that
> exists depends on the nature of policy networks. (1993: 67)

Some scholars, particularly in Britain (see Jordan and Richardson, 1987), have explored the extent to which it is possible to identify both a variety of policy networks and stronger variants of this phenomenon, which have been called 'policy communities'. Networks may cohere into communities and communities may disintegrate into networks. There may be some issues where communities are more likely than networks and vice versa.

Kickert et al. say: 'Until recently the concept "policy network" had often been negatively evaluated. It was seen as one of the main reasons for policy failure: non-transparent and impenetrable forms of interest representations which prevent policy innovations and threaten the effectiveness, efficiency and democratic legitimacy of the public sector' (1997: xvii). They indicate that they do not agree with that view. We do not need to take sides in that argument here. What is important is that, as Scharpf states in his essay, a realism about networks requires us to recognize two points. First, that networks may be crucial for the sort of 'implementation deficit' that Pressman and Wildavsky were so concerned about. And second, that effective implementation, as suggested by Hjern and his colleagues, may depend upon the development of collaborative networks. Certainly, the British network literature recognizes that they may be very important for successful policy formation and implementation and it suggests that governments have sought to foster policy networks and policy communities. M.J. Smith (1993), drawing on Jordan and Richardson (1987), identifies four reasons for this:

- They facilitate a consultative style of government.
- They reduce policy conflict and make it possible to depoliticize issues.

- They make policy making predictable.
- They relate well to the departmental organization of government.

This British network literature has shown little interest in implementation *per se*, but implicit in much that has been said about this subject is a specific suggestion, namely that the discontinuity between policy formation and implementation that is perceived as problematic by the top-down theorists is largely eliminated through the continuity of the relationship that exists between the government and its specific partners in a policy network (such as the agriculture or the health policy network). We do not need to examine the evidence for such a view here. The point is that this is a theoretical approach that does not see implementation in terms of the realization or non-realization of hierarchically determined goals.

On the other hand the questions about effective implementation remain relevant. They re-emerge in new forms as concerns about network management (as in the concerns of Kickert et al.'s book – this is explored further in a section explicitly devoted to the work of these authors and their colleagues on pp. 77–9). The questions also appear as the reservations about policy outcomes expressed by those excluded from these consensual modes of action. The orientation is more one of external management than of policy making; horizontal rather than vertical.

Network theory thus contributes to a recognition of the need for new ways to formulate implementation issues and highlights the difficulties of the policy formation/implementation distinction.

Randall Ripley and Grace Franklin: specifying policy types

A similar strong emphasis upon networks, though framed rather more in traditional pluralist terms echoing Lowi's (1979) emphasis on 'interest-group liberalism', is a contribution by two American scholars, Randall Ripley and Grace Franklin: *Bureaucracy and Policy Implementation* (1982). Ripley and Franklin see themselves as very much concerned with 'what is happening and why' rather than with asking the top-down question 'whether implementers *comply with* the prescribed procedures, timetables and restrictions' (p. 10). They regard as inevitable what the top-downers call 'implementation deficit' and are concerned rather to explore implementation processes, which they see as having five features, set out by them in a long sentence with appropriate emphases:

Implementation processes involve *many important actors* holding *diffuse and competing goals* who work within a *context of an increasingly large and complex mix of government programs* that require *participation from numerous layers and units of government* and who are affected by *powerful factors beyond their control.*
(1982: 9)

It is important to note that Ripley and Franklin make it quite clear that their concern is with American bureaucracy and particularly with federalism. They note that '[a]lmost no national or federal programs are implemented wholly or directly by the national government in Washington' (p. 25). That is emphasized, not in criticism, but because of the importance of questions about the extent to which generalizations about implementation need to be seen in their institutional or cultural contexts. At least Ripley and Franklin are quite explicit about where their work is grounded, emphasizing issues on federalism that concern others (notably Goggin et al., see pp. 66–9 Ferman, see pp. 70–1 and Stoker, see pp. 72–3).

In various ways Ripley and Franklin emphasize the political nature of the implementation process – 'no less political than any other set of policy activities' (p. 6). They also stress that, while it may be appropriate to model the implementation process in terms of a flow of activities, there is not necessarily a logical sequence and the interventions of interest groups are not structured in hierarchical terms. Ripley and Franklin's approach, in this respect, owes a great deal to Eugene Bardach (see pp. 48–9).

Hence, Ripley and Franklin may be seen as amongst the writers who have sought to inject a political realism into the top-down approach, without at the same time embracing a bottom-up perspective. But the most important reason for highlighting their work here is that they give particular attention to the relevance of policy type for the policy process. They classify policy types into:

- distributive;
- competitive regulatory;
- protective regulatory; and
- redistributive.

Many scholars have sought to develop policy typologies (see Parsons, 1995: 132–4). Ripley and Franklin's classification owes a great deal to earlier work by Lowi (1972), though it lacks one category, 'constituent policy' (concerned with the design of institutions), and it divides regulatory policy into two categories. The latter distinction is one between 'competitive regulatory' policies, which 'limit the provision of specific goods and services to one or a few designated deliverers' (Ripley and Franklin, 1982: 72), as with the granting of airline routes or television channels, and 'protective regulatory' policies, controlling potentially harmful activities. Essentially the classification is designed to help the elucidation of the factors that influence implementation success. Implicitly this suggests that underlying the question of whether some kinds of policy may be harder to implement than others lie issues about the probability of conflict and outside interference.[1]

The actual classification used is obviously open to challenge. The distributive/redistributive distinction implies, illogically, that distributive situations are ones in which the state gives without having to derive an income from someone, whilst with redistributive ones there are both winners and losers. Obviously this distinction really rests on the extent to which the losers can readily identify themselves. Significantly Ripley and Franklin partly acknowledge this illogicality by indicating that they confine their redistributive concept to shifts of resources from advantaged to disadvantaged groups, whilst acknowledging that the reverse does apply. They justify this in terms of ideological perceptions in the United States (we would want to say 'dominant ideology').

The basis for the distinctions between the distribution and redistribution types, on the one hand, and regulation, on the other, can also be challenged on the grounds that regulatory activities also have winners and losers. Again, as with the distributive/redistributive distinction, there is a presumption that Ripley and Franklin's classification is at times influenced more by what they want to say about implementation difficulty than by logic. 'Affirmative action', for instance, they give as an example of a redistributive policy rather than a 'regulatory policy'. Finally it should be noted that it has been commented that in actual policies the various types are often mixed (Ingram and Schneider, 1990: 69). However, this is in many ways simply an extension of the earlier ground for criticism. Were the types logically grounded, empirical variety could be handled.

Ripley and Franklin and others are raising important questions about the extent to which policy type makes a difference, and connecting this significantly to the extent to which an intense and conflictual 'implementation politics' is likely to emerge with some policies. However, there are grounds for questioning whether the typology they derive from Lowi is satisfactory for a systematic analysis of this issue.

The final issue that Ripley and Franklin's book discusses quite fully is the meaning of 'implementation success'. Their perspective on this is that successful implementation *'leads to desired performance and impacts'* (1982: 200), seeing this as superior to defining success in terms of either compliance or a lack of disruptive activity. That still leaves the question 'desired by whom?' Furthermore, to link performance and impact in that way is to mix two very different criteria. Performance may be as desired but not the impact (the operation was a success but the patient died!), or of course vice versa. There is a link here with the discussion of outputs and outcomes in Chapter 1, a theme that will be picked up again when we look at methodological issues in Chapters 6 and 7.

Paul Sabatier: towards the advocacy coalition approach

An essay published by Paul Sabatier in 1986 represents an important attempt to bring the various theoretical threads together. We have already identified Sabatier as a key figure in the establishment of the 'top-down' approach to implementation. His later essay, together with work that followed it (particularly that on the 'advocacy coalition approach' with Hank Jenkins-Smith, 1993), involves some fusion of the various approaches, particularly with respect to methodological issues.

In the 1986 essay Sabatier is willing to concede some of the methodological strengths of the bottom-up approach: its effective approach to the study of networks, its strength in evaluating influences on policy outcomes other than government programmes, and its value when a number of different policy programmes interact. Hence he suggests that choice of methodology might depend upon whether there is or is not a 'dominant piece of legislation structuring the situation' (Sabatier, 1986: 37).

Nevertheless Sabatier's essay hardly responds to the critique made by the bottom-uppers of his normative assumptions. He speaks of the latter as 'free to see all sorts of (unintended) consequences of governmental ... programs' (p. 34). He argues that bottom-uppers 'overemphasize the ability of the Periphery to frustrate the Center' (p. 34). What the bottom-up critique does, however, is precisely to question this language of intentions and consequences.

Sabatier is particularly critical of those, like Barrett and Fudge, who tend to obliterate the distinction between policy formation and implementation. He argues:

> First, it makes it very difficult to distinguish the relative influence of elected officials and civil servants – thus precluding an analysis of democratic accountability and bureaucratic discretion, hardly trivial topics. Second, the view of the policy process as a seamless web of flows without decision points ... precludes policy evaluation ... and the analysis of policy change. (p. 31)

But if those he criticizes are right about real processes, his alternative imposes an artificial distinction. In other words, his (normative) concern with accountability (and he is not alone here) seems to obscure his judgement on what actually happens. In the light of his strong feelings on this issue it is interesting that Sabatier argues that the approach he had earlier adopted with Mazmanian 'did not provide a good conceptual vehicle for looking at policy change over periods of a decade or more'. As a reason he states that it 'focused too much on the perspective of program *proponents*, thereby neglecting the strategies (and learning) by other actors' (p. 30). His later works endeavour to rectify this error. It looks as if Sabatier's new approach falls foul of his own criticism of Barrett and Fudge's perspective. There is of course a real dilemma here; a problem for implementation studies about steering a course between the Scylla of a narrowly conceived rigorous study and the Charybdis of a broad and shapeless study of a long and complex process. These are important points to which we will have to return.

In the last part of the 1986 essay Sabatier outlines what he sees as the way forward, involving the 'advocacy coalition framework', adopting the bottom-uppers' unit of analysis – a whole variety of public and private actors involved with a policy problem – as well as their concerns with understanding the perspectives and strategies of all major categories of actors (not simply program proponents). It then combines this starting point with the top-downers' concerns with the manner in which socio-economic conditions and legal instruments constrain behavior. It applies this synthesized perspective to the analysis of policy change over periods of a decade or more. (p. 39)

In more recent work Sabatier has shifted his attention to the development of his 'advocacy coalition' approach (see particularly Sabatier and Jenkins-Smith, 1993), offering a more holistic view of the policy process. He rejects the 'stages' heuristic within which much implementation work is embedded (see further discussion in Chapter 8. In many respects this takes him much closer to the bottom-up perspective, because the 'advocacy coalition' can be seen as comprising actors from all levels. There remains, however, a question about the extent to which the concept of 'coalition', like the concept of network, to which it has obvious links, can highlight the significance of conflict within the policy process.

Jan-Erik Lane: clarifying the normative issues

Jan-Erik Lane is important for picking up the normative issues, to which his Swedish compatriot Benny Hjern made such a distinctive and provocative contribution. Lane questions the search for an integrated theory of implementation by drawing attention to what he sees as a problem embodied in the meaning of the word. He suggests that implementation is seen as involving both notions of an 'end state or policy achievement' and 'a process or policy execution' (Lane, 1987: 528).

Whilst the dichotomy Lane is making has much in common with the top-down/bottom-up distinction, it does not exactly parallel it. Perhaps (like Hjern and Hull distinguishing between 'policy output analysis' and 'organization-theory inclined' work, see pp. 54–5) it rather highlights the normative as opposed to the methodological distinction in the latter dichotomy. That is clearly explained when Lane goes on to emphasize two alternative considerations in relation to his dichotomy: responsibility and trust. He argues that the 'responsibility' concerns are about the 'relationship between objectives and outcome' (Lane, 1987: 542) while the 'trust' concerns refer to 'the process of putting policies into effect' (p. 542). Lane argues that top-down models are particularly concerned to emphasize the 'responsibility side' while bottom-up models 'underline the trust side' (p. 543). He then argues:

An implementation process is a combination of responsibility and trust.... Without the notion of *implementation as policy accomplishment* there is no basis for evaluating policies and holding politicians, administrators and professionals accountable. On the other hand, *implementation as policy execution* rests upon trust or a certain amount of degrees of freedom for politicians and implementors to make choices about alternative means for the accomplishment of goals....

Implementation theory has thus far been the search for some pattern or way of structuring the process of implementation in such a manner that there will be a high probability of policy accomplishment. This has resulted in a controversy between those who believe in control, planning and hierarchy on the one hand, and on the other those who believe in spontaneity, learning and adaptation as problem-solving techniques. A reorientation of implementation theory would be to inquire into how accountability is to be upheld in the implementation of policies and how much trust is in agreement with the requirement of accountability. (p. 543)

Malcolm Goggin, Ann Bowman, James Lester and Laurence O'Toole, Jr: aiming at systematic research

In the next section we will discuss the independent contribution that Lawrence O'Toole has made to implementation theory. Here, however, we are concerned with his joint work with American compatriots Malcolm Goggin, Ann Bowman and James Lester. In their *Implementation Theory and Practice: Toward a Third Generation* (1990) they describe themselves. as engaged in pioneering a more systematic approach to research on implementation. Their earlier 'generations' are not the same as those covered by the earlier sections of this book. Rather Goggin and his colleagues call the first generation the pioneering 'accounts of how a single authoritative decision was carried out' (Goggin et al., 1990: 13), amongst which Pressman and Wildavsky's book is the prime example. Their second generation are all those before themselves who were engaged in 'the development of analytical frameworks' (p. 14). They see the third generation that they are helping to bring into life as engaged in 'scholarship ... to develop and test explanatory and predictive implementation theories of the middle range' (p. 15).

Hence, the aim of Goggin and his colleagues is to further a 'more scientific' (p. 18) approach to the study of implementation. To that end they set out what they call a *'communications model'* for the analysis of implementation, with a very strong emphasis upon what affects the acceptance or rejection of messages between layers of government (see Figure 4.1). Issues about measuring variables are carefully addressed in each case. To help to explicate this model and the hypotheses, they use material from three American case studies in which they have been engaged.

Clearly it would be inappropriate for us to set out all of the hypotheses formulated by Goggin and his colleagues. They fall into the following groups:

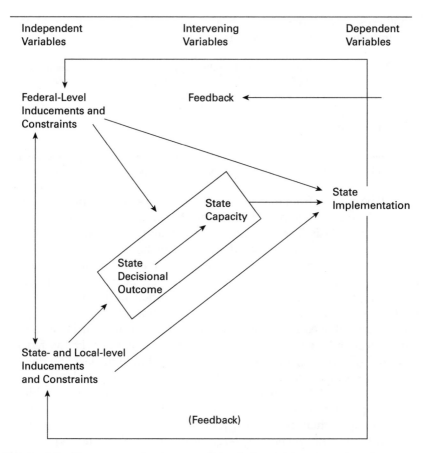

Figure 4.1 *The communications model of inter-governmental policy implementation*
Source: Goggin et al., 1990: 32

Independent variables

- Federal-Level Inducements and Constraints.
- State- and Local-level Inducements and Constraints.

Intervening variables

- Organizational Capacity.
- Ecological Capacity.
- Feedback and Policy Redesign.

(This list is based upon section headings in their eighth chapter.)

There are seventeen hypotheses in all, but most of these are quite elaborate and contain sub-hypotheses within them. To give a little more indication of what is involved in this approach, here are two examples of hypotheses drawn from the two groups. From the group State- and Local-level Inducements and Constraints:

> H5: The more legitimate and credible the supportive state or local senders of messages in the eyes of state officials, the more likely the state's implementation is to proceed promptly and without modifications. (p. 179)

From the group Organizational Capacity:

> H7: The more personnel a state devotes to implementing a program, the greater the likelihood of prompt implementation without modifications. (p. 182)

It will be evident from this discussion that issues about communications between layers of government – federal, state and local – are very important for this analysis. The case studies Goggin and his colleagues use are in many respects preoccupied by federal/state relations in the United States. They all concern federal Acts that depend very much upon implementation at state level; indeed they may even be seen as about issues that under some interpretations of the American Constitution would be regarded as no business of the federal government at all.[2] Quite appropriately Goggin et al. are critical of earlier American studies for their disregard of activities at state level. But more significantly they discuss national policy as 'federal messages' (Chapter 3), a usage that seems to highlight the fact that there is a problem about assuming a capacity to command at federal level.

The concern of Goggin and his colleagues to cope with problems related to political-administrative layers in a federal system has a significant effect upon their methodology, making the specification of variables rather difficult and generating large numbers of elaborate hypotheses. They are struggling with the tension between a need to satisfy the practical demand for propositions about implementation success or failure and the complex nature of the phenomena with which they are concerned.

Clearly *Implementation Theory and Practice* is a careful and elaborate attempt to specify a scientific framework for implementation studies. It escapes from the static nature of earlier studies that have difficulty in handling feedback between implementation and policy formation and from the rigidity of top-down efforts to specify particular 'rules' for those who want to control implementation. Yet, as has already been suggested, it focuses on one particular aspect of the implementation: communication between layers of government (with particular reference to the version of this issue that arises in American federalism). Because of this, it may be asked to what extent it offers a comprehensive and universally applicable framework for the study of implementation.

On the other hand that last remark suggests that a more universal framework will include even more hypotheses, and an alternative criticism of the approach adopted by Goggin et al. is that in practice it will be very difficult to work with all, or even most, of their hypotheses and handle the way they offer interacting explanations of events. An approach that offers a way towards fewer, more situationally limited hypotheses is offered by Matland's work, to be discussed below.

Laurence O'Toole, Jr: implementation in networks

Laurence O'Toole has the special distinction of making contributions to the implementation literature across the period from the very early days of implementation research (he gave a conference paper with Robert Montjoy in 1977 and published an article with him in 1979) until the time this book is being completed. He will doubtless write much more in the years to come. It is quite difficult to separate out his special contribution to the literature from his role as a wide, and broad-minded, observer of the scene. Indeed the latter comment is very pertinent, since he is a scholar who, on many occasions, has stressed the need to take a broad rather than a narrow view of the implementation literature. His biography for the 1979 article describes him as 'a student of organization theory as well as public administration and democratic theory' (Montjoy and O'Toole, 1979: 465), and in much of his work he makes connections between the concerns of the implementation literature and the contributions of organizational sociologists. In his 1986 review of 'policy recommendations for multi-actor implementation' one of his key conclusions is that '[s]ince implementation research of necessity draws from numerous subfields of social science ... more effort should be undertaken to devise links and develop comparisons across them' (p. 204). That comment is echoed in his assessment of the field published in 2000, which has a section on 'indirect contributions to implementation research' (2000a: 273–82). But Laurence O'Toole's work has also been marked by a particular interest in the exploration of the problems about studying, or making recommendations on, implementation involving multi-actor collaboration. In his 1986 article he showed how few recommendations were emerging, and how often actors had been offered quite conflicting 'proverbs'. He returned to that theme in an article published in 1993, drawing heavily upon his studies of waste-water privatization (see also O'Toole, 1989a, 1989b). In the 1993 article he demonstrated the limitations of contingency theory's suggestion that it is possible to match inter-organizational arrangements with policy objectives so that the best way to implement can be 'read off' from the latter. What is particularly noted here is the difficulties that arise because of competing policy goals.

O'Toole's work later in the 1990s took him even more deeply into complex implementation situations when he carried out studies in Hungary as that country emerged from Communism (1994, 1997). We find him here arguing that the implementation process was complicated by the fact that the country was engaged in a process of 'constitutional choice'

(1994: 516), and that therefore theories about policy implementation 'as developed in the West are of limited use' (p. 493).

That work by O'Toole, and perhaps also his earlier research on waste-water privatization, raises questions about the ambition of implementation theory to handle complicated change processes. At the end of the 1990s he became involved in work with the much more specific objective of trying to model inter-organizational processes, and particularly the management of networks, in such a way as to facilitate quantitative empirical work (O'Toole and Meier, 1999; Meier and O'Toole, 2001).

Laurence O'Toole remains a scholar who is eager to keep alive the tradition of implementation studies; as such we owe a great deal to him. We will return to some of his recent contributions to the assessment of the field, and the exploration of ways forward, in Chapters 7 and 8.

Dennis Palumbo and Donald Calista: placing implementation in the policy process

The next contribution to the literature we will look at is an edited collection by two Americans, Dennis Palumbo and Donald Calista's *Implementation and the Policy Process* (1990c). Edited collections rarely have a unified stance on theoretical issues. Inasmuch as this one has a stance, it is that it aims to 'place implementation in the broader policymaking process' (1990a: xii). Though this leaves open the possibility that implementation and policy formation are analysed separately, the view that this should not be done seems to be taken by some of the contributors to the book. The main concern of the volume is set out in Palumbo and Calista's own essay. Here they argue:

> There is no doubt that implementation research has finally laid to rest the politics–administration dichotomy. Early implementation research fostered this view when it assumed that implementers were supposed to simply carry out previously made policy directives. More recent research demonstrates that implementation is a legitimate part of the policymaking process – a part that can be neither diminished empirically nor de-legitimized normatively. (1990b: 14)

This position particularly rests upon the argument that 'implementers are involved in every stage of the policy cycle' (p. 15), a case that partly involves producing evidence – certainly long present in British literature on the role of the civil service – that bureaucrats contribute to policy design (Chapman, 1970). It is reinforced by an argument that policy design is seldom initially clear and that renegotiation of details with the multiplicity of actors affected by that policy is an accepted part of the policy process.

Later in the book an essay by Ferman goes even further, asserting that 'implementation politics is an integral part of the American political system as envisioned by the Founding Fathers' (1990: 50). Ferman highlights the divisions in the American system, stressing the connections between fragmentation between legislature and executive and that between the federal government and the states. She argues that

> the factors that contribute to the gap between policymaking and implementation are manifestations of the Madisonian system of American politics and government. The implication of this finding for implementation theory is that we should view implementation in a very different light – implementation is another check in the American system of government. (p. 39)

Hence she argues that James Madison's 'victory' in creating a system of government in which centralized power was prevented created different demands and incentives for policy makers and implementers and thus two different 'types of politics' (p. 40). Ferman's emphasis on this last point is interesting. On the one hand she accepts the evidence for a 'gap between policymaking and implementation'. On the other she argues that this can be seen as a legitimate check upon executive or legislative power. An alternative perspective, such as that embodied in some of the bottom-up work (particularly that of Hjern and of Barrett and Fudge), would be to emphasize the extent to which negotiation between levels in practice closes that gap.

One contribution to the Palumbo and Calista volume, by the Dane Søren Winter, sets out a model for implementation research in which emphasis is given to issues about the impact of the policy formulation process upon implementation. This is an issue that was earlier given attention in a paper written by Susan Barrett and one of the present authors (Barrett and Hill, 1981) that emphasized the extent to which political compromises were built into policies, and the fact that these compromises are not once-and-for-all processes but may continue on throughout the history of the translation of policy into action (quoted in Hill, 1997a: 134, 139). Hill elsewhere went on to argue further that this process may be encouraged by the policy formers to enable them to evade decision problems or to shift responsibility for policy failure on to implementers (Fimister and Hill, 1993; Hill, 1997a).

Some of the contributors to Palumbo and Calista's book (particularly Fox and Yanow) raise questions of a clearly postmodernist kind about the extent to which positivist models can be used for the study of implementation. Fox supports the arguments for a wide view of the policy arena and a broad time-span, along the lines set out in Sabatier's 1986 essay, and also argues for the consideration of 'multiple standpoints'. He rejects a total shift away from positivism, but argues that 'to the positive benefits of modern social science must be added respect for the disciplined employment of sound intuition itself born of experience not reducible to models, hypotheses, quantification, "hard" data, or little pieces of incorrigible fixity' (1990: 211). Yanow (1990) develops a related argument for an 'interpretive' approach – with an emphasis on 'interpretations of policy language, legislative intent or implementing actions' (1993: 55) – to the study of implementation, questioning the quest for one best way of studying the subject.

Robert Stoker: analysing the implications of layers of government

Robert Stoker's monograph (1991) deals explicitly with issues about the implementation of federal policy in the United States. In recognizing, like Ripley and Franklin, that issues about federalism lie at the centre of the preoccupations of much of the American literature, there is a need to ask (as will be done at the end of this section) whether what he has to say has resonances outside his home country.

Like Ferman, Stoker identifies as a crucial flaw in the American top-down literature the extent to which it is concerned about failures to exert federal authority in a system of government that was designed to limit that authority. He highlights as the leading expression of that view what he calls the 'disability thesis', that the 'U.S. government is disabled by design' (p. 50). He therefore contrasts two alternative approaches to the solution of implementation problems, which to a large extent parallel the normative aspects of the top-down and bottom-up views. Taking his lead from Lindblom (1977), he labels these approaches 'authority' and 'exchange'. The authority approach involves suggesting ways to simplify or circumvent the barriers to compliance. The exchange approach requires the achievement of co-operation.

Stoker's emphasis on the importance of the division of powers within federalism, and his endorsement of the case for limitations upon government power, leaves little doubt about where he stands on the case against trying to solve implementation problems through the use of the authority approach. What is important about his analysis, however, is that he also sees shortcomings in the exchange approach. He recognizes, like Barrett and Fudge, the way this confuses policy formation and implementation. While that comment does not in itself invalidate the exchange approach, Stoker goes on to stress how this leads to an analysis in which what results from an exchange process is seen as inevitable, regardless of the interests or moral ends that may be involved. He suggests instead that this is to disregard the extent to which co-operation needs to be seen as a device to handle conflicts rather than one that can only succeed if they are eliminated. Hence he argues: 'The flaw in the disability thesis, and the implementation literature that reflects it, is that it may be possible to manipulate the conditions of the implementation process to encourage co-operative responses to conflicts of interest. This possibility has received scant attention in the literature' (p. 50).

Thus, as a third alternative to 'authority' and 'exchange', Stoker sees 'governance' as an activity in which 'reluctant partners' are induced to collaborate. In this sense he takes up an argument from Clarence Stone (1989) that it is important to give attention to 'power to' accomplish collective goals as opposed to 'power over' recalcitrant others. This leads him on to an exploration of the extent to which different 'implementation regimes' can arise, or be created. Here he uses game theory, drawing particularly upon scholars who have developed this to explore relationships between nations (Axelrod, 1984; Axelrod and Keohane, 1985; Oye, 1985). What is important for Stoker is the extent to which games are repeated, and occur in contexts in which there is a 'history of interaction between participants' and 'the expectation of future interaction' (Stoker, 1991: 74). We find a similar emphasis upon seeing games within structures in Scharpf's *Games Real Actors Play* (1997a). There he writes of them as 'within the shadow of the state' (1997a: chap. 9).

Stoker designates a number of kinds of 'implementation regimes'. One dimension for these may be outside actors' control – inasmuch as they are not themselves engaged in the creating of constitutions. The other dimension involves choices of 'action sectors' (bureaucratic, joint or quasi-market). In that sense governance can occur through choice of ways of 'bringing together ... essential elements in an otherwise fragmented world' (here Stoker quotes C. Stone again, 1989: 227).

It was noted above that Stoker is quite explicitly dealing with American federalism. It therefore may be objected that what he has to say has no relevance to more unitary systems of government. It is important to recognize that the federal/state relationship in the United States may often be more appropriately viewed as one in which a collaborative policy-formation process rather than implementation process is occurring. However, issues about securing the collaboration of 'reluctant partners' are by no means absent from other, possibly simpler, constitutional structures of inter-governmental relations. It is important, for example, to note:

- many central/local government relationships in which the latter lay claim to a measure of autonomy;
- policies that require collaboration between separate ministries or agencies; and
- the factors analysed by Lipsky, discussed above (see pp. 51–3), that convey a measure of autonomy to street-level bureaucrats.

These are recognized by Stoker himself: making a contrast between the 'centralized', 'shared' and 'diffuse' distribution of public authority in different constitutional or institutional contexts. Hence, whilst Stoker makes a particularly important contribution to arguments about federalism, his work must be seen as making a contribution to the normative arguments about co-ordination and control that preoccupy so much of the implementation literature.

Richard Matland: specifying implementation contexts

In an article published in 1995, Richard Matland, an American scholar, has offered an interesting alternative approach to those who have seen the way forward for implementation studies as involving the accumulation of large numbers of hypotheses. His comment on a literature review by O'Toole (1986) that identifies a large number of key variables is that a 'literature with three hundred critical variables doesn't need more variables: It needs *structure*' (Matland, 1995: 146).

In his article Matland reviews the top-down and bottom-up models and the main efforts to synthesize them. He is critical of Sabatier for his shift away from a specific attention to a policy to a policy field, arguing that a 'policy field followed over many years can change so radically that it bears little resemblance to its initial form. If implementation research is to retain a meaningful definition, it should be tied to a specific policy rather than to all actions in a policy field' (p. 152).

Central to Matland's argument is a view that instead of simply producing lists of variables to be taken into account, implementation theorists must specify 'the conditions under which these variables are important and the reasons we should expect them to be important' (p. 153). He suggests that these conditions must be derived from a coherent approach to the concept of 'successful implementation'. Perhaps another way of putting this is to argue that there needs to be a clearly specified 'dependent variable'. Matland sees disagreements about the concept of successful implementation as very fundamental for the top-down/bottom-up argument, with the former much more likely to want to use specific outcomes as the dependent variable while the latter 'prefer a much broader evaluation' (p. 154).

Matland refers to a discussion of this topic by Ingram and Schneider (1990) that looks at the top-down/bottom-up debate as an argument about how discretion should be assigned to implementers. Ingram and Schneider distinguish:

- the strong statute approach, with the whole policy design task tackled at the top (as highlighted in Davis's attack on discretionary power (see Chapter 2, p. 25));
- the 'Wilsonian Perspective' (1990: 77), picking up on Woodrow Wilson's concern about efficient but unpoliticized administration, in which clear goals are set but administrative agencies have discretion on the organization of administration;
- the 'grass-roots approach' (1990: 79), in which street-level staff and even 'target populations' have discretion over 'all the elements of policy logic'; and
- the 'support building approach' (1990: 81), in which policy content is bargained between top and bottom.

While this seems a useful way of conceptualizing how policies are actually made, the peculiar feature of this analysis is that it is all set out in terms of questions about how they *should* be made. The political realism of other writers, who suggest ways discretion emerges as a result of struggles over policy goals, is entirely disregarded and these alternatives are presented as choice options for the 'top'.

The approach actually adopted by Matland largely avoids that problem by noting a variety of plausible definitions of successful implementation:

- compliance with statutes' directives;
- compliance with statutes' goals;
- achievement of specific success indicators;
- achievement of locally specified goals; and
- improvement of the political climate around a programme.

In relation to these there are decisions to be made about the extent to which the values of those who design policy are to be accorded primacy over those of others. But then crucial to this argument is the question whether or not policy goals have been explicitly stated in some official policy document. If this is the case, Matland argues,

> then, based on democratic theory, the statutory designers' values have a superior value. In such instances the correct standard of implementation success is loyalty to the prescribed goals. When a policy does not have explicitly stated goals, the choice of a standard becomes more difficult, and more general societal norms and values come into play. (1995: 155)

But there does not seem any intrinsic reason why rigorous implementation studies cannot be based around alternative goals to those of the 'statutory designers', particularly as what democratic theory suggests may itself be contested territory. However, that does not detract from Matland's central point about the distinction between clear and unclear goals.

Matland goes on from that last point to argue that there is a tendency for top-down theorists to choose relatively clear policies to study whilst bottom-uppers 'study policies with greater uncertainty inherent' in them. He then suggests that this difference has two features – ambiguity and conflict. These two concepts perhaps rather tend to interact, and can obviously be related back (as he acknowledges later in the essay) to issues about goal conflict (on which the criticism set out in the last paragraph may be pertinent). Nevertheless Matland is pointing us towards an important issue for separating different kinds of implementation studies. In particular, in treating ambiguity and conflict as intrinsic features of policy rather than as phenomena that good policy designers should try to eliminate, he gets away from a specific contradiction embedded in top-down recommendations for those who design policy. This contradiction

TABLE 4.1 *Matland's analysis of the impact of conflict and ambiguity upon implementation*

	Low conflict	**High conflict**
Low ambiguity	Administrative implementation Resources Example: Smallpox eradication	Political implementation Power Example: Busing
High ambiguity	Experimental implementation Contextual conditions Example: Headstart	Symbolic implementation Coalition strength Example: Community action agencies`

Source: Simplified version of the table in Matland, 1995: 160

entails that they are being urged to control the very things that they are least likely to be able to control, or perhaps want to control (see Hill, 1997a: 133–4).

Matland uses his distinction to develop the matrix set out in Table 4.1. In that table 'administrative implementation' needs little explanation. Matland describes this as where there are the 'prerequisite conditions for a rational decision process' (1995: 160), the ideal situation for the application of the top-down model. With 'political implementation', he says, 'implementation outcomes are decided by power' (p. 163). In this case, theories that emphasize interactions and policy/implementation feedback are particularly applicable, whilst those that stress decision making at the micro-level are less so. In the case of 'experimental implementation', 'contextual conditions', meaning environmental influences on outcomes, are likely to be important: 'Program mutations arise as different organizations implement different policies in different environments' (p. 166). There are complex feedback and learning issues to consider in this case, and bottom-up approaches to analysis are particularly likely to be applicable. 'Symbolic implementation' involves high conflict despite the vagueness of policy. The strength of coalitions, particularly at the local level, tends to determine outcomes. Professional values and allegiances may be important for these. It is a pity Matland does not have more to say on this point. His example of 'community action' is very much an area where programmes have not satisfied the aspirations of participants either at the top or at the bottom. Much more significant examples may occur in areas where ambitious but ambiguous aspirations to effect health improvements or crime reductions offer significant opportunities for policy development through the implementation process by professional coalitions.

Matland's article offers some important suggestions about the need to think about implementation very differently in relation to different policies. At the same time his distinctions between different types of policies cannot be deduced, as Ripley and Franklin suggest (see pp. 61–3), from a simple categorization of policy types based on Lowi's work. Matland also avoids seeing the level of policy discretion as something explicitly chosen by policy formers, recognizing how it may be a function of policy conflict. The question about his argument is then: How easy is it to *label* policies in the way he does?

Walter Kickert, Erik-Hans Klijn and Joop Koppenjan: elaborating network analysis

A book edited by three Dutch authors, Walter Kickert, Erik-Hans Klijn and Joop Koppenjan, published in 1997, offers a particularly cogent exposition of the importance, for implementation, of issues about the management of networks. This section will refer to that work, and other work closely linked to it. The idea that policy processes are in general an interplay between various actors and not centrally governed by government is now broadly accepted (Kooiman, 1993; Rhodes, 1996a). This point is explored more in Chapter 5. Some speak of a pluricentric view replacing a unicentric one (Klijn and Teisman, 1991). This view is central to the policy network approach.

Earlier in this chapter it was shown how Scharpf and others developed the network concept in implementation studies. The theoretical roots of the approach lie in inter-organizational theory and the interactive perspective on public policy (Hufen and Ringeling (eds), 1990; Klijn, 1997). The policy network approach has developed a distinctive framework. Its central assumption is 'that policy is made in complex interaction processes between a large number of actors which takes place within networks of interdependent actors' (Klijn and Koppenjan, 2000: 139). The actors involved are mutually dependent because they need each other's resources to achieve goals (Scharpf, 1978; Benson, 1982; Rhodes, 1988). Patterns of interaction emerge around policy problems and resource clusters. So policy networks can be defined as (more or less) stable patterns of social relations between interdependent actors, which take shape around policy problems and/or policy programmes (Klijn and Koppenjan, 2000). In time, rules are developed in the networks that regulate behaviour and resource distribution. In this way, they influence the regulations in which the rules and resource distribution are gradually shaped, solidified and altered (Giddens, 1984). Policy networks thus form a context in which actors act strategically.

Series of interactions take place around policy and other issues, which can be called games (Crozier and Friedberg, 1980; Rhodes, 1981; Scharpf, 1997a). Series of games thus form policy processes. During a game, actors operate within the established resource distribution and set of rules. The existing, ambiguous rules are interpreted (March and Olsen, 1989; Klijn, 1996). Actors select strategies based on their perceptions of the nature of the problem, their desired solutions and those of the other actors. Different actors have different perceptions.

In policy networks, co-operation is a necessary condition to achieve satisfying outcomes. However, this does not mean it is established without conflict, since there is tension between interdependency and the diversity of goals and interests. This tension needs to be solved in any policy game. To achieve co-operation, steering is needed. So network management is focused on the improvement of co-operation between involved actors (O'Toole, 1988). Two types of steering strategies can be distinguished: process management and network constitution. Process management has as its aim the improvement of interaction between actors in policy games, taking the structure and composition of the network as given. Network constitution aims at changing the network. Since this means institutional change, these strategies are time consuming (Klijn and Koppenjan, 2000).

Because co-operation between actors is central in the policy network approach, explanations for the success or failure of policy processes are based on the extent of co-operation achieved. Explanations are found, on the one hand, in process variables, like the degree to which actors are aware of their mutual dependencies; the degree to which interactions are balanced favourably or unfavourably with perceived outcomes of the interaction; and the degree to which game management is foreseen. On the other hand, success or failure is explained by the structural characteristics of the network, such as the degree to which actors possess veto power because of indispensable resources and the degree to which actors in a game belong to the same network. The latter means that they also interact with each other and that they have developed reciprocal rules (Klijn and Koppenjan, 2000).

In policy networks, actors are relatively autonomous; they all have their own objectives. There is no central, co-ordinating actor. This is why the process and outcome cannot be evaluated in terms of the objectives of one actor. Furthermore, initial problem definitions or objectives, even when established collectively, change during the interaction processes. Another problem is the fact that interests and preferences of non-participating parties are most probably not represented. In the network approach, the evaluation of success or failure of policy is based on the process used to arrive at a possible common problem formulation. For this, the *ex post* satisfying criterion (Teisman, 1995) and the win-win situation criterion are used. Furthermore, process criteria like openness, carefulness, reliability and legitimacy must be included in the evaluation, as well as external effects of the process (Kickert et al., 1997).

Although governments are considered to be actors in policy networks, this does not mean they are like other actors. Governments have a special position, which in most cases cannot be filled by others. They have unique resources and unique objectives. They have considerable power because of their resources, but this also limits their possibilities. For example, it is exactly their tasks that to a great extent define interdependence. As Klijn and Koppenjan (2000) state, a government can take up different roles in a network-like situation. In the first place, it can choose not to participate. As there are existing dependencies that need to be dealt with and the power of opposition needs to be broken, this option requires a huge investment in decision-making and implementation activities and has high risks. Second, a government can choose to carry out tasks in co-operation with private, semi-public and also other public actors. The two other roles are those of process manager and of network builder. Governments seem to be eminently suited for the latter role, given their special resources and their role as representative of the common interest. It is essential that government in concrete game situations does not confuse these different roles. In the words of Klijn and Koppenjan: '[c]onfusion of roles can lead to misunderstandings and conflict among actors and can prove to be costly in terms of effectiveness and efficiency, but especially with regard to the reliability and legitimacy of government' (2000: 154).

Bo Rothstein: elaborating the normative issues

A valuable discussion of implementation theory by a Swedish scholar, Bo Rothstein, is set out in his book called *Just Institutions Matter* (1998). In that book he tackles some fundamental questions about the role of the state, particularly in relation to social welfare. The sub-title is *The Moral and Political Logic of the Universal Welfare State*. This book links philosophical questions about what the state should do to questions about what the state can do effectively. Rothstein's approach to 'just institutions' is rooted in the longstanding defence of universalism in social policy, which sees citizens' interests as best enhanced and unfairness and discrimination as minimized where entitlements are clear and thus rights are self-enforcing. The problem then to be addressed is: How should public services be organized when the nature of the activity – the benefit or service to be provided or the behaviour to be regulated – makes it difficult to realize this model of state action?

Rothstein shows that the study of implementation can contribute to answering the above question. His aim is then to fuse 'empirical state theory' with 'normative state theory'. This means that his principal contribution to the study of implementation is towards the resolution of the prescriptive arguments, but that what he has to say also has bearing upon the methodological arguments. Hence Rothstein's interest in implementation research arises because it 'poses the question of how different ways of organizing public administration affect the prospects for carrying out programs successfully' (1998: 7).

Rothstein first reviews the implementation literature, describing implementation research as 'to a great extent … misery research, a pathology of the social sciences, if you will' (p. 62), echoing the famous Pressman and

Wildavsky sub-title about the frustration of expectations. Rothstein suggests that there are three problems embodied in that view of implementation research. The first is a tendency for research to focus on programmes that fail. The second is that, even when that is not the case, there nevertheless tends to be an interest in programmes of considerable complexity with high ambitions in the face of limited knowledge. The third problem is that 'implementation research has taken an excessively mechanistic and rationalistic view of the process of implementation' (p. 64). The result is, as has been said in various ways in this and the previous chapter, the accumulation of checklists of factors that may affect success in the implementation process. Hence, like Matland, Rothstein aims to sort out the factors rather more effectively.

Rothstein seeks to follow Winter (see p. 71 above) in separating policy design issues from policy execution issues. We will not follow through his exploration of design issues in detail. His essential concern in this part of his analysis is to sort out conditions under which policies may be designed to minimize implementation problems. This leads him to struggle with issues about policy taxonomies, with in his case a particular concern to explicate those policies for which the simple 'universalist' model can be argued to be the most appropriate. When this is not possible he recognizes, as have most of the more modern implementation theorists, that admonishments to policy designers to have clear objectives and work with valid causal theories are often unrealistic. He notes that 'the state must take measures even when certain knowledge is not to be had' (p. 75). This leads Rothstein on to the exploration of 'policy execution', in which he stresses that the best ways to organize policy implementation depend on 'the type of *task* the organization must carry out' (p. 90). Here he is building on a substantial body of organization theory: (particularly contingency theory: see Burns and Stalker, 1961; Woodward, 1965; Hickson et al., 1971; Greenwood et al., 1975).

Rothstein identifies as a central concern of the 'top-down' literature the notion of 'responsibility drift' (1998: 93) as policies are implemented in complex networks. He recognizes the Hjern solution of control through networks as vulnerable to leaving policies liable to capture by special interests. We have already noted Rothstein's preference for simple targeting; the issue here is: What should happen when this is impossible? What he sees as important in these cases is (like Lipsky, see p. 53) the development of street-level accountability systems. At the same time he endorses some of the ideas about the creation of choice for consumers, traditionally associated with the New Right attack upon capture of policies by 'providers'. But he also explores the limitations of the market model, making the comment that its feasibility depends upon 'how the implementation of the freedom of choice program is structured' (p. 209).[3]

In analyzing the alternative approaches to accountability, Rothstein explores issues about legitimacy and trust, which he claims (like Lane, see pp. 65–6) have been rather neglected by implementation researchers. He goes on to point out that '[w]ithout citizens' trust in the institutions responsible for implementing public policies, implementation is likely to fail' (1998: 100). This is an important point, which perhaps helps us to understand some of the differences between the dominant American implementation literature, involving very high expectations in a relatively low-trust context, and some of the rather different European contributions.

Rothstein identifies six ideal-typical models for policy process legitimization:

- legal-bureaucratic;
- professional;
- corporatist;
- user-oriented;
- politician-oriented; and
- lottery-based.

His argument is that all these are applicable. Which should be applied (alone or in combination with others) will depend crucially upon the policy programme involved. Emphasizing, as noted above, that the state must act even when it does not know what will work, Rothstein argues that '[s]uccessful policy implementation is often a question of so organizing the implementation process as to accommodate the need for flexibility and the uncertainty in the policy theory' (1998: 113). He goes on to stress that the greater these are, 'the stiffer the demands on organization and legitimacy' (p. 113).

Rothstein's concern with implementation theory is largely prescriptive – in two senses. First, he aims to resolve the top-down/bottom-up argument about accountability by drawing attention to the multiplicity of ways policies may be legitimated. Second, he wants policy formulators to learn from implementation analysis that, where policies cannot be kept simple, attention must be given to the structuring of the relationship 'between the partially autonomous *producer* and *the citizen*' (1998: 115). However, in advancing these prescriptive arguments he draws our attention to some of the complexities in the accountability relationship that have to be addressed when we endeavour to describe and study the implementation process.

Conclusions

Table 4.2 charts the main contributions to the implementation literature, showing how the debate around the top-down and bottom-up perspectives developed over time.

TABLE 4.2 *Contributions to the study of implementation discussed in this and the previous chapter, by year*

Year	Top-downers	Bottom-uppers	Synthesizers etc.
1973	Pressman and Wildavsky		
1975	Van Meter and Van Horn		
1977	Bardach		
1978	Gunn		Elmore
			Scharpf
1979	Sabatier and Mazmanian		
1980		Lipsky	
		Elmore	
1981		Hjern and Porter	
		Barrett and Fudge	
1982		Hjern and Hull	Ripley and Franklin
1984	Hogwood and Gunn		
1986			Sabatier
			O'Toole (multi-actor implementation)
1987			Lane
1990			Goggin et al.
			Palumbo and Calista
1991			Stoker
1995			Matland
1997			Kickert et al.
1998			Rothstein

The table shows that there are good grounds for regarding the debate between the top-down and the bottom-up perspectives as now rather dated. However, we regard it as still a useful way of looking at the implementation literature as it highlights two important issues: about methodology and about the normative or ideological perspectives that influence the study of implementation. The case for comparing alternative methodologies, rather than regarding one approach as being the right one, was made very early in the 'debate' by Elmore (1978). Furthermore, at least since the Sabatier article of 1986 there has been little dispute with the proposition that choice of methodology may depend upon the subject and circumstances of a research study. As in so much other social research, the remaining still disputed methodological issue concerns the extent to which a positivist methodology is seen as feasible and appropriate. This was discussed in Chapter 1 (see pp. 10–11).

Table 4.3 offers a rough classification of the various theorists whose work has been explored, in terms of their methodological stances, the extent to which they highlight issues about networks or attempt to distinguish between policy issues, and their commitment to prescription.

A number of contributors to the top-down/bottom-up debate identified the way in which normative and methodological perspectives interact – viewpoints on key considerations of authority and legitimacy dictating how implementation problems are studied (and perhaps sometimes vice

TABLE 4.3 *Theoretical approaches to the study of implementation*

General approach	'Positivist' methodological stance	Strong emphasis on (a) networks	(b) policy types
Primarily descriptive			
Pressman and Wildavsky		x	
Van Meter and Van Horn	x		
Lipsky	x		
Elmore	x	x	
Scharpf		x	
Kickert et al.		x	
Ripley and Franklin	x		x
Sabatier	x	x	
Goggin et al.	x	x	
Palumbo and Calista			
Stoker	x		
Matland	x		
Essentially prescriptive			
Bardach		x	
Gunn			
Rothstein		x	x
Mixed			
Sabatier and Mazmanian	x		
Hjern and Porter		x	
Barrett and Fudge		x	
O'Toole	x	x	
Lane	x		x

versa). What comes out of the normative debate as indicated in Chapter 3 must be that how we approach the analysis of implementation issues (like so many other issues in social research) is influenced by who we are, whom we want to influence and who is paying for our work.

With those arguments for both methodological and normative selectivity we might perhaps reach the conclusion, after reviewing the implementation literature, that there is little more to be said. As was suggested right at the beginning of Chapter 3, we see no case for a 'general theory of implementation'. That is something else, however, from arguing that there are not better and worse ways of studying this important subject. Furthermore, the case for selectivity does not mean that it is irrelevant to develop more effective ways to deal especially with two clusters of variables that seem to complicate implementation studies: the nature of the substantive policy issue and the relevance of the institutional context. The contributions by Matland and by Rothstein particularly indicate their importance. These factors, then, need to be related to issues about a choice of a dependent variable.

In Chapter 6, when we review actual implementation studies (as opposed to efforts to theorize about it), we explore these issues further. We do so by relating them back to issues about choices of methodology and to the underlying normative issues from which this subject cannot escape. Before that, in Chapter 5, the development of implementation research, as exposed in this and the previous chapters, is positioned in its societal context.

Notes

1 This is a development of an argument deployed by Hargrove (1983), who also used Lowi's approach to categorization. Hargrove argues that the case for a typology is that different types of issues will involve different kinds of participants.
2 They are hazardous waste policy as influenced by the Resource Conservation and Recovery Act of 1976, family planning services under the Family Planning and Population Research Act of 1970, and municipal waste-water treatment as amended by the Clean Water Act of 1972.
3 Rothstein explores some of the widely deployed arguments on this topic; we will not digress into these here.

5

The Rise and Decline of the Policy-Implementation Paradigm

Introduction

Some contemporary observers of social change speak of the 'fate of the state' (Van Creveld, 1996), 'phantom states' (Derrida, 1993) or even of the 'end of the nation state' (Ohmae, 1995). The 'information society' (Drucker, 1995) or 'network society' (Castells, 1996) has no ideological, institutional or political centre attributed to it. Guéhenno went one step further when he gave his book the title *La Fin de la Démocratie* (1993). Talking of postmodern politics, Smith sees a 'political system disorientated, deficient and out of sorts with itself' (1994: 137). An alternative is presented by some writers in the form of the rise of the 'virtual state' (Frissen, 1999; Rosecrance, 1999).

In the context of such 'postmodern' perspectives a phenomenon like the implementation of public policy looks a bit out of date. If the flourishing period of the national state is over, is there still something like 'implementation' to be observed and studied? Do new forms of governance affect how we examine matters of implementation, and make them less or more relevant? These questions are central in this chapter. In order to position implementation theory and research in its societal context, the chapter's focus is on developments in both the practice and study of public administration after the Second World War. The first part of the chapter examines, side by side, what in the successive periods has happened in the real world and the academic responses to it. We aim to do justice to these responses, but, of course, complement them with an inter-pretation and judgement of our own. In the second part of the chapter the linkages between the study of implementation and the practice of public administration are further explored.

A distinction between three phases is made. The first was the era of great expectations (the 1950s, 1960s, 1970s; with origins in the 1930s). The second was the period of government retrenchment (the 1980s and 1990s). Then in the third, and current phase, we see developments with a particu-larly mixed character. Developments in the practice of public adminis-tration and implementation of public policy are sketched for each phase. The account of these cannot be comprehensive or universal in their cov-erage; our focus is particular upon developments in the United States, the United Kingdom and the Netherlands. From the United States there are particularly important influences on the literature. The exploration of developments in the latter two countries – whilst naturally to be expected here because of the locations of the authors – offers, given their somewhat different system characteristics, a valuable contrast (see Esping-Andersen, 1990; Hupe and Meijs, 2000). These descriptions of public administration in practice form the background for a sketch of developments in imple-mentation theory and research that can be interpreted as characteristic of each phase. After these primarily descriptive sections an overall assess-ment of the social history of the practice and study of public policy imple-mentation is made. The chapter ends with a concluding prognosis.

The first phase

The age of interventionism: 1930 to 1980

With his 'New Deal' the American President Franklin Roosevelt, in the early 1930s, offered policies to face the social consequences of a major economic crisis. Public works were undertaken, employment programmes were developed, social policy measures were enacted (Weir et al., 1988; Skocpol, 1995). It was in this period that many talented individuals sought to liberate American administration from the constraints of American politics (Schlesinger, 1960; Leuchtenburg, 1963). Government, in particular federal government, promoting social welfare, took on an active role. When the Second World War started, the high level of government activity stretched to sectors of society that were formerly seen as completely private. After the war, government expenditure for obvious reasons declined, but in the Truman and Eisenhower years the general confidence in the public sector remained relatively high (Reichard, 1988). In 1961 President Kennedy attracted 'the best and the brightest' to Washington to participate in federal government (Halberstam, 1972). Johnson, his successor, undertook his 'Great Society' project, aiming at the reduction of income and class inequalities. He declared a 'war on poverty' (Zarefsky, 1986).

As in the depression in the thirties, the Second World War led to efforts to liberate administration from the constraints of politics. In the Americans scarcely had to face the demands of total mobilization so desperately imposed upon the European nations. For Americans an understanding of the inefficiency of the governing system came perhaps even more from the anxieties of the 'cold war' (the fear that Russia would overtake them) and difficulties in Vietnam. It also came in a recognition for some that the war against poverty at home (which had not been fought very effectively by Roosevelt in the 1930s) needed fighting more efficiently again in the 1960s and 1970s. It was explicitly out of this 'war' that implementation studies emerged.

Thanks to American Marshall Aid, Western European countries like the Netherlands were, after the Second World War, rapidly put on their feet again. In a material sense the Netherlands was rebuilt. Alongside financial aid, American influences were visible in the way the rebuilding took place. Industrialization, planning and consumption were key elements in the underlying thinking of policy makers, which was explicitly macro-economic. A similar kind of 'thinking-from-the-top' was expressed in rural and urban planning. Despite the societal segmentation called 'pillarization' (Lijphart, 1975), all parties accepted the necessity to 'roll up their sleeves' in reconstructing the country. The organized employers offered stable employment in exchange for moderated wage demands from employees, while both wanted government to invest in the physical and social infrastructure of the country. With differences along lines of religious denomination as far as specific variants were concerned, there was consensus about the need to extend social security into a comprehensive system. The steadily developing economic prosperity made such an extension possible, while the Keynesian axiom of keeping up purchasing power provided the rationale (Cox, 1989). The creation of a nation-wide net of motorways, processes of sub-urbanization and the large-scale introduction of American household gadgets had direct consequences for the lifestyles of various social layers. From 1958 there was a rise in the number of lower class students entering higher education (Schuyt and Taverne, 2000). Many of these students fulfilled the demand of the ministries – increasing until deep into the seventies – for academically trained civil servants to make public policies at the various domains of the extending 'Verzorgingsstaat' (zorg = care; verzorging = taking care of) (Van der Meer and Roborgh, 1993).

Whilst the United Kingdom did not, like the Netherlands, suffer invasion, it experienced total mobilization in face of that threat. But during the war it also began to prepare for the peace. In particular Beveridge set out the principles for what was generally seen as a decent social security system. After the war, whilst developments had much in common with those in the Netherlands, administrative change was less fundamental. Although the Labour government elected in 1945 saw a need to continue many of the approaches of wartime administration to effect social change after the war, it saw less need to change the way that government itself was organized. Despite the fact that the United Kingdom's role in the world was much changed, the fact that the country had not been occupied and that it was one of the victors perhaps made it reluctant to re-examine traditional approaches to public administration. In any case, the practice of public administration in the UK has been traditionally rather distinctive. Unlike the USA, with its strong Constitution, but also unlike continental Europe, public administration and government in the United Kingdom are linked within a framework of administrative law that is to a large extent not formalized. Referring to the values that have been attributed to the British civil service, Gray and Jenkins state that these

> represent an ideal and perhaps idealized world where the administrative practice is set in a traditional structure of parliamentary accountability. This almost Weberian model of administrative structures – hierarchical, neutral, salaried, pensioned and rule-bound – was perhaps not often analysed as such but was seen as an adequate and necessary model for the UK political system. (1995: 77).

Gray and Jenkins go on to observe that the practice of British public administration took place for a substantial period in a consensus regarding both the context of political–administrative relationships and its underlying basic values. Young speaks of the 'mandarin world of Whitehall, in which skepticism and rumination (are) more highly rated habits of mind than zeal or blind conviction' (1989: 155). Dunsire characterizes the values leading the practice as equity, justice, impartiality and conspicuous uprightness, with liberty and participation relegated to representative organs. He speaks of a 'paternalist, statist canon, with emphasis on collective action and faith in bureaucratic rationality and professional autonomy' (1995: 28).

In the 1960s and 1970s challenges emerged to the 'gentlemen amateurs' in Westminster and Whitehall (Fulton Committee, 1968; Thomas, 1968), which led to incremental changes. Gray and Jenkins (1995) mention a focus on strategic planning in local government and the National Health Service, the introduction of rational techniques of budget reform and an increased emphasis on the strategic management of the public services. According to these authors, rather than questioning the fundamental links between political and administrative structures, the role of government and the value basis of the public service, these reform efforts remained within the accepted consensus. The reform objectives were not a smaller state, but better service delivery. Nevertheless, Gray and Jenkins observe in retrospect that 'the argument that the state was badly managed was common' (p. 79).

Implementation research and social engagement

By the time the Second World War began, according to Kettl, the study of public administration in the USA had acquired 'remarkable prestige and self-confidence' (2000: 10). Many prominent public administration theorists came to Washington to help manage the war. Afterwards, in the light of the war's experience, argues Kettl, such a simple administrative principle as the separation between administration and politics (see Chapter 2, p. 30 above) seemed shallow. Some time after the war the rise of graduate programmes of public affairs at American universities could be observed. In these programmes the strict separation between politics and administration was replaced by a mixed focus.

Robert McNamara, Secretary of Defense in both the Kennedy and the Johnson administrations, invited the Rand Corporation to introduce the 'Program Planning Budgeting System' (PPBS) into his department. As a follow-up, this system was introduced by President Johnson into other departments as well. Thus a demand arose for what are called 'policy analysts': civil servants academically trained in the application of policy analysis techniques. Harvard, transforming its Littauer School of Public Administration into the John F. Kennedy School of Government, was one of the first universities to offer a 'public policy program' . Berkeley, too, founded a 'Graduate School of Public Policy' (Kickert, 1996). 'Contrary to the traditional Public Administration more oriented as it has been towards the "nuts and bolts" of the practice of management in government, the new "public policy analysis" relies more on the "hard" analytical sciences' (Kickert, 1996: 130).

It was against this background that Pressman and Wildavsky in 1973 carried out their study *Implementation*. Curious about what had happened in Oakland to the good intentions expressed in Washington, these authors formulated a distinctive approach for what would be called implementation research (see Chapter 3, pp. 44–5). As has been made clear above (Chapter 3 and 4), an ongoing stream of studies followed. Whether there was – seen from 'the top' – disappointment about the outcomes of policy implementation or – observed at 'the bottom' – concern about the operational problems experienced in implementation processes, normative and methodological stances were seldom treated as needing distinct identification and elaboration. At the same time, in either instance, the social engagement of the implementation researcher was often great.

The study of public administration in Great Britain, Rhodes states (1996b), has long been insular, dominated by an institutionalist tradition characterized by an interest in administrative engineering but a distaste for theory. Dunsire speaks of an 'old style of purely narrative-descriptive academic writing about public administration' (1995: 33). Hogwood points out the specific British feature that apart from the study of public administration there is the discipline of social administration or social policy. Before the rise of academic interest in public policy in the 1970s there was already a substantial literature on social policy. Much of that was 'descriptive of current provisions or the development of each set of provisions, and often with an explicit or implicit normative support for the maintenance or further development of welfare provisions' (Hogwood, 1995: 60). Hogwood observes that, though there are older British examples of public policy studies, from the mid-seventies British writers begin to adapt or incorporate insights from American writers, and develop their own case studies (p. 62). The impact of this, as far as the study of implementation was concerned, was the elaboration of British contributions to theory influenced both by the Americans and by developments in Germany and Sweden (the work of Hjern and of Scharpf, for example, discussed in Chapters 3 and 4, pp. 53–5 and pp. 59–61). In Chapter 3 significant British contributions from both a 'top-down' and a bottom-up' perspective have been examined (see the discussion of the work of Hogwood and Gunn pp. 50–1 and Barrett and Fudge pp. 55–6 respectively). One of the current authors was heavily involved in this British work (Barrett and Hill, 1981; Ham and Hill, 1984).

Nevertheless, in the United Kingdom, the links between the study of public policy and the practice of public administration did not become as close as they became in the late sixties in the USA and, slightly later, in the Netherlands (Kickert and Van Vught, 1995). Though the study of public policy is institutionalized in public administration and political studies, the inter-disciplinary drive behind the policy orientation of the 1960s did not take hold in Britain (Hogwood, 1995: 70). Whitehall civil servants remain sceptical about formal policy analysis, stating that much of what they do is policy analysis in itself. At the same time training by social science academics of public servants particularly working in local government and the National Health Service fulfilled a demand for a policy focus. According to Hogwood, it can be no coincidence that the call for a more 'bottom-up' approach to implementation came from an academic unit, the School for Advanced Urban Studies at the University of Bristol, which was heavily engaged in the study of local government (1995: 69).

Distance in prosperity

Market and corporate government: the 1980s and 1990s

There have been many attempts to explain the way public administration changed in the phase of government retrenchment that occurred in the 1980s and 1990s; it would be going well beyond the brief of the current book for us to attempt to add to them (see Pollitt and Bouckaert, 2000, for an overview). Whilst the development acquired in due course a more or less global character, and saw some of its most extreme manifestations in New Zealand, its emergence was seen initially as very much linked to the acquisition of power by two determined right-wing politicians, Margaret Thatcher and Ronald Reagan. Thatcher became Prime Minister of a Conservative government in Britain in 1979. Across the public sector large structural changes were initiated: in central government, local government, the health service and the public utilities (Dunsire, 1995). As a follow-up of the Ibbs Report the so-called 'Next Steps' agencies were established in central government. Dunsire describes them as involving 'the relatively wholesale adoption of structural separation of political responsibilities from executive responsibilities, the former remaining with ministers assisted by small "policy" departments, the latter divested to new executive agencies each with its chief executive and required to produce mission statements and performance targets in a "framework document"'(1995: 24; see also Gains, 1999). Business methods were introduced into government, changing both external (privatization, contracting out) and internal relationships (performance measures). This created a 'genuine clash of cultures' between the world of Whitehall as described above and an 'almost Cromwellian impatience with the status quo' (Young, 1989: 155). Referring to the work of Fry (1984), Dunsire speaks of a 'gulf between the mandarins' rooted understanding that their job was to advise on policy; and the new Prime Minister's idea that their job was to execute policy and to manage their departments efficiently' (1995: 27).

Gray and Jenkins (1995) explain the drastic changes in the political agenda that took place in the United Kingdom in the eighties in terms of the failure of the efforts to control the economy in the previous decade. The rejection of the old solutions for the management of the state was followed by a search for new methods of control, accompanied by a changing political ideology that broke with the existing consensus. In Gray and Jenkins' view this focus on management and control, particularly of resources, explains also the political rejection of policy analysis in the mid-1970s. They observe: 'Faced with deepening crises of public expenditure the prime policy goal of government in the United Kingdom and elsewhere became the control of public finances' (p. 87). In all parts of the public sector, at various levels and in different modes, changes accompanying the realization of this primary goal were initiated. Gray and Jenkins indicate that confronting the public sector with market concepts like costs, prices and performance measurement implied the creation of different relations of accountability and, in fact, power relations, at the expense, for instance, of professional groups. Not only were these new labels introduced into the vocabulary, but they also changed the practice of administration. Rhodes (1996b) speaks of an integrated and sustained attack on what was perceived as the 'failure' of traditional government and administration.

John Major, succeeding Margaret Thatcher in 1990, added new elements to the ideology and practice of corporate government when he stressed 'giving more power to the citizen'. With his 'Citizen's Charter' he aimed at setting standards for the quality of public service in terms of prompt action, delivery dates, courtesy, with a final possibility of an entitlement of citizens to compensation payments (HMSO, 1991). Referring to the work of Richards (1992), Dunsire stresses the new patterns of legitimation that were being introduced here:

> Empowering the 'consumer' of public services creates new forms of controlling also the middle and lower ranks of public bureaucracy, while at the same time it disempowers the 'citizen' as participant in collective decision making at the macro – level. The Charters do not compensate for the loss of power by representative institutions, or the 'democratic deficit'... . (1995: 31)

Having been administrators during the period of the steady growth of public expenditure that gave birth to the modern welfare state, public servants in the eighties and nineties became 'managers'. Among other things this implied that a specific public task might be fulfilled via a contract: a system of 'management of outputs' emerged. The delivery of the public services became perceived as the production process of such outputs. What we call 'implementation' was thus taking place at a distance from a centre of government, even more invisible than it was for the directors of the former policy programmes. The difference was furthermore that the public 'administrator-turned-public-manager' now had a legitimation for not being interested in the internal process of implementation. It was only the results that counted. If the outputs deviated from what had been agreed upon, this had consequences for the contract and hence, in some cases, for the financing of the organization involved. 'Policy' and 'implementation' were being disconnected. The couplings, particularly in the form of contracts, were loose.

A year after Margaret Thatcher became British Prime Minister, Ronald Reagan won the American presidency. His predecessor, President Carter, had earlier declared war on Washington 'red tape' and created the President's Reorganization Project. It became a débâcle (Wamsley, 1990a). In his first inaugural address President Reagan stated: 'In this present crisis, government is not the solution to our problems. Government is the problem' (20 January 1981). Whilst it was more difficult to change the machinery of public administration in the United States than it was in Britain, the criticism of 'Big Government', articulated by the head of government himself, did not remain without effect. Though the material consequences in terms of (re-)privatization of government offices and services became visible slowly at a later stage – and perhaps with a more mixed character than hoped for by its originators – it seems less the effect on existing policies that was overwhelming than the influence on potential policies. It was especially the rhetorical side of the market ideology that was valued highly, both in politics and in administration. The breaking of a general post-war consensus gave room to forces aiming at 'reinventing government' (Osborne and Gaebler, 1992) in a rather fundamental way. Fundamental by effect, though simple in essence, the core of the retrenchment philosophy was that the mode of operation seen as usual for business corporations, and also the norms and values related to the private sector more generally, should similarly apply in the public sector. At all layers of government, and almost on a global scale, public officials embraced an 'away with us' attitude (Ringeling, 1993).

At the core of this development was the fact that government reduced its own service delivery capacity to a minimum and, instead, preferred contracting out operational activities. Milward and his collaborators observe that 'even though health and human services are funded by public agencies, the distribution of these funds is controlled and monitored by non-governmental third parties, who themselves determine which agencies to subcontract with for the actual provision of services' (1993: 310). Just as in private businesses, the functions of the headquarters of an organization became primarily focused on retaining 'system integration skills' (T.J. Peters, 1990: 13). The already famous business example was that of the Nike corporation. Instead of manufacturing sports shoes itself, the main office of this firm 'produces' them by contracting with various firms all over the world, directing its attention entirely to research and development, design, marketing and financial control. Milward (1996) describes the degree of separation between a government and the services it funds as a measure of the 'hollowness' of the state, indicated by the number of layers between the source and the use of funds to secure outputs. On various policy domains, on different layers of government and in numerous countries, similar examples of this 'hollowing out of the state' can now be observed.[1]

'Government is broken' remarked President Clinton after reading the eight hundred recommendations to improve federal government that were contained in Vice-President Gore's report *From Red Tape to Results: Creating a Government that Works Better and Costs Less* (Moe, Iggy: 111). Clinton and Gore had launched the National Performance Review, in which Osborne's and Gaebler's (1992) conception of 'reinventing government' was adopted. The 'steering, not rowing' notion of Osborne and

Gaebler led to the imperative to governments: Do the things you are good at. For you that means: Govern! And leave the operational side to others.

In the Netherlands comparable trends occurred. In national public administration a new axiom was embraced: 'the separation of policy and implementation'. It led to the reduction of the ministries to 'nuclear departments' responsible for 'agencies' that from there are 'steered at a distance'. Several implementation organizations that used to be directly subordinated to a certain ministry now perform a specific (financial, inspection or other) function for several ministries at a time, having gained in relative autonomy (see Kickert, 1998).

The latter phenomenon – the similarity to the British 'Next Steps' exercise may be noticed – provides an example of the creation of new public–public steering relationships. The notion of hollowing out is appropriate here because the nucleus became smaller while the archipelago of agencies around it was extended. Relationships of chain-like hierarchy and control were replaced by contract relationships or, at least, acquired a mixed character. Nevertheless, many of the arrangements referred to by the term 'hollow state' in an American context were of a public–private nature. So-called third-party organizations created new layers between government and citizen or corporation. In countries with a (neo-)corporatist tradition like the Netherlands, traditionally there has been an extended societal midfield between the state and the citizen, consisting of organizations of 'private initiative' stemming from various denominations, but fulfilling public tasks, while being to a large degree publicly funded (Dekker, 1998). In countries with a different tradition, such as the USA, hollowing out in some respects may imply the creation of a societal midfield with such a character. Kickert distinguishes three main ingredients of *public managerialism* as: business-like management, client-orientedness and 'market-like' competition (1997: 732). As each of these three fit better or worse in different national systems, in the various countries they get a different degree of attention. Similarly the pace at which both the intended and unintended effects of the developments as pictured became visible varied from country to country.

Implementation research and shifting agendas

Gray and Jenkins (1995) trace the rise of public management in Britain as a threat to the study of public administration, starting as far back as the late 1960s and early 1970s. They observe that an orientation towards reform in the practice of public administration then was accompanied by academic efforts to place the study of it on a firmer theoretical footing; among other things by the development of policy analysis and policy studies (Hogwood and Gunn, 1984; Hogwood, 1995). As indicated above, Whitehall remained sceptical about the adoption of policy analysis, while the beginning of the Thatcher era in 1979 meant a change in the political as well as academic agenda. Public management became the new theme (Flynn, 1993), while as 'new managerialism' it was also criticized (Pollitt, 1990). The intellectual sources used in academic work changed, too. Though in Britain the links between political science and public administration, on the one hand, and (organizational) sociology and social policy, on the other, had traditionally been stronger than, for instance, those with law, now (micro-)economic thinking (rational choice, principal–agent theory, and so on) became an important source. The principal embodiment of this is Dunleavy's influential *Democracy, Bureaucracy and Public Choice* (1991), offering a critique of mainstream public choice theory but showing how a more robust analysis of the private interests of public officials might be developed.

In the USA similar developments took place. Under the heading of 'the new public management' (Hood and Jackson, 1991; Kettl, 2000) an approach was introduced both to the practice and to the study of American federal government that was substantially different from the more traditional public administration. In an assessment of the state of the field, Kettl, referring to the work of F. Thompson (1997: 3), sketches the elements that distinguished the new public management itself: 'It focused on management rather than social values; on efficiency rather than equity; on mid-level managers rather than elites; on generic approaches rather than tactics tailored to specifically *public* issues; on management rather than political science or sociology' (2000: 27). In a reinforcing relationship of causes and consequences, the penetration of the ideology of managerialism in Western democracies, hardly leaving any layer or policy domain untouched, was accompanied by changes in the way in which analysts of government and administration approached the object of their studies. After Waldo's *The Administrative State* (1948), some authors now speak of the 'increasingly organizational state' (Laumann and Knoke, 1987) or the 'entrepreneurial state' (for instance, Eisinger, 1988). British writers have picked up this theme, writing of the 'contracting state' (Harden, 1992) or the 'managerial state' (for instance, Clarke and Newman, 1997).

We have shown in Chapters 3 and 4 how implementation studies mushroomed after the initial challenge thrown down by Pressman and Wildavsky. As O'Toole (2000a) observes, policy implementation moved from nowhere to a position of prominence in the seventies and early eighties. There was, as we have seen, a proliferation of studies that, in turn, brought

> an explosion in types of research designs, varieties of models, and – especially – proposals for adding a bewildering array of variables as part of the explanation for the implementation process and its products. The cornucopia of investigations catalyzed, in turn, a set of sectarian disputes: qualitative and small-n versus quantitative, large-n investigations; top-down versus bottom-up frameworks; policy-design versus policy-implementation emphasis, and so forth. Implementation was even seen by some worried students of traditional public administration as a theme posing a hegemonic threat to the field. (O'Toole, 2000a: 264)

Despite the emergence of new agendas it was exactly in the early eighties that – as shown above – European scholars joined the implementation debate. Dunsire (1995) presumes that these were, relatively separated from the new agendas, a reaction to policy failures in the seventies. However, there was a strong 'bottom-up emphasis' in much of this work. In a 'bottom-up' view implementation becomes 'a kind of bargaining activity between the objectives of the keepers of organizational resources and the perceptions of need by street-level executants' (Dunsire, 1995: 18). Though British studies of the implementation of public policies would continue to appear, after the bottom-up contributions, according to Dunsire, the 'theoretical urge apparently lessened'. He explains this as follows: 'Postulation of an "implementation gap" as the key to delivery failures may have suddenly seemed *de minimis* in face of the trumpeted claims of the New Right impugning the whole institutional structure of services ...' (p. 19).

Furthermore, Dunsire points at the sociological rather than political science roots of the British bottom-up contributions. More generally, he suggests, the number of British scholars of public administration is relatively small, hence individuals, having made a contribution in one area of the discipline, may want to move on to something else.

Not only in Britain, however, was there, from the mid-1980s, a decline in the academic interest in theory and research on public policy implementation as a central scholarly theme and perhaps sub-discipline of political science and public administration. In the premier policy schools in the USA the scale of implementation research diminished (Lynn, 1996a). Implementation scholars like DeLeon (1999a) speak of the implementation literature as 'lacking in any consensual theory', consequently labelling implementation studies as an 'intellectual dead-end'. O'Toole (2000a) observes in retrospect that, indeed, the spate of scholarly research aimed explicitly at the implementation theme had abated.

The comments above are about a relative decline, which is difficult to chart exactly, given that – as will be shown in Chapter 6 – implementation studies come in many forms and within various disciplines. No comprehensive bibliometric study is available.

Pragmatism in the new millennium

The age of pragmatism: from the 1990s to the present

The Netherlands has been traditionally known for its struggle against the sea. That same sea enabled the Dutch to gain profits as a nation of merchants and traders. The 'Golden Age' of the seventeenth century produced not only the picturesque canal centre of Amsterdam, but also painters like Rembrandt and Vermeer (Schama, 1987; Israel, 1995). Later, painters like Van Gogh and Mondriaan would add to the reputation of this small country near the North Sea. It would be in the 1990s that the Netherlands would attract attention for what is called 'the Dutch model' or 'the Dutch miracle' (see below).

Given the segmented character of Dutch society, divided in 'pillars' along lines of denomination, there has been a longstanding tradition of consensus making. Because of the need for a collective defence against the water (see Daalder, 1966), because of the possibilities of trade (on the combination of the merchant and the cleric see Ter Braak, 1931), or just because of the logic of class behaviour (Lijphart, 1975), the members of the Dutch elites – pillarized as they are – have long been accustomed to meet, deliberate and negotiate with each other (see also Hupe, 1993b). Usually the result of this giving and taking is a compromise acceptable to the parties involved. In social and economic affairs this consensus making has to a large extent been institutionalized. In the tripartite Social Economic Council, founded in 1950, representatives of employers' organizations and employees' organizations regularly meet, together with independent experts appointed by the Crown. This Council, the highest organ of advice in governmental social and economic affairs, is the epitome of Dutch labour relations and, as such, symbolic of the more general culture of consensus characteristic of Dutch society, state and the relations between them (Hupe and Meijs, 2000).

Consultation, decentralization – in both its territorial and functional variants – and participation are key elements in the contemporary practice of Dutch public administration. Changes in the National Assistance Act, a cornerstone of the Dutch *Verzorgingsstaat*, imply major qualitative alterations in the relationships of the governmental and other actors involved in the delivery of this type of social services. In this context the metaphor of *overturned relationships* between national and local government is used, while one of us speaks about *implementation as partnership* on all levels of the delivery system of national assistance (Hupe, 1996). Particularly in the last decade direct-participatory ways of public decision making – as complementary to indirect-procedural ways like voting as practised in the formal system of representative democracy – have spread over other policy fields as well as that of social and economic policy. Under headings like 'interactive policy making' the direct involving of citizens, in one way or another, has become more or less standard practice (for overviews see Pröpper and Steenbeek, 1999; Edelenbos and Monnikhof, 2001).[2]

Against this background, in 1982 an agreement was made involving the offer of moderate wage demands made by the organized employees, in exchange for employment offered by the employers' organizations, both enabling government to reconstruct government expenditures. The positive results of this agreement, in terms of cuts in public finance, economic growth and a recovery of job growth, form the essence of what is called 'the Dutch miracle' (Visser and Hemerijck, 1997). From 1982 Christian-Democrat Ruud Lubbers led three successive coalition cabinets. In the first two the Christian-Democrats governed together with the Liberal party, while the latter in the third cabinet in 1990 were succeeded by the Social-Democrats. Wim Kok, then Minister of Finance, gave particular attention to the task of 'getting government spending sound'. He managed to do so without losing touch with his – socialist – electorate. Since 1994 he has chaired a coalition unprecedented in Dutch parliamentary history before: a partnership between the Social-Democratic and the two Liberal parties. In this so-called 'purple' cabinet (a mix of red and blue) the traditional opposition between 'labour' and 'capital' seems to have been eliminated.

The emergence of a more pragmatic approach in Britain after the replacement of Thatcher by Major was described by Dunsire as follows: '[T]he erosion of the public–private distinction, and towards purchasing rather than supplying, towards enabling "voluntary" and community provision rather than delivering services, toward harnessing self-policing associations rather than enforcing regulations … and so on' (1995: 34). In Dunsire's view, there is a kind of inevitability in the shifts in social mood underlying these trends: from hierarchism to individualism, from both of these towards egalitarianism. Using the 'grid/group' cultural theory-framework (Schwarz and Thompson, 1990; M. Thompson et al., 1990), Dunsire sketches an actual way of life marked by 'a critical rationality, by general loss of faith in politics, by loss of trust in "authorities", by the enhanced sensitivities behind the silly face of "political correctness", and by "Green" forms of global awareness' (1995: 33). These cultural shifts imply a need for 'more complex, subtle conceptions of control' in which management 'has to be conceptually divorced from its residual associations with hierarchical authority' (Bellamy and Taylor, 1992: 39). In that respect Dunsire sees the trends he observes not so much as outcome of Thatcherite policies but of these more deeper, one could say sociological and almost universal, socio-cultural changes. He observes a shift in attention away from linear processes 'from policy to bureaucratic action', to the 'methods and outcomes of purposive social control eschewing the primary use of either coercive regulation or an extensive public sector'. Hence he argues that governments, regardless of their political 'colour', will be 'likely to search more for indirect administration-saving ways of discharging their inalienable duty to guard against external threat and internal disruption, and of achieving their electorally legitimated policy programmes; the outcome may be described as "governance" rather than "government" ' (Dunsire, 1995: 34).

In the 1990s progressives took office as government leaders in various Western countries; either as Prime Minister of a coalition cabinet, like

Schröder in Germany, Jospin in France and Verhofstadt in Belgium, or chairing a one-party government like Blair in the UK and Clinton in the USA. The latter two in particular took an interest in the Dutch *'polder-model'*. They saw it as an example of the 'third way' they were aiming for in their respective countries (Giddens, 1998).

The approach of the Blair government in Britain has been to embrace the administrative changes of the Thatcher/Major era inasmuch as they are believed to deliver good public services, but to reject the dogmatic commitment to privatization that had characterized much of the approach of their predecessors. Two typical developments have been the response to the 'private finance initiative' and the replacement of compulsory competitive tendering by best value.

In the former case, Labour had been expected to reject the Conservative policy of encouraging private investment in public services, particularly the scheme under which new hospitals were developed on that basis. In practice the government has merely reshaped the scheme under a new name of 'public–private partnerships', arguing that what is important is to get new resources into health care in a context in which there are constraints upon public borrowing (stemming from macro-economic policy).

In the latter case, the 'best value' policy for local government is described as follows:

> Best value will be a duty to deliver services to clear standards – covering both cost and quality – by the most effective, economic and efficient means available. In carrying out this duty local authorities will be accountable to local people and have a responsibility to central government in its role as representative of the broader national interest. Local authorities will set those standards – covering both cost and quality – for all the services for which they are responsible. But in those areas such as education and social services where the Government has key responsibilities and commitments, the Government itself will set national standards. (Department of the Environment, Transport and the Regions, 1998, para 7.2)

The 1999 Local Government Act imposes this duty on all local authorities except parish councils. The process started in 2000. Local authorities are required to establish the following for all their services:

- specific objectives and performance measures;
- a programme of fundamental performance reviews; and
- local performance plans.

Their efforts to secure 'best value' are required to be very much in the public domain. But in addition to general public scrutiny, the government itself set up a system of auditing and inspection. Hence there is a system of reporting back to central government, which has given itself powers to intervene if the evidence suggests what it regards as below-standard services.

Implementation research and governance

As was noted in Chapter 4 (p. 66), Goggin and his colleagues saw implementation studies as consisting of three generations: the first generation
described single cases; in the second generation, analytical frameworks
were developed; while scholars of the third generation, like themselves,
aim at explaining variety. They argued: 'Clearly, the challenge for the next
generation of scholarship is to develop and test explanatory and predictive implementation theories of the middle range' (Goggin et al., 1990: 15).
Writing in 1998, Lester and Goggin seemed to have remained optimistic
when they spoke of a 'rediscovery of implementation studies', wanting 'to
stimulate a renaissance of interest in policy implementation research' (p. 2).
Earlier, Lester and his colleagues observed that the ' "critical" variables
have not been identified' (Lester et al., 1987: 200).

Kettl (2000), in his assessment of the state of the field of public administration around the beginning of the third millennium, develops an argument relevant to the study of implementation. He stresses the importance
of the political culture present in a specific political system as far as sus-
ceptibility to a specific ideology of reform is concerned. Speaking about
the USA, Kettl focuses on the various political norms and policy expectations implied by four different political traditions: Hamiltonian,
Jeffersonian, Wilsonian and Madisonian. The essence of these different
political traditions can be summarized as follows. Wilson's politics–
administration dichotomy is relatively well known; Hamilton sought a
strong and effective executive branch; in the Madisonian tradition the
principle of balance of power is central; while in the Jeffersonian one there
is a strong commitment to a small government protecting individual
autonomy. On the basis of this variety Kettl constructs a typology of
administrative ideas, using the Wilsonian (hierarchical) and Madisonian
(balance of power) political traditions on one dimension, against the
Hamiltonian (strong executive/top-down) and Jeffersonian (weak executive/
bottom-up) traditions on the other (p. 17).

Kettl acknowledges that the new public management frames three
important issues for American public administration. With its focus on a
strong top-down executive this reform ideology fits the Hamiltonian
tradition. At the same time, in its separation between management and
policy functions it is more Wilsonian than Hamiltonian, Kettl observes.
Next, what President Clinton aimed at with his National Performance
Review Kettl sees, on the one hand, particularly as far as reducing government's basic jobs is concerned, as less sweeping, but, on the other, as more
ambitious than the new public management. With regard to the latter,
Kettl refers to the incorporation of outcome-based measures and cus-
tomer service standards for all government programmes (p. 27).
Furthermore, though the National Performance Review has been heavily
influenced by new public management thinking, Kettl stresses its own

character, based on the specificity of American institutions and political traditions. Not every country has the same kind of parliamentary system as New Zealand embodying the separation of policy and administrative responsibilities, or government policy makers willing to specify clearly the goals they want managers to pursue, Kettl observes (p. 27). New Zealand-style management contracts therefore cannot simply be transplanted into a different institutional context. From these distinctions Kettl draws some conclusions about American public administration. First, it follows the political norms and policy expectations embedded in a specific political culture. Reform ideologies like 'Westminster new public management', as Kettl calls it (p. 28), do not fit the patterns of American political traditions. Therefore they either are ignored or must be tailored to fit the American system. Second, the values and norms of the various political traditions inevitably conflict.

Kettl (2000) explores three questions, fundamental for the field of public administration, upon which the new public management has cast fresh light:

- What should replace the field's reliance on hierarchy (p. 28)? Gradually hierarchy's theoretical preeminence has slipped. Instead of having evaporated, hierarchy continues, however, 'to describe how most complex organizations organize themselves and how elected officials think about holding government bureaucracies accountable' (pp. 28–9). Kettl regards organizational theories of networks and political theories of governance as promising here, because they offer possibilities, both empirical and normative, to incorporate the continued importance of hierarchical authority into broader models of public administration.
- What should be the field's approach to the policy–administration dichotomy (p. 29)? Kettl observes that, while since the 1950s policy decisions and administrative action have been mainly seen as seamlessly connected, the new public management reformers, aiming at the promotion of efficiency, have resurrected this dichotomy.[3] In the new public management theory the 'principal' hires 'agents' to perform the government's work. Contracts concern expected results; flexibility is given with regard to how to achieve them. 'The practice, however rapidly it is spreading, raises all the knotty questions about political accountability and administrative effectiveness that traditionally have needled public administration theory' (p. 29).
- There has long been criticism of public administration for a lack of rigour in theory and research, Kettl observes. How can this discipline advance the state of theory, ensuring the systematic testing of its theoretical propositions? For Kettl, game theory and statistical analysis are particularly relevant here.

Kettl concludes that these three questions 'shape the core puzzles in American public administration' (p. 30). The differentiated ways in which public administration and political culture are related can explain many of the conflicts among scholars with competing theories, for because of its relation to a specific political tradition, after all, 'every theoretical proposition is also implicitly a political argument' (p. 30).

For the sub-discipline of public policy implementation theory and research O'Toole (2000a) undertook an exercise similar to that carried out by Kettl for the field of public administration as a whole. In his assessment of the state of implementation research his point of departure is that the practical world is now just as much in need of valid knowledge about policy implementation as it has ever been. If scholarship has not simply solved the problem, what has happened? Where has all the policy implementation gone, or at least the scholarly signs of it (p. 265)? O'Toole's answer is that the evidence is mixed. Though the top-down/bottom-up debate has been superseded, the number of approaches to synthesis remains limited, while there has not really been an attempt to winnow the overwhelming number of variables toward parsimonious explanation.[4]

When Kettl makes his observations about the state of public administration, it is obvious that he is looking at the subject in the context of the specific American political-administrative setting and culture. Nevertheless, his argument has wider implications. Among British authors a further development of the field can also be observed. The shift in British work away from public administration to public management in the 1980s has already been noted. But in the 1990s the small number of British scholars in this field readily returned to a pragmatic stance that recognized the wide range of approaches to their subject. Christopher Hood's *The Art of the State* (1998) provides both an expression of that stance and a useful exploration of relevant ideas. He argues that 'variation in ideas about how to organize public services is a central and recurrent theme in public management' (p. 6). He suggests that grid/group cultural theory (Douglas, 1982; M. Thompson et al., 1990) can be used to encapsulate these different ideas. Here 'grid' refers to alternatives that public organizations should be constrained or, by contrast, that managers should be 'free to manage' (Hood, 1998: 8). 'Group', on the other hand, refers to debates about who should provide services. Hence Hood arrives at four 'styles of public management':

- High 'grid'/low 'group' – 'the fatalist way' where rule-bound systems are developed and low levels of co-operation are expected
- High 'grid'/high 'group' – 'the hierarchist way' involving socially cohesive rule-bound systems
- Low 'grid'/low 'group' – 'the individualist way' involving a high emphasis on negotiation and bargaining
- Low 'grid'/high 'group' – 'the egalitarian way' with high participation expected. (1998: 9)

Hood argues that these four approaches represent choices, each with built-in strengths and weaknesses. Then, in a way that is consonant with the logic of his argument but perhaps surprising in relation to what may be observed in the real world, he argues that any balance between them 'is likely to be problematic and precarious because each of the approaches involves an underlying logic which, if taken to its limits, will tend to destroy all the others' (p. 209). Hence Hood seems to be acknowledging contemporary diversity yet doubting that it can be sustained, a curious position perhaps qualified a little by the parenthetical comment 'if taken to its limits'. This analysis contributes little to the consideration of implementation other than to highlight the various models considered for its control.

Looking particularly at implementation theory and research, Hogwood (1995) sounds optimistic when he remarks that he would not have time enough to read all the third-wave implementation studies that have been published. Simultaneously, however, he observes that within British political science and public administration in general, the quantitative analysis of policy is underdeveloped, and he admits that much of contemporary implementation literature is concerned with 'refinement, refutation, and the construction of artificial debates' (p. 70). In the second half of the 1990s British interest in implementation theory seemed to have declined seriously. One of the few reviews of the topic was published by one of us, asking whether it was 'yesterday's issue'. It noted that

> the 1980s and 1990s saw the emergence of an approach to the policy/implementation process in which the 'top' (and particularly the politicians) have sought to inculcate dramatic value shifts at the lower level through institutional changes particularly directed at changing incentive structures. It has been prepared to carry these through rapidly and without experiment at the outset, apparently not worrying much about the way in which these changes might actually impact upon practice, but has then moved in with a variety of devices to try to control the behaviour of the implementers. (Hill, 1997b: 383)

The article went on to assert the continuing importance of implementation studies so long as it was noted 'how slippery the concept of implementation is' and 'the strong normative elements in the implementation debate' were recognized. Hence, it ended:

> If we want to have a debate about accountability by all means let us have one – after all the issues about the need for new approaches to public accountability are of enormous importance – but let us not confuse attempts to analyse how policies are put into practice with that debate. If we want to do the latter let us take our methodological lead from the organizational sociologists who have argued that an analysis of sources of power and influence must avoid either privileging or demonizing particular sources of that power and does not therefore require the prescription of a correct starting point, at the top or bottom. (p. 383)

In this perspective it is relevant to notice, for instance, that recently the UK Economic and Social Research Council financially enabled a series of seminars organized from management schools of the Universities of Aston and Cambridge on the very subject of public policy implementation.

What, in any case does seem to have increased since the self-proclaimed first 'third-generation' study of Goggin et al. (1990) is the consciousness of the multi-dimensional character of the object of implementation theory and research. In a way, and perhaps reinforced by those authors' endorsement of the use of multiple measures and multiple methods, their programmatic stance has been working as an 'intimidating standard', as O'Toole acknowledges. Yet, in the end, O'Toole views the glass as half full: 'There is more than meets the eye...'. 'A considerable quantity of provocative, well-conceived, and well-executed recent scholarship bears quite directly on salient issues of policy implementation, even if not explicitly and obviously framed in such terms' (2000a: 265). O'Toole's major message is that nowadays one can see more 'implementation research' when one looks *beyond* investigations with a self-proclaimed focus on implementation. He refers here to Meier:

> My biased survey of literature suggest[s] that a wide range of journals publish articles that inform the study of policy implementation – the mainstream sociology journals, most of the public administration journals, the professions journals (public health, social work, sometimes law or medicine), many of the economics journals, and on rare occasion a political science journal. Much of this literature is not intended to directly answer questions of policy implementation, but it addresses concerns that are central to policy implementation. (Meier, 1999: 6–7)

O'Toole, however, distinguishes four indirect contributions to implementation research coming from outside implementation studies but from within political science and public administration: formal and deductive approaches; institutional analysis and development; networks and network management; and the study of governance. The latter three themes are seen by Frederickson (1999) as having infused the subject of public administration more generally, while it may be noticed that the latter two themes are recognized as promising by Kettl, too, in his assessment of the field of public administration. Both networks and governance therefore justify closer attention here. Kettl observes that particularly since the Second World War much governance has involved 'heavy and increasing use of multi-organizational teams and partnerships with non-governmental tools' (2000: 23). In Kettl's view, network theory (see the discussion in Chapter 4 of this book, pp. 59–61 and 77–9) has provided a framework for 'understanding the growing interconnections among varied organizations that find themselves working together to implement public policy' (p. 24). This framework has helped public administration 'escape the pathologies of theory deeply rooted in hierarchical authority' (p. 24), bringing theory closer to administrative practice. This has led to new approaches to co-ordination. Besides, according to Kettl, network theory has helped to provide the foundation for linking the study of governance with an understanding of the workings of government. Referring to the work of Frederickson, Kettl sees this last contribution as the most important one, because network theory provides the connection 'to the big issues of democratic government. It is in governance theory that public administration wrestles with problems of representation, political control of bureaucracy and the democratic legitimacy of institutions and networks in the time of the fragmented and disarticulated state'. (Frederickson, 1999: 19)

What is attractive about the contemporary use of the concept of governance is its broad scope. Moving away from a concentration on government as a locus, using this concept as a focus draws attention to relevant forms of actions aimed at governing that were not looked at as such before. These actions are practised by government, but also by corporate and non-profit actors. Irrespective of contexts, in principle they all, in their own way, fulfil public tasks in the overarching public domain. Away from a merely hierarchical perspective on the exercise of authority, the concept of governance opens up a view of a more 'horizontalist' way of governing. What is particularly relevant here is that the concept provides a different, but continued, focus on implementation. At the same time, however, this broadness is problematical, for both research and practice. Instead of diminishing the number of variables seen as relevant for the explanation of implementation behaviour, implementation processes, policy outputs or policy outcomes, it seems to enlarge that number. As O'Toole observes: '[T]he variety of arrangements embraced by the governance notion defies parsimonious theory building' (2000a: 279). So, under the governance heading the 'too many variables' problem (see p. 74 above) re-emerges. In the practice of public administration the container character of the governance concept may mislead policy makers. Pragmatic logic both in implementation research and in policy practice may imply that the governance concept can be used in a productive way if applied in a contextualized form; we will explore how to do this in Chapter 8.

Evaluation

Differentiation

Though the objective is not causal explanation here, there is a need to interpret and understand what we have found so far. As in the entire chapter, moving to and fro between the study of implementation and the practice of public administration sheds light on relevant linkages. Evaluating the 'evolution of implementation studies', Lester and Goggin (1998) position the various implementation scholars within a typology. Their dimensions are:

- whether a specific scholar is positive (or not) about the continuation of implementation studies; and
- whether he or she advocates (or not) the modification of the conceptual or methodological approaches used in those studies.

On the basis of this typology Lester and Goggin distinguish the following types of scholars: 'reformers', 'testers', 'skeptics' and 'terminators'. Inspired by Lester and Goggin's effort, but aware of the limits of classification, we can explore developments in the field of implementation research within their societal context. The questions set out at the beginning of this chapter concerned the relevance of implementation theory and research and the possible changes in that relevance, given certain developments in state and society. Therefore it may be useful to distinguish between, on the one side, the scientific and, on the other, the normative or political orientation the various implementation scholars express in their work. On the scientific dimension they may be distinguished in terms of their particular epistemological stance, between, at one end of the continuum, a more positivist one and, at the other, a more interpretative/hermeneutic one. On the political or normative dimension authors vary in the extent to which they favour the procedural, indirect, form of democracy called representative democracy, or the alternative, participation-oriented, more material and direct forms of democracy, called deliberative or discursive democracy (Dryzek, 1990; Elster, 1998; see also pp. 28–32 in this book). When a study of the implementation of a specific policy is aiming to explain an 'implementation gap', its normative stance may be characterized as one in favour of representative democracy. Depending on the stated research objective and some related elements to be taken into account, the epistemological stance may be called positivist here.

Thus a variety of leading perspectives in implementation theory and research are distinguished in Table 5.1. Operationalization of the dimensions of this typology makes it possible to position any specific implementation study within it. Though this is not the place to carry out such a bibliometrical exercise, we can facilitate it by giving some illustrative examples. Studies like Pressman and Wildavsky's *Implementation* (see Chapter 3, pp. 44–5 above) and much of the early work by Sabatier (see, for example, his comment quoted on p. 64) may be characterized as being written from a combination of amazement about what is happening with good intentions formulated as policy and a drive to contribute to improvement by producing knowledge of the facts: the 'reform' perspective. We see a similar preoccupation in the more recent work on 'mandates'

TABLE 5.1   *Leading perspectives in implementation theory and research*

	Epistemological stance	
Stance on democracy	**Positivist**	**Interpretative**
Representative democracy	'Reform'	'Description'
	'Testing' 'Explanation'	
Deliberative democracy	'Criticism'	'Activism'

(see Chapter 6, pp. 125–6). Contrastingly, an activist challenging of 'top-down' policy makers can be observed behind the statement that 'the policy–action relationship needs to be considered in a political context and as an interactive and negotiative process, taking place over time, between those seeking to put policy into effect and those upon whom action depends' (Barrett and Fudge, 1981a: 29; see the discussion of their work in Chapter 3, pp. 55–6). A similar stance can be noticed in Hanf and Scharpf's (1978) plea for looking at the world – perceived as being inter-organizational – fundamentally in a 'horizontal' rather than hierarchical way (see the discussion in Chapter 4 above, pp. 59–61). Lipsky's seminal work on street-level bureaucracy (see Chapter 3, pp. 51–3) has sometimes been taken for a demonstration of 'bureaucrat bashing'. There are reasons, however, to read the book as the opposite: a, finally political, charge against high-ranking policy makers who from 'top-floor suites' impose financial cuts on lower-level functionaries and for the rest leave them alone in their 'crowded offices' (1980: xii). Faced with an increasing work-load, these front-line bureaucrats cope with their dilemmas in an individual way, trying to make the best of it. Thus Lipsky, in fact, as we noted, makes public heroes of officials required to represent government in direct contact with citizens. His book therefore can be seen as emblematic for the 'criticism' perspective. Later, the perspectives of 'activism' and 'criticism' seem to be continued in the work of some interpretivist scholars. As we showed in Chapter 2, rather than focusing upon high-ranking government officials, the focus in some of those publications is on citizens or public servants and their participation in processes of (self-)governing (compare Stivers, 1994). Other contemporary studies imply, for instance, a critical analysis of administrative language (see Yanow, 1993, 1996).

Many implementation studies still focus upon a single policy process, in a mainly descriptive way. Sometimes the authors are explicitly aiming to explain what is perceived as a policy or implementation 'failure', though both their epistemological and normative stances may vary. These descriptive-explanatory kinds of studies still form the most numerous category of studies (see O'Toole, 1986); they can be called the mainstream of implementation theory and research. Ahead of that stream there are contributions purposively designed to accumulate knowledge, deducting hypotheses and performing empirical research in as systematic a way as possible. In a small number of cases, notably those in which Kenneth Meier has been involved (see p. 122, 125 etc.), hypotheses are tested on large aggregates of data, with the use of formal models. The epistemological stance in those cases is clearly positivist (in any variant) here, while the normative stance – almost by definition, because of the theory-driven aim of testing – is neutral or unarticulated.

On paradigms

The typology presented here does not say anything about the relative importance of the various types, neither in terms of, for instance, explanatory value – a scientific dimension; nor in terms of use in the public domain – a societal dimension. However, in this chapter it has been suggested that links can be made between the study and practice of public policy implementation. Our assumption is that such patterns can only be found if the developments in both worlds are observed in relation to each other. Kuhn's conception of a 'paradigm' (1970), in amended form, may be helpful here.

Kuhn argues that if, in a certain domain of science, the practice of theory and research for a certain period is guided by a legitimate and more or less coherent set of problems and methods, this practice can be called 'normal science', while the set can be labelled as a specific 'paradigm'. Scientific progress is made when that particular set of problems and methods is changed and one paradigm is succeeded by another; then a paradigm shift takes place. When raising the question whether there is or has been an 'implementation paradigm', we refer to the more or less coherent and in a certain period legitimate set of problems and solutions connected with turning public policies into actions, as perceived by both practitioners and analysts of implementation. A paradigm shift, then, would mean that the legitimacy and coherence of such a specific set at a specific time seems to have diminished in favour of other sets of problems and solutions. In order to be able to make such observations with an eye on the future, it may be appropriate to go back to the practice of implementation again, looking at some recent developments.

Paradigms and contexts

On 13 May 2000, in Enschede, a middle-sized city in the eastern part of the Netherlands, a fireworks factory exploded. Twenty-two people were killed and 600 were wounded. Because the factory was located in the heart of the city, in a densely populated district, hundreds of houses were completely destroyed (*NRC Handelsblad*, 10 May 2001). This disaster shocked the entire country. How could this have happened? Moreover, which officials had tolerated the location of a fireworks factory in the centre of the city? The former National Ombudsman led a major investigation. His conclusion was that the management of the factory was primarily responsible for the disaster, but immediately in connection to that, all government officials along the administrative chain from the local authorities, via the Army, to the Ministry of Environmental Affairs were to blame. The former Ombudsman called for a 'cultural revolution' in government, implying that, on any administrative layer, rules need to be enforced and responsibilities taken. Though the Mayor remained in office, the two aldermen most responsible for the permits given to the director of the company resigned.

Within a deeply vested administrative culture of pragmatic 'wheeling and dealing', disasters like this in contemporary Netherlands lead to pleas for 'strong government'. At the same time, the intended but also unintended consequences of the privatization of several former government organizations have become visible (Algemene Rekenkamer, 1987, 1998). The backlash from these privatizations has led to the foundation of various institutions of oversight (Hupe and Klaassen, 2001). This 'new normativism', manifested at the political level, seems a reaction to what may be perceived as a pragmatic public-administrative practice. It is argued that too many adverse consequences of this practice have now become apparent. Amongst the opposition to the seven years of two 'purple' social–liberal coalition cabinets, a number of aldermen, local politicians from the Christian-Democratic and Green Left parties, presented a political pamphlet against the 'excessive economization of societal life'. Expressing their discomfort with the 'dominant thinking in public administration – with its stress on government retrenchment, privatization and market philosophy' – they purposively anticipate the possibility of a new, social-capital-oriented, political coalition of the Labour party, the Christian-Democrats and the Radical Left party (*NRC Handelsblad*, 23 March 2001).

In Britain, which was, as we saw, prominent and early in embracing a comprehensive market ideology in the 1980s, one now can observe the succession of that ideology by a more pragmatic 'It does not matter how, as long as it works' orientation. It is illustrated by the 'best value' approach to surveillance over local government outlined on p. 99. After eight years of Democrat administration it is unclear yet what changes in the American government may be expected. However much, on a comparative scale, there may seem to be doctrines of administrative reform showing certain similarities, they are implemented with specific accents, at a varying pace, into political and cultural environments that may fundamentally differ. What seems to remain, however, becoming apparent in cases of fiascoes, crises and disasters, is the public need to get answers to two questions: 'What went wrong? 'and: 'Who is responsible?' The consequence seems to be a context-bound but continuing attention to an 'hierarchical' mode of governance.

The policy-implementation paradigm and beyond

Dunsire, looking at the development of the study of public administration, states: 'Having been "public administration" in the 1970s, and become "public policy and management" in the 1980s, the name of the discipline may well become "governance" in the 1990s' (1995: 34). Analysing theory–practice links in the evolution of public management and public administration, Gray and Jenkins relativize the 'numerous claims of a paradigm shift [that] have been made' (1995: 76). In their view the rise of new public management implied less a revolution in paradigm, supplanting traditional public administration, than a 'competing vision' remaining in many ways 'separate and distinct' (p. 92). In our view it seems as if in the practice and study of government and administration in a certain period the dominant way in which problems as well as solutions are framed is specific, while, over time, this dominant frame is 'succeeded' by another one.

When one looks more in particular at the development of the study and practice of public policy implementation one can see it coming onto the agenda in the 1970s, in the context of the extension of Western welfare states, which had grown rapidly after the Second World War. As sketched above, government, in almost all Western countries, initiated sometimes very ambitious policy programmes. At the same time, particularly within the academic disciplines of political science and public administration, new public policy schools were founded. After 1973, when Pressman and Wildavsky discovered and explained the possibility of a gap between the intentions and outcomes of a policy, a major new part of the research agenda was filled by the study of implementation. Therefore, one may speak more specifically of a *policy-implementation paradigm* as growing from post-war economic prosperity, with roots in the anti-crisis actions of government in the thirties, enhanced by wartime government performance, and at its peak in the seventies.[5]

At the beginning of the eighties – the Thatcher–Reagan era – this paradigm, which had been so closely connected to large-scale policy programmes of an interventionist central government, was replaced. Or, rather, the prevailing problem/solution mind-set lost its ideological dominance. This happened both in the practice and in the study of policy implementation. Implementation was defined away; it was management that mattered instead. More precisely, with the contractualism embodied in what can be called the *new public management (NPM) paradigm* the ins and outs of implementation were left to the managing 'agent', with whom the 'principal' makes a contract specifying expected outputs. In that paradigm, implementation was being contracted away; and with that, the responsibility for possible failures related to it. It may, however, be said that another aspect of the implementation issue emerged with this: the implementation of effective regulatory policy. Though the vertical orientation inherent in the policy–implementation distinction remained intact, the stiff 'chain' became a 'rope'. It is in this period that implementation studies no longer dominated the research agendas of political science and public administration. Nevertheless, interesting contributions appeared, particularly ones written from a critical or activist perspective, in the first half of the 1980s. In any case there was an inevitable 'time lag' inasmuch as academics continued to publish work inspired by the concerns of the earlier era. Moreover, the introduction of new public management was a slow process, opposed by many. Gradually, and relatively separated, new themes, like the importance of networks, arose, away from the main part of the stream, while at the same time broadening it.

It is important not to characterize this development as one from hierarchy via markets to networks, as Lowndes and Skelcher say: 'A crude periodization of modes of governance can also carry with it the myth of progress – bureaucracy is all - bad, markets as a necessary evil and networks as the "new Jerusalem"' (1998: 331). Yet, in the 1990s the traditional relevance of the central political institutions began to be relativized. There was more attention to government's dependency upon other societal actors. Steering these actors as objects may have become more difficult. Some people argue that this is not a problem, on the grounds that private actors are quite capable of recognizing public responsibilities for themselves (Bozeman, 1987). While the *locus* of traditional politics in 'government' to a certain extent became more empty (Bovens et al. [1995] speak of the 'relocation of politics'), the *focus* of 'the political', on the contrary, gained relevance (see Hupe, 1994). Thus one can speak of a *governance paradigm*, emerging in the 1990s. Its difference from the previous paradigms is, first, the greater attention to relations of dependency, implying that (central) government is not expected to do everything always on its own. Second, there are more and other values relevant than just the ones connected with the market, particularly those related to the specific public character of governing and government, like justice, equity, equal treatment of equal cases, and so on. Third, there is a case for a rehabilitation of the hierarchical model of governing – though not a sufficient condition, since appropriate application necessarily depends on the *context* involved. Under this governance paradigm implementation is still there, but as under the NPM paradigm, in a hidden form. Other than in the policy-implementation paradigm, implementation is not seen as following formulation-and-decision in a vertical chain-like relationship. Neither is it hidden behind contracts, as under the new public management paradigm. In the governance paradigm, inasmuch as the focus is on the new more 'horizontal' mode of governance in the form of network management, this can be seen as an externalized process of policy formation in which government acts together with a variety of public and private actors. The nuts and bolts of implementation – in a narrow sense – are defined further away, located in one of the 'latest' parts of a policy-making process that has been made longer in the 'early' parts. The vertical *chain* and *rope* here have become a lightly *woven thread*, loosely coupling societal actors of various sorts. It is because of that variety that implementation and the managing of it will vary from case to case.

In the succession of the different paradigms, the traditional anchor-point for implementation, located in the making of public policies as for-mulated and decided upon by organs of representative democracy, has become less visible. With that, scholarly attention has moved to other agendas. Undue emphasis on a dominant administrative ideology at the macro-level may exclude appropriate responses to problems at the micro-level. The disaster of the exploding fireworks factory in Enschede, reported above, shows that the broad legitimacy of a particular way of handling public-administrative affairs in the real world may have serious adverse consequences. This refers to the fact that in a paradigm, defined on a *macro*-level as it is, certain norms and values are highly estimated at the expense of others. In any specific configuration of factors at the *micro*-level, others might have been more appropriate. In the case of Enschede this means that a more hierarchical mode of governance, dealing with municipal permits, could have been seen as more appropriate than the consensual, negotiating mode of governance that was actually practised. The prescriptive consequences of this notion are further explored in Chapter 8.

The future of implementation studies

All the categories of implementation studies, as typified in Table 5.1 above, seem to be ongoing, still producing contributions to the knowl-edge on public policy implementation. Nevertheless, in the successive periods what may be seen as mainstream and what not has changed. The rise of new issues to scholarly attention has broadened the agenda sub-stantially. When we link national backgrounds with the history of leading perspectives in implementation theory and research presented above, it can be observed that the policy-implementation paradigm and its connected 'reform' perspective originated in the USA, and it is that country that currently evidences the 'testing' perspective most frequently. Undoubtedly the time factor plays a role here. Given the sheer number of mainstream implementation publications, it is clear that if anywhere a practice of 'normal science' in this field could have developed, it is in the USA. At the same time it seems to be in the UK where a fertile soil was present for the establishing of the new public management para-digm. The Whitehall tradition could be persuaded, under pressure from market ideology, to accept pragmatic, and intellectually relatively shal-low, management discourse where it had been unwilling to accept the public policy orientation. Since the late eighties, after several outspoken contributions particularly written from an 'activist' perspective, it looks as if the British have become less visible in the field of implementation studies, while at the same time they are prominently present in the development of the scholarly theme of new public management. In the Netherlands attention has been given to both perspectives, which are perhaps less seen as alternatives. Given the Dutch tradition of consensualism, it may not be a coincidence that it is particularly the theme of networks, network management and governance, on which a substantial and steadily growing contribution from Dutch academics to the international debates has been important (see Chapter 4, pp. 77–9).

Looking at each of the leading perspectives in implementation theory and research, it can be expected that the mainstream of studies in which the implementation of a specific public policy is described and analysed will continue. The critical and activist stream will, in a different way, persist in the form of the attention given by some postmodern(ist) implementation scholars to citizens' and participatory perspectives. The fact that most postmodernists seem to have other interests than implementation research can now be explained. For them the phenomenon of 'implementation' in the narrow sense has become obsolete, something belonging to a past era. Besides, postmodernists, as was argued in Chapter 2, pp. 37–9, are uninterested in causal effects. Nevertheless, central to the study of implementation are questions why something did happen or did not happen.

The 'new normativism' may involve a return to earlier perspectives on implementation. Under the influence of crises and disasters, for instance, the shadow sides of privatization (the NPM paradigm) or the adverse consequences of an ultimately pursued pragmatism (the network mode under the governance paradigm) may become visible. This may lead to appeal for oversight and other forms of appropriate institutional design. Possible links with institutional theory may provide fruitful perspectives for contextualized research here, both in a descriptive and a prescriptive sense (see, for instance, Hoppe et al., 1987).

In addressing the question of the future of implementation studies a distinction between a broad and a narrow agenda should be made. As far as the former is concerned, the developments on the level of multidisciplinary attention continue as before. Just as there was practice and study of implementation before it became something that could be called a paradigm, this will be the case after that paradigm has declined. The kind of research recognized by Kettl (2000) and O'Toole (2000a) as promising and, actually, advancing 'implementation studies' therefore can be valued as broadening perspectives and enhancing chances for the development of new insights and the use of new sources of knowledge.

There is a possible risk, however. Paraphrasing what Wildavsky once said about planning, it may be that if implementation research seems to be everywhere, perhaps it may be done nowhere. Therefore, the narrow implementation studies agenda remains important; if not in the scholarly terms of scientific progress, then certainly because practitioners continue to ask for evidence-based advice. The systematic research that some scholars, particularly American ones, do makes a substantial theoretical-empirical contribution to the accumulation of knowledge on what still can be called the sub-discipline of public policy implementation. One of the character- istics of these studies is that, instead of theorizing about what should be the elements of a comprehensive, overarching theory (constantly adding new variables), they focus on confronting existing knowledge about a relatively narrowly defined subject, in a systematic way, with relevant sets of data. Next to this kind of study, it can be expected that, if certain requirements are met (see Chapter 7), the linking of large quantities of data with parsimoniously formulated formal models (Meier and O'Toole, 2001; see also Torenvlied, 1996a, 1996b) may advance the field – at least in the narrow sense.

Bringing the mainstream of implementation studies to a higher level of scientific sophistication does not happen automatically, however. Therefore some methodological issues of a general kind need further attention. We will deal with them in the next two chapters. There we shall also formulate some programmatic considerations.

Notes

---

1 Specific research on the hollow state was reported in a symposium of the *Journal of Public Administration and Theory* (April 1996). Scholarly inquiry there concerned case studies of mental health services (Milward et al., 1993; Lynn, 1996b); human services collaboratives (Bardach and Lesser, 1996); revolving loan programmes for waste-water treatment infrastructure (O'Toole, 1996); child care regulation (Gormley, 1996); public use of information technology (Milward and Snyder, 1996); and substance abuse services (S.R. Smith and Smyth, 1996).

2 Even in defence policy – traditionally seen as a policy field suited only for a hierarchical way of governing – sometimes direct citizens' participation is sought (for a case description see Hupe, 2000).

3 What in this book is called the *implementation follows formulation and decision theorem* (as explained in Chapter 1) certainly has been – and still is – a central element in the usual image of public policy making seen as a cycle or stage model. A logical and a normative justification should be distinguished here. As far as policy formulation and decision making were seen as taking place 'at the top' of the public-administrative system, this view at the end of the 1970s and beginning of the 1980s was challenged by 'bottom-up' implementation

theorists. These theorists showed, though rather implicitly, that the situating of formulation and decision 'at the top', that is to say, in the centre of national government, involves a normative or political view; not one that is logically necessary. The 'bottom-uppers' (particular Hjern) contrasted this normative view with an alternative one. Their picture of empirical reality, in which the connection of implementation action with policy decisions in fact appeared to be much looser than expected, formed the basis for their implicit view that this *should be* so. What, later in the eighties, the new public management theorists did also implicitly concerned a specific normative-prescriptive view: implementation proceeds better if separated from policy formation and managed by contracts (see also Chapter 3).

4 As examples of efforts aiming at synthesis, O'Toole (2000a: 268) mentions Mazmanian and Sabatier (1983), Bressers and Ringeling (1989); Goggin et al. (1990); Stoker (1991); Matland (1995); and Ryan (1996).

5 It is not the 'implementation paradigm', because the object – what is implemented – always presupposes a subject: what has to be implemented; usually a policy goal. This is not a normative, but a logical matter.

6

Implementation Research:

The State of the Art

CONTENTS

Introduction

This chapter explores how implementation theory is used in research into implementation. In talking of a body of theory and of the practice of research a reference point for many is the model of 'normal science', in which hypotheses derived from more or less generally accepted theories are tested. This activity leads on to the establishment of a series of propositions, which can be re-tested and modified over time. Only very exceptionally do new theories emerge that cut across the mainstream work and lead to a 'paradigm' shift in the established body of knowledge (Kuhn, 1970). We recognize that some political and social scientists deny that their discipline can be described in these terms, and indeed that some are unhappy about the use of the word 'science' in connection with their activity. Nevertheless most political scientists and analysts of public administration think that it is feasible to frame their work, at least in broad terms, within the 'normal science' model. Moreover, there is an expectation from the wider public for the social sciences that findings will be specified in terms of propositions supported by evidence. This is particularly important in relation to a topic like implementation, where there is an expectation that the discipline will make a contribution to questions about 'what is feasible' or 'what will work'. It is therefore appropriate to ask, in this chapter, to what extent it is possible to make statements about the *state of the art* of implementation research. In the next chapter we will go on from this to some suggestions as to considerations that those doing implementation research should take into account.

The tentative nature of this introduction perhaps already conveys to readers the fact that we have, here, set ourselves a substantial task. There have been two earlier reviews of the empirical literature that have made partial attempts to carry out this kind of task. One of them was Paul Sabatier's use of a review of studies to help him explore the relative strengths and weaknesses of the top-down and bottom-up approaches to the study of implementation (Sabatier, 1986 – see also Chapter 4, pp. 63–5). The other one was Laurence O'Toole's examination of multi-actor implementation published in the same year (1986). To help us with the development of this part of the book we undertook a systematic survey of articles published in political science, public policy and public administration journals between 1991 and 1998 (this is described in the Appendix). We will not confine what we say in this chapter to the evidence that emerged from that study, but it is appropriate to discuss the questions we encountered in setting up and analysing that survey in order to highlight the issues that complicate the assembling of a systematic picture of contemporary implementation research.

Any attempt to delineate the literature reporting studies of implementation encounters two major interlocking facts. One is that findings relevant to the understanding of the policy implementation process have been, and are being, made by researchers in a wide range of disciplinary or sub-disciplinary areas. The other is that those findings are reported to the world in a wide range of ways in a multiplicity of different kinds of publications.

Chapter 2 addressed the various ways in which implementation issues are also explored either in other areas of political science or in organizational sociology or studies of law. Within political science and public administration the longstanding concern about the basic relationship between politics and administration continues to be examined by researchers. Active Presidencies in the United States have led to a variety of studies that have been concerned not just with the respective influences of President and Congress but also with the successes and failures of the efforts of the President to influence behaviour in regulatory agencies and other administrative bodies (see the discussion below, p. 125). Though many of these studies are not presented as drawing upon implementation theory, they clearly make contributions to implementation studies. Conversely, to add to the confusion, a British study of the impact of Margaret Thatcher (Marsh and Rhodes, 1992) is quite explicitly presented as a study of implementation but is very largely concerned with ideological influences upon initial policy *formation*.

In an era in which classical economic theory became much more important for political rhetoric, the analysis of politics, government and administration took on board all kinds of economic approaches. The particular implication of this for the study of implementation was that the top-down perspective, as well as propositions about the politics–administration relationship, was re-framed in terms of propositions about relationships between 'principals and agents'. Bureaucratic interests were expressed in terms of the self-interests embodied in rational choice theory (see Dunleavy, 1991, for a critical review and development of the original theory). Propositions derived from game theory were also developed in efforts to model implementation processes. In Chapters 3 and 4 some observations have been made about the problems of applying to the implementation process the formalistic propositions derived from these sources. Here we merely note that some contemporary empirical studies take these sorts of propositions, rather than more complex implementation theory, as their starting points.

However, it is elsewhere in the study of implementation that it is more difficult to disentangle the contributions of explicit 'implementation studies' from those made by work with other theoretical perspectives. Since a great deal of the analysis of complexity within the implementation process stresses inter- and intra-organizational relationships, it is inevitable that important contributions to the understanding of these processes come from writers whose theoretical underpinning stems from organization theory, or more precisely from organizational sociology. The more detailed analysis of these relationships concerns issues about actual behaviour at 'street level', where the links between research inspired by Lipsky and research rooted in the sociology of work are very close. Moreover, these two veins of research mingle closely with a socio-legal concern with issues about discretion and rule application. This is seen most particularly in studies of police behaviour, but there are related concerns for the study of service and benefit delivery and for the study of regulation (this topic is discussed further below).

If relevant research for our topic is conducted under a variety of theoretical and disciplinary rubrics, it will inevitably be difficult to define a clear range of publications in which relevant outputs may be found. But the task of delimiting a relevant literature is compounded by other factors. First, in addition to the direct disciplinary literature – in political science, sociology, and so on – there is a considerable amount of work on implementation issues that is published in books and journals defined in terms of their substantive area of concern rather than in terms of a disciplinary one: social policy, housing policy, health policy, environment policy, criminology and policing, planning, and so on. Second, since much implementation research is carried out for specific customers with explicit practical concerns, a substantial 'grey' literature of pamphlets and reports has been generated. This literature may contain much that can advance our understanding of implementation, but it is hard to locate, and when located there may be a need to translate its specific concerns into 'evidence' that can be related to more general hypotheses. Third, the factors that determine what gets published and where it gets published may be unrelated to whether findings advance our understanding of implementation or not. It has, for example, been alleged that much early implementation research was essentially 'misery research' (Rothstein, 1998) highlighting disasters and implementation failures and providing a distorted impression of implementation difficulties. But it is probable that studies of failures are more likely to be published. More recently, changing political concerns and administrative fashions may have affected awareness of implementation issues (as was shown in the previous chapter). Additionally, academic agendas, language and labels change over time, and the decisions of journal editors and publishers reflect those changes. New studies with new insights are given more attention than studies that replicate earlier ones, and old ideas may be dressed up in new concepts.

In this chapter we bring together a range of key findings. According to the 'normal science' model, which was indicated above as a possible approach to this subject, the aim should be to sort through the literature as a whole. The comments above show some of the complications of such a task. In practice there is still comparatively little that can be said to be distinctly 'known' about implementation in a way that adds to or departs from the deductive statements of the theorists set out in Chapters 3 and 4. For example, propositions about the importance of resourcing new policy initiatives properly or about clarity when one group of actors seek to mandate another are essentially statements of the obvious. As a consequence, many of the findings to be presented involve the establishment of useable methodologies rather than 'facts' generalizable across all fields. Instead of trying to be comprehensive, we will deal with the issue about the relationship between a core literature on implementation and other relevant literature, delineated above, by means of cross-references to some key sources. We see the 'core' implementation theorists discussed in Chapters 3 and 4 as having a clear concern to explain the presence or absence of a 'gap' between what is observed and what was desired or expected (or retrospectively what might have been expected). We will come back to this methodological issue in the section looking at 'dependent' variables. A good example of this is work that is concerned with policy evaluation, but that seeks to look at how events between policy formation and a studied outcome may have had an influence.

Hence, to sum up the above discussion and introduce what is to follow: we start from the position that a sub-discipline concerned with policy implementation seems to have been established within political science and public administration. Within that sub-discipline scholars need to be able to advance some propositions about how this process can be researched. These need to involve testable propositions about influences upon the policy process between an initial stage that we call 'policy formation' and the ultimate policy output.

We recognize that this approach to the topic – with testable propositions and probably causal assumptions – has been challenged by some writers on implementation. As was made clear in the discussion of this issue in Chapter 1 (see pp. 10–11), we do not share that perspective. But we do acknowledge the importance of that challenge inasmuch as we certainly do not equate a positivist standpoint with a rejection of qualitative methods, and even recognize that some situations will be best analysed in interpretative terms. An examination of actual empirical studies suggests that in fact the challenge to positivist methodologies has had little impact upon research practice. Indeed it may only have had the effect of inhibiting empirical research.

The framework we use below highlights some of the key issues about ways to segment or separate empirical analyses of implementation, and ways to frame hypotheses. It lists the independent variables in a way that corresponds to a top-down or stagist perspective. However, whilst (as will be shown) the choice of the dependent variable may be influenced by perspectives on the old top-down/bottom-up argument, there is nothing intrinsic to the framework that locates 'policy' definition at any particular part of the political-administrative system. On the contrary, a great deal of the more innovatory literature sets out to deal with questions about the role of staff at or near the bottom of the system or about how they receive and transform the efforts of others to 'mandate' them. In other words, there is always a 'top' in the sense that somewhere is formulated and decided what has to be implemented, but the location of that 'top' may vary: it may even be 'at the bottom'. In the last analysis it is important to try to develop the systematic study of implementation, separating theoretical and methodological questions from the normative one about who *should* exercise authority within the policy process. This is what we do in this chapter and the next. We will return to the normative question in Chapter 8.

Dependent Variables

The extent to which it is possible to identify a dependent variable depends upon both the methodological stance of the author and the topic he or she was studying. In the 88 articles from journals during the 1990s that were reviewed (see Appendix), 53 worked with an explicit dependent variable and in a further 21 there could be said to be an implicit one. Many of these studies identified more than one dependent variable.

Clear identification of dependent variables may depend upon two considerations examined below in the discussion of independent variables: policy characteristics and the extent of policy formation. Definition of dependent variables raises questions about the extent to which legislative intentions can be readily identified. Some of the early top-down literature has been noted as involving an uncritical acceptance of objectives specified in the policy-formation process. However, this is not implicit in the process of identification of dependent variables; these may emerge during various stages of an implementation process or be attributed to the policy process by the researcher (or any outside observer).

A good example of some of the issues about the choice of dependent variables is provided by research on child support legislation. An American article about this topic (Keiser and Meier, 1996) uses 'successful enforcement' to define its dependent variables. These are then further defined in terms of 'total impact' (dollars collected per head of population), 'effectiveness' (dollars collected per case) and 'efficiency' (dollars collected related to dollars spent on administration). But a later study from one of the same authors focuses instead on bureaucratic discretion within the enforcement system (Keiser and Soss, 1998) and uses 'good cause exemptions' from applications of the policy as its dependent variable. A British study of the same subject, while not using an explicitly implementation research methodology or setting out quantified findings, shows that phenomena such as error rates, appeals and complaints about the system might be appropriate dependent variables for a study of this subject (G. Davis et al., 1998).

The various alternatives to the dependent-variable definition identified in the previous paragraph illustrate some of the options in relation to an apparently similar case. Problem definitions are important here. Divergences between these may occur even when the implementation process is considered from a 'top-down' point of view, let alone when a wider perspective is adopted in which the points of view of, in the child-support case for example, those required to pay maintenance are taken into account. Yet amongst the dependent variables identified there are no ultimate-outcome variables included, unless money collected or the saving of public money is deemed to be such. In the political debate about this policy area child-maintenance enforcement is justified (and attacked) in terms of its impact upon family poverty and its long-run influence upon marital behaviour. Clearly these studies could have used dependent variables based upon these arguments.

Many studies use outcomes as dependent variables. In these cases it may be that policy 'goals' have been made very explicit, but equally they may have been attributed by the researcher. The extent to which the latter is problematical may depend upon the extent to which there is seen to be an uncontroversial shared goal. Examples of outcome variables used by implementation studies include:

- unemployment levels;
- child employment;
- equal education opportunities;
- pollution levels;
- crime levels; and
- road accidents.

What makes the use of 'outcomes' difficult is the fact that these may be determined by factors other than the policy under scrutiny. Policies may aim at outcomes like those identified above by initiating a variety of activities: increasing inspection and policing, developing education and training, providing official guidance and/or coercion, and so on. Implementation may be judged a success in 'output' terms if these activities occur (or are increased). But more police may have no impact on crime, curbing some emissions may increase others, training may not reduce unemployment, health education may have no impact on behaviour, and so on.

What this implies is that, where implementation studies use outcome measures for their dependent variables, there is a particularly important need to consider factors independent of the implementation process that may influence them. There has long been an awareness of the importance of taking into account wider economic factors in the explanation of policy outcomes in relation to efforts to prevent unemployment (Metcalf, 1982) or reduce pollution (Blowers, 1983). But controlling for these independent variables external to the policy process may require some ingenuity. For example, in Meier and McFarlane's study of family planning (1995) the outcome measure they are interested in is impact upon unwanted pregnancy. This cannot be measured directly, so two alternative outcomes are identified: abortion and poor maternal and child health. Since both of these may be explained by factors unrelated to the impact of policy implementation, 'environmental' variables that may offer alternative explanations are put into the regression model: namely levels of Catholic religious adherence and socio-economic deprivation.

Where the dependent variables are outputs, they are generally administrative decisions of some kind: enforcement actions in regulatory policy, determinations of applications for particular benefits or services, and so on. It is interesting to note amongst the outputs used the presence of indices that might, in other studies, register as independent variables (see the fourth category in the list below) – in particular, attitude studies that identified changes of perspective on the part of street-level staff as their dependent variables.

One special group of dependent variables are indices of policy system change – administrative reorganization, privatization, and so on – where what was being monitored was meta-policy making or in Lowi's term 'constituent policy making', with no concern to explore what the ultimate public impact of this change might be. A study by O'Toole (1989b) shows how particular problems of 'goal multiplicity' are likely to arise, complicating dependent-variable analysis in relation to policies of this kind. He takes the example of waste-water treatment privatization and shows how, along-side the goal of increased efficiency, there are concerns about the impact of the measure on technical capacity at the local level, on the encouragement of innovation, on equal opportunities and on labour relations.

O'Toole's concern is pertinent to all implementation analysis but his message is particularly significant in an age when (a) governance change is on the agenda (as was shown in the previous chapter) and (b) that change is justified in terms of its capacity to lead to valued 'outcomes'. There is certainly no lack of implementation studies that look at privati-zation (Wistow et al., 1992; Wistrich, 1992; O'Toole, 1994; Ryan, 1995b) or organizational restructuring (Denis et al., 1993; Ranade, 1995; Thompson and Jones, 1995; Flynn et al., 1996). It should be noted, however, that many of these are qualitative in nature and do not attempt any analysis that can be expressed in terms of impacts upon a dependent variable.

Independent Variables

Introduction

It was shown in the theoretical chapters that there have been many attempts to specify an essential checklist of independent variables. These variables can perhaps be specified in seven categories:

- policy characteristics;
- policy formation (in much of the literature seen as efforts to structure policy from the 'top');
- issues about 'layers' in the policy transfer process, or what we call 'vertical public administration';
- factors affecting the responses of implementation agencies (their organi-zation, their disposition, and so on) – these may be subdivided into issues about the overall characteristics of the agencies and issues about the behaviour of front-line (or street level) staff;
- horizontal inter-organizational relationships (relationships between parallel organizations required to collaborate in implementation);
- the impact of responses from those affected by the policy; and
- wider macro-environmental factors.

Whilst it is recognized that it is not always easy to draw distinctions between some of these categories, and that much implementation theory is about interactions between them, it is possible to explore approaches to empirical work looking at each separately. This discussion will do that.

Policy characteristics

Many writers have suggested that the characteristics of policy will affect its implementation. The most common approach to this issue has been to try to work with or develop Lowi's taxonomy of policy types (1972) – distributive, redistributive, regulatory, constituent. This, however, runs into problems because the distinctions between the types are difficult to draw. There seems *prima facie* to be a case for identifying some policies as inherently harder to implement than others. In practice, however, this can perhaps only be boiled down to the contrast Matland (1995) draws between 'ambiguity' in policy characteristics and the likelihood that 'conflict' will arise in implementation. In principle, the fact that we are able to survey a wide range of different articles on different topics should mean that we can supplement this by drawing up some sort of matrix in which policy types and implementation consequences are compared. In practice, the variety of ways in which implementation studies are formulated and the diversity of the methods they use make this impossible.

We have noted above how policy characteristics may affect the identification of a dependent variable, but that is merely to suggest that policy substance will affect methodology, not that it will have an impact upon implementation. The comments that have been made about the special problems for identification of the dependent variable when 'constituent' policy is involved are also clearly pertinent.

But the overall problem central in this section can be seen by going back to the underlying concerns of Matland and Rothstein (see Chapter 4), which are to predict whether or not particular policies will run into implementation difficulties. This cannot necessarily be predicted from the intrinsic characteristics of the policies, but rather depends upon an interaction between those and the other factors in the categories discussed below.

Advance on this topic, by other than deductive approaches, may perhaps await studies that compare distinctly different policies. These would be likely to be difficult to formulate. In practice the fact that researchers tend to have interests in specific areas and funders are unlikely to be sympathetic to wide-ranging studies across policy areas means that there is an absence of material we can use to take forward these very general comments on this issue.

Policy formation

In Chapter 2 it was recognized that one of the literatures that implementation studies emerged from was that concerned with the relationship between politics and administration. It remains the case that there are many modern studies that address this issue, by sophisticated exploration of the respective power of the executive, legislature and bureaucracy. The

American literature (see, for example, T.M. Moe, 1982; Nathan, 1983; Wood, 1988, 1991, 1992) has been stimulated by renewed political activism from Presidents like Ronald Reagan. Some of these studies have involved the use of quantitative studies using time-series data, which explore the ways in which political impacts may occur, and therefore raise questions about implementation. For example, a study of US regulatory agencies uses statistical time-series data to show that 'political appointments – a shared power of the president and Congress – is the most important instrument of political control; changing budgets, legislation, congressional signals, and administrative reorganizations are less important' (Wood and Waterman, 1991: 801). In other countries explorations of these themes have been more qualitative in nature (for example, Hennessy, 1989, on the UK and Pusey, 1991, on Australia).

But the literature mentioned in the previous paragraph is concerned with the impact of policy formation upon implementation only in the most general terms. More pertinent is work that is concerned with the shape given to policy by any initial formation processes. It was shown in Chapter 3 that one of the concerns of the implementation theorists has been to give advice to policy formers on the contents and shape policy should take to ensure its successful implementation (see, for example, Hogwood and Gunn, pp. 50–1 above). The ingredients of this literature are best expressed by Van Meter and Van Horn's specification of the importance of policy standards and objectives. The latter 'elaborate on the overall goals of the policy decision ... to provide concrete and more specific standards for assessing performance' (1975: 464). These authors also identify the importance of the resources and incentives made available, a variable emphasized by Goggin and his colleagues as top-down 'inducements and constraints' (1990).

If independent variables are to be specified under this heading, it is necessary to develop criteria that will enable policies to be distinguished from each other in terms of the extent to which they are clearly specified, resourced and supported. During the 1980s and 1990s a very distinctive vein of research of this kind was developed – which may be described as 'mandate' studies (Fix and Kenyon, 1990). A good example of these is a study by Meier and McFarlane (1995) that compares a number of policy initiatives all with the same apparent objective, where in practice one statute set policy goals much more clearly than any of the others. Peter May (1993, 1994, 1995; May and Burby, 1996) has carried out a number of studies that explore 'mandates' supplied by one level of government to another. The substantive policy area he studies is flood and erosion control, and he has explored the impact of state laws on the behaviour of local governments in both the United States and Australia. A particular interest is in a comparison of the extent to which, in different situations, mandates that are either coercive or seeking co-operation produce significant responses. However, salient amongst May's findings is evidence that choices between these options may need to take into account the problem to be solved and the predisposition of the agencies being mandated. In other words both the previous topic in this chapter – policy type – and one to be discussed below – agency disposition – have to be taken in to account in arriving at an operationalizable conclusion.

The latter point draws attention to the fact that any propositions about the effectiveness of mandates are likely to depend upon the extent to which the layer of government doing the mandating is seen as a legitimate policy maker for those being mandated. It is a theme to which we will return in the next section.

One of the more complex issues in relation to policy formation concerns the extent to which feedback occurs (an important feature in Goggin et al.'s model, see Chapter 4, pp. 66–9) and policy adjustments are made over time. This is a theme that tends to provide difficulties for quantitative studies. Whilst time-series data may enable some attention to be given to this issue, the underlying questions about the nature of the 'game' being played between layers tends to require a more qualitative approach. This is seen, for example, in Castellani's (1992) study of the closure of mental health care institutions in New York state or Clark's (1997) study of the negotiations between the Australian federal government and the states over changes to the assessment of need for geriatric care. In the latter we find the question being raised: 'why should we help them solve their problem?'

Vertical public administration

Issues about the impact of vertical links in the chain from policy formation to the street level have been on the agenda of implementation studies ever since Pressman and Wildavsky's effort to model this mathematically (1973). In Chapters 3 and 4 we explored the work of various theorists who have struggled with this issue. Amongst them Goggin and his colleagues (1990) are most relevant to this chapter as they developed their analysis using a number of empirical studies. All of these concerned federal government/state relationships in the United States. What that book brings out very clearly is the methodological complexity inherent in multi-layer implementation research. A major factor contributing to that complexity is the fact that often intervening levels, as layers in the political-administrative system, have a legitimate claim to engage in policy formulation and decision making: Where does 'policy formation' end and 'implementation' begin? It is in recognition of this that Goggin et al. refer to federal 'messages' to states rather than federal policies.

This levels/layers distinction may be important. Given the notion of 'three worlds of action', as developed by Kiser and Ostrom (1982), it is possible to speak of *levels* to indicate the distinct parts of the policy cycle as logical-analytical constructions, while using the term *layers* to refer to separate co-governments exercising legitimate authority with relative autonomy and probably controlled by democratic representative organs. Thus it may happen that an American state, as a formal 'layer' in the political-administrative system, fulfils a task on the 'level' of implementation regarding policy A, but on the 'level' of policy formation as far as policy B is concerned.

On the whole, empirical studies avoid the need to handle too many difficulties of this kind by limiting attention to the relationship between two levels in a policy-making process, preferably together connected to one single political-administrative layer. In a certain case both the formation of a specific policy and the implementation of it may take place within the domain of judicial authority of, for instance, an American state. In other cases, what is seen as 'implementation' of a policy may involve separate layers. Many of the studies from the United States are in practice either about federal/state relationships or about state/local government ones. In such cases 'gaps' between two bodies may be misleadingly seen as 'deficits' when the 'lower' tier has clear rights to adapt or even disregard policies emanating from the 'upper'. In fact both layers then have *policy-formation* prerogatives. In several US and Australian studies concerning federal/state relations there is little doubt that the language of implementation deficit is relevant if states are failing to carry out clearly *mandated* federal policies. But in a policy area already shown above to involve multiple and to some extent competing goals, Keiser and Soss observe of a US federal law on child support that '[o]ur analysis indicates that levels of bureaucratic disentitlement are shaped by partisan control of state governments, by the values of the state bureaucracy, by the funding decisions of elected officials, and by the levels of demand placed on the bureaucracy' (1998: 1152). Similarly, Scholz et al. (1991) highlight local political influences upon responses to a federal measure within one particular US state, and Cimitile et al. (1997) explore the limited local impact of unfunded federal mandates.

A related issue is the study of the impact of policies where the initial formation activities are outside the nation state. There is a growing volume of studies of the implementation of European Union policies that indicate very distinct processes of reformulation within individual nation states. What is called 'implementation' in those studies in fact could be seen as 'policy formation'. Lampinen and Uusikylä (1998) note widespread variation in the implementation of EU directives. They hypothesize that political institutions, political corporatism, public support for EU membership and political culture will influence implementation. But they find that only two of those variables seem to be important: political institutions (high stability) and political culture (high levels of trust). A deeper analysis of this issue is provided by Knill and Lenschow (1998), who compare the implementation of EU environment policy directives in Britain and Germany. They hypothesize that different administrative traditions will affect implementation, with nation states showing a tendency to reject regulations embodied in a form that is alien to those traditions. They find in fact that reality is more complex: changing political and administrative agendas also have an impact.

Clearly within the international relations literature this topic secures wider coverage, in terms of the factors that affect the reception of international initiatives and agreements by national governments (see, for example, Hurrell and Kingsbury, 1992; Kellow, 1997). Particularly interesting in this field is the rise of a theme of 'multi-level governance'. The further integration of the European Union has not only changed the relationships between the member states and the EU, but also enabled direct institutional contacts between the latter and regional and local authorities. Recently this development has been described among political scientists as 'multi-level governance' (Jachtenfuchs, 1995; Scharpf, 1997b; A. Smith, 1997). B. Guy Peters and Jon Pierre define this phenomenon as referring 'not just to negotiated relationships between institutions at different institutional levels but to a vertical "layering" of governance processes at these different levels' (2001: 132). Though somewhat distant from implementation theory and research, this theme has relevance for our methodological discussion. However, whilst the terms that are being used ('levels', 'layering') suggest a resemblance with our view on vertical public administration, the approach is different from ours. The concept of 'multi-level governance' seems to refer to an analytical cut from the whole of inter-institutional relations and processes, eventually to a policy. Looking at implementation, our cut goes the other way around: from a specific policy (programme) to the system of intergovernmental relations. While some policies are formed and implemented within one domain of judicial authority (for example an American state, using state agencies for implementation), in other policy processes a variety of political-administrative layers are concerned, on several of which the (co-)formation of the policy involved takes place. Thus, one could, alternatively, introduce the concept of 'multi-layer policy formation' here.

Influences on implementation agency responses

This section will explore implementation agency responses in terms of:

- overall characteristics and disposition of agencies; and
- issues about the behaviour of front-line (or street-level) staff.

Sub-sections within this section deal separately with these two.

Agency characteristics and disposition   This is an issue that has been given much attention by theorists. Van Meter and Van Horn identify various aspects of this topic, separating them into two different categories (see Chapter 3, p. 46, for the other variables they mention):

- the characteristics of the implementation agencies, including issues like organizational control but also, going back to inter-organizational issues, 'the agency's formal and informal linkages with the "policy-making" or "policy-enforcing" body' (1975: 471); and
- the 'disposition' or 'response' of the implementers, involving three elements: 'their cognition (comprehension, understanding) of the policy, the direction of their response toward it (acceptance, neutrality, rejection) and the intensity of that response' (p. 472).

Overall organizational rigidity and resistance to new initiatives is highlighted in some studies, such as – for example – the study by Koppenjan of problems with the development of a new Dutch passport (Koppenjan, 1991). It also appears in studies of the relative ineffectiveness of new US Presidential initiatives (see, for example, Durant, 1993; Krause, 1996). In the light of the heavy emphasis upon intra-organizational characteristics in the theoretical literature it might be expected that many studies would be found that operationalized these. The absence of this is perhaps an indicator of the extent to which a division of labour has occurred in which much of this work has been done by organizational sociologists developing the propositions that emerged from Max Weber's theory of bureaucracy (1947) into various forms of contingency theory and neo-institutional theory (see Hickson et al., 1971; Di Maggio and Powell, 1983; Scott, 1995). Relevant empirical studies – see, for example, Goodrick and Salancik's study of the relative influences of organizational characteristics and risk assessments on the incidence of caesarean births (1996) – are more likely to come within this rubric.

Studies that can compare the responses of a number of similar agencies – states, counties or cities – clearly offer scope for an exploration of the influence of agency characteristics in a systematic way. In practice we find elements of analysis of agency characteristics mixed in with issues about disposition. A good example of such a study is one by Harbin et al. (1992) of services for handicapped children that developed what is called an 'assessment of influential characteristics scale' to analyse agency characteristics. This has four key subdivisions:

- climate (history of services and levels of support from decision makers and advocacy groups);
- resources (financial, qualified personnel, existence of specialized facilities);
- policies (current interagency agreement and existing legislation); and
- system (experience with inter-agency services).

Note in this case the particular importance of a predisposition to carry out inter-agency work (a theme to which we will return).

The question of agency disposition is addressed in some studies not in terms of implementation theory but with exploration of a much older theoretical approach that clearly has something to say about the 'disposition' of implementers: the theory of 'representative bureaucracy' (see Chapter 2, p. 29). A study of equal educational opportunities explores this issue in a sophisticated way, showing that

> [p]olitical forces ... were able to influence policy outputs to benefit minority students. This political influence is indirect. Black school board members influence the selection of black administrators who in turn influence the hiring of black teachers. Black teachers then mitigate the impact of bureaucratic decision rules and provide black students with better access to educational opportunities. (Meier et al., 1991: 173–4)

Similarly a study of loan allocations for rural housing shows the impact of variations in the number of staff from minority groups, between different offices, upon loans to people from that group (Selden, 1997). But that really takes us on to the other sub-theme of influences upon the behaviour of street-level staff.

Before leaving the topic of institutional disposition, a connection with another literature needs to be noted. This is the study of the relationship between the social, political and economic characteristics of *local* governments and public policy outputs (key examples of work on this theme are Boaden, 1971; Newton and Sharpe, 1977; Danziger, 1978; Valente and Manchester, 1984; Hirsch, 1995). Where local government is in the role of implementer of policy formed elsewhere, this literature is surely relevant. In practice a specific study may have many of the characteristics of a mainstream implementation study and there may be things to be learnt from it.

Hence, Choi (1999) studied a British central government initiative designed to increase the privatization of local government services: legislation requiring local authorities to put out certain local services for tender by private companies. The system set up was known as Compulsory Competitive Tendering (CCT). Local authorities were not required to privatize but they were required to set up a procedure facilitating private tendering for services, which could be in competition with tenders from 'in-house' free-standing business organizations known as Direct Service Organizations (DSOs). The government's idea was that there should be a fair competitive process between private organizations and DSOs, in which tenders would be won by the lowest tender meeting all the specifications necessary for the efficient performance of the task. Choi observed that there was great variation between authorities in the extent to which services went either to private companies or to DSOs, and set out to explain that variation. The crucial variable for Choi's study was one measuring the 'disposition' of the implementing agencies: political control of the authority. His study showed that in 1991 the most significant independent variable was political control of authorities – with Labour-controlled authorities more likely to have given contracts to DSOs and Conservative authorities more likely to have privatized.

Here we have a simple conclusion on the influence of political disposition. But Choi went on in case studies to explore how that had an impact in the light of the fact that central government had taken considerable steps to prevent an authority 'disposed' to ignore the policy from doing so. The legislation required a visible tendering process. It expected that in any competition between DSOs and privatized organizations there should be, to use terms from the related jargon, a 'level playing field'. Choi carried out some case studies to examine the 'strategies' used by local authorities to influence the 'slope' of that 'playing field'. These revealed both strategies by Labour authorities to make tendering more difficult for private companies and the reverse from Conservative-controlled authorities.

This case study takes us, as does the work of Harbin and his colleagues, quoted above, into, first, the more detailed study of organizational behaviour and, second, inter-organizational relationships. These are discussed below.

Influences on the behaviour of street level staff   At least since the seminal book by Michael Lipsky (1980) (see pp. 51–3) it has been recognized that any attempt to explain implementation must look within agencies at the factors that affect the behaviour of street-level staff. Empirical research on implementation contains at least four variants on this theme:

- single-agency case studies where behaviour is examined qualitatively;
- studies of the attitudes of bureaucrats that are used to deduce their impact upon actual behaviour (in this case attitude is the dependent variable);
- single-agency studies where quantitative analysis of individual bureaucrat behaviour is possible; and
- studies that take an already recognized implementation 'gap' and seek to explain this by an examination of the bureaucratic task and the bureaucrat/client interaction.

Examples of the first category include Satyamurti's study of British social workers (1981); Bowe et al.'s study of the implementation of education reform in Britain (1992); Ryan's examination of influences on Australian industry policy (1996); Khademian's exploration of bank regulatory activities in the US federal government (1995); and O'Toole's exploration of influences on Hungarian environment policy (1997). A particularly interesting study in this category is a Californian one of the implementation of policy reforms requiring 'welfare' recipients to increase their labour-market participation. This involved observational techniques and showed that workers were primarily concerned to carry out normal eligibility interviews. In the course of these they might give information about policies that would be applied if clients secured work. But most responses about work were prompted by questions from clients, and this was only in a small minority of cases. There was very little evidence of efforts to direct people towards training opportunities (Meyers et al., 1998).

It may be noted that again we encounter a boundary with other areas of research activity, in this case particularly hard to delineate, sociological studies of the determinants of behaviour by workers in organizations of all kinds. Lipsky's theoretical work drew heavily upon studies of this kind, particularly studies of police behaviour. The latter has developed into a substantial research industry (for reviews see Holdaway, 1983; Grimshaw and Jefferson, 1987; Reiner, 1992).

An example of the second category is Chan et al.'s study of Chinese environment policy (1995), attributing a 'gap' to the attitudes of officials who recognize alternative local economic considerations. Rather further from actual policy is a study that explores the theories of justice held by street-level bureaucrats (Kelly, 1994).

It is the third category that involves, in methodological terms, the most adventurous approach to this issue. Chaney and Saltzstein (1998) show that female representation in police forces is positively correlated with active responses to domestic violence. A study by Weissert (1994) of Medicaid spending shows that office managers' 'activism' in the community influences the generosity of local spending decisions. Maupin (1993) includes some data on street-level attitudes in an exploration of the activities of parole offices. In a study to which we will return in the next section, Provan and Milward (1991) collected data on the attitudes of street-level staff to help to explain collaboration in networks. Clearly also, as noted above, there are studies to be found of this kind within the literature on the sociology of organizations too. A classic study in the latter genre, which was very much about public policy implementation, was Blau's study of a public employment service (1955).

There were some interesting articles in the fourth category, taking a known implementation gap as the starting point (and therefore not really working with a dependent variable) and seeking to explain it. We highlight here two studies of the ineffectiveness of a new provision in the US AFDC ('welfare') law that expected beneficiaries to be penalized if their children did not attend school regularly. Ethridge and Percy (1993) show that the policy was premised upon a 'rational actor' theory in which quite complex linkages were expected. They set this out in terms of steps in a logical chain: parents want to maximize AFDC payments; parents are able to monitor the school attendance behaviour of their children and interpret messages about this; parents are able to control the behaviour of their children; and the threat of sanctions will lead parents to take action. They go on to question these assumptions and illustrate their problematic character using evidence about practice on the ground or derived from litigation about the law. Stoker and Wilson (1998) focus more precisely upon flaws in the verification process for this policy, using evidence from interviews of staff. They explore the weaknesses of the two alternatives essential for verification: depending upon the transfer of administrative information or getting clients to produce the evidence that they had complied with the requirements of the legislation.

Horizontal inter-organizational relationships

It was noted in the theoretical chapters that many policy-implementation issues are seen as rooted in problems of inter-organizational collaboration at the horizontal level – that is, collaboration between organizations that are in no sense in hierarchical accountability relationships. It was noted that this is a theme to which O'Toole has given particular attention (see Chapter 4, p. 69). In an article published in 1986 he reviews both the theoretical and the empirical work in this field. He provides cogent evidence on 'the considerable difficulties that plague the field' (p. 205), and much that he has to say about designing the research agenda more carefully will be echoed in Chapter 7 of this book. O'Toole found few examples of empirical work that advanced knowledge in the field, singling out perhaps only the work of Durant (1984, 1985), whom he sees as adding the time factor to 'other frequently-cited implementation variables' (O'Toole, 1986: 204). Later, in a study of efforts to prevent traffic accidents, Durant and Legge (1993) went on to demonstrate the importance of analysing how policy effects wear off over time.

In the sample of 88 articles reporting empirical studies reviewed in the preparation of this book, 24 concerned issues where, in significant respects, there was a need for inter-agency working. However, quantitative causal analysis in these situations was almost totally absent; the one clear exception to that generalization being Provan and Milward's article mentioned in the previous section. That study looked at services for mentally ill adults; it used involvement in a collaborative network as its dependent variable and collected attitude data to measure the commitment of the staff of individual organizations to that network.

As was noted earlier, an analysis of other literature – in this case particularly the organization studies journals – might have led to the discovery of other statistical studies on this topic. Again there is a very clear incidence of overlap between the academic disciplines since relationships between organizations have been given considerable attention in the sociological 'branch' of neo-institutional theory.

When we shift our attention to qualitative studies, we find discussions of inter-organizational collaboration in, for example, case studies of military base redevelopment, milk marketing, the designation of toxic waste dumps, food programmes for children, water basin clean-up, erosion control, preservation of rare species and several general articles on environment policy. In the light of British concerns with inter-agency collaboration in areas like health and social care this topic has been given substantial attention in a range of studies (Pettigrew et al., 1992; Wistow et al., 1994; Flynn et al., 1996; Hudson et al., 1997; Powell et al., 2001). On the whole these studies do not draw upon implementation theory (see Hudson, 1987, and Hudson et al., 1999, for a discussion of the relevant literature). However, a key theme in much of this British work has been the importance of relationships between street-level workers for collaborative initiatives imposed or encouraged from 'above'.

The impact of responses from those affected by the policy

It is important to recognize that implementation processes are influenced by the responses of those affected by the policy. This is seen most evidently in studies of regulatory policy, particularly where those regulated are powerful (large companies for example). There is a literature here that sees the policy process as co-production, involving negotiation and bargaining (Whitaker, 1980; Parks et al., 1981; Kiser, 1984; Hanf, 1993). But even the responses of weaker actors – the clients of welfare programmes – may feed back into the policy-implementation process.

A range of studies may be noted where powerful *objects* of regulation are 'visible' as potential influences on implementation, as follows:

- studies by Hawkins and his associates on water pollution control in Britain (Richardson et al., 1982; Hawkins, 1984), which focus upon the way discretion is exercised in enforcement activities;
- Blowers' study of efforts to deal with pollution from brickworks in England (1983, 1984);
- a study of occupational safety regulation in New York state where it is suggested that there is greater scope for discretion in relation to the regulation of construction than of manufacturing (Scholz et al., 1991);
- an examination of the views of Chinese implementation staff that shows how they take the views of polluters into account (Chan et al., 1995);
- a study of networks in relation to the acidification issue in Hungary (O'Toole, 1997);
- an examination of varying 'advocacy coalitions' in relation to river pollution and the protection of endangered species (Ellison, 1998); and
- case studies of Swiss regulatory policy that emphasize the importance of 'social learning in policy networks' (Knoepfel and Kissling-Näf, 1998).

These studies are, of course, embedded in a wider literature that emphasizes the impact of powerful actors upon policy making – stressing phenomena such as regulatory capture and the influence of corporate power (see *inter alia* Lukes, 1974; Lindblom, 1977). It should perhaps be taken as self-evident that actors that can influence the policy-formation process may also influence the implementation process.

Turning to issues about individuals as influences providing a feedback into policy, attention obviously needs to be given again to some of the studies that focus upon the behaviour of street-level bureaucrats, in particular the studies of efforts to build regulatory controls into American 'welfare' policy (Ethridge and Percy, 1993; Meyers et al., 1998; Stoker and Wilson, 1998). Hupe (1993a) has explored the way in which discretionary behaviour in welfare administration may involve co-production (see also Knegt, 1986). Reference has been made above to the importance of police studies for exploration of street level behaviour. The interaction between police officers and presumed law breakers has been shown as important for 'disposal' decisions (Fielding and Fielding, 1991; Campbell, 2001).

There is an interesting theoretical and methodological issue here about the extent to which this theme – of the response of those affected – should simply be seen as a variant on the inter-organizational collaboration theme discussed in the previous section. Where modern governance involves inter-organizational collaboration in which private organizations may be as involved as public ones, the distinction between the two sections can be challenged. The conceptualization of this target-group involvement has been examined under different headings, each referring to a different aspect. The concept of co-production, as used, for example, by Parks et al. (1981), Kiser (1984) and Hanf (1993), refers to the joint contribution delivered by partners in a system. Depending upon institutional culture and style of regulation, the interaction between government officials and business corporations may take some form of negotiation (for examples in the field of environmental regulation see Hanf, 1993). The concept of co-production is also used in relation to the participation of citizens, for instance in the form of client councils around municipal social services departments (Hupe, 1993a). Some authors use the concept to refer to citizens' participation in general (Tops, 1999). But then, of course, there are all kinds of conceptual equivalents available, like 'citizenship' (Van Gunsteren, 1998), 'local democracy' (Daemen and Schaap, 2000), 'discursive democracy' (Dryzek, 1990), 'deliberative democracy' (Elster, 1998) and also 'participatory policy making' (Edelenbos, 2000).

In a country like the Netherlands the phenomenon of 'interactive policy making' can be observed as a contemporary expression of a longstanding tradition of consultation and consensus making (Hendriks and Toonen, 1998). This tradition, so characteristic in Dutch water management, rural and local planning and social economic affairs (Visser and Hemerijck, 1997), has now spread to other parts of the public domain. Citizens are sometimes invited to have a say in, for instance, the formulation of a plan for enhancing traffic safety, the sale of social housing or the location of a centre for asylum seekers. In its broadest definition co-production is used as an approach to policy making in which a national, local or other government involves citizens, non-profit organizations, business companies and/or other governments in the making of a specific policy. Inasmuch as co-production particularly concerns the extension of the 'early' parts of the policy process, the implication for implementation may be a limited one.

There is a need to distinguish between situations in which collaboration is central to the policy activity and those where essentially there is an attempt to influence, regulate or benefit some outside party. In this sense co-production of social services – involving private or voluntary organizations as service-delivery agencies under contract – does largely belong to our 'horizontal relationships' category. On the other hand, co-production meaning a negotiative relationship in which a powerful polluter's compliance with regulation depends to some extent upon its consent does not.

The environment or policy context

Inasmuch as implementation studies are concerned with policy outcomes, there are some difficult questions about the policy environment that have to be dealt with. These are about the extent to which policies can effectively address issues that may be influenced by phenomena over which governments can have little or no influence: changes in the moral climate of a nation, demographic change, global economic forces, and so on. As suggested earlier, these factors are important where implementation studies seek to explain outcomes, and some of the issues and methodologies for dealing with them were explored there (see pp. 121–2).

There is an issue here about change over time – an issue that has been noted as affecting all implementation studies. The development of techniques to incorporate changes into regression studies, with appropriate lags, has been significant in the recent development of quantitative implementation studies. Hence we find studies incorporating variation in migration pressures into the study of the implementation of French immigration policy (Hollifield, 1990) and changes to agricultural markets into a study of the evolution of agricultural policy (Meier et al., 1995).

Conclusions

In the introduction to this chapter it was suggested that an analysis of the *state of the art* of implementation studies was more likely to yield interesting evidence on advances in methodology than substantive findings that could be assembled as established 'truths' about the implementation process. The former will be explored further, and shaped into some recommendations, in the next chapter.

Nevertheless, many studies have suggested issues that deserve close attention by those who want help in determining what they should or should not do. To take the topics in the order in which they have been explored here, research has, in particular, highlighted:

- the need for recognition of the complexity of the output/outcome relationship in policy implementation;
- issues about the need to give attention to the nature of the relationship between policy formers and policy implementers when the former frame mandates;
- the importance of the 'street level' in the implementation process, something that cannot simply be dissolved into a series of propositions about ways to impose stronger control;
- the continuing importance of inter-organizational relationships for implementation; and
- the importance of co-production involving clients, customers and regulatees, often even where they are comparatively powerless.

Notwithstanding the need to subdivide or sub-categorize parts of the implementation process to assist careful analysis – whether by researchers or practitioners – it is important to recognize the extent to which the many variables interact, and therefore the need to grasp the process as a whole. This whole, moreover, is one of which in certain cases it may be inappropriate to separate implementation off from the policy-formation part of the policy process.

7

Doing Implementation Research

Introduction

This chapter follows on from the description of the state of the art of implementation studies to set out methodological and programmatic issues that need to be dealt with by researchers. Its starting point will be a restatement of the view that there are important questions to which researchers can supply answers, about what happens within the imple-mentation process and about things that are seen to have 'gone wrong'. This will be followed by an examination of some of the issues that then have to be tackled. The chapter will end with the examination of a specific real issue to explore how implementation research may proceed.

The perspective here is that it is feasible to attempt to use research designs that will contribute to causal explanations of events. Under normal circum-stances this involves the exploration of the factors that may influence a dependent variable, along the lines used to explore research findings in the previous chapter. Reference was made there, and earlier in this book, to the views of those who do not see this as a feasible activity, and therefore suggest that researchers cannot attempt to generalize or offer causal explanations but can only give accounts of events or of actors' perspectives on events. We do not share that view and will not explore it in this chapter. Nevertheless we will indicate, at various places in the chapter, situations in which the policies under examination or the contexts in which their implementation occurs are such that it is not possible to do more than offer an account of events and of actors' perspectives on those events, in as systematic and neutral a manner as possible. In other words, we recognize difficulties about achieving objectivity but our perspective is that this is a function of the situations and circumstances that have to be observed and recorded, not something that can be rejected out of hand as inherently unrealizable.

The concepts used in this book were defined in Chapter 1. We do not want to go back over the same ground but do need to emphasize some implications of those definitions for our perspective here. In that chapter a distinction was made between, on the one hand, formulation and decision making as, together, policy formation; and, on the other hand, implementation. Clearly therefore it is the latter that has to be given attention in the design of research. But this may be difficult in situations where there is a particularly strong 'iterative' process between implementation and formation – this is where implementation is essentially an experimental or evolutionary process where strong feedback is actively expected (what Wildavsky and Majone call 'implementation as evolution', see Chapter 3, p. 12). In such a situation any attempt to look at implementation *per se* must involve the study of a 'moving target'. Here a descriptive approach may be all the researcher can attempt, but it may be the case that it is more appropriate to decline to study implementation because of an extreme lack of clarity about 'what is being implemented'.

A policy may be no more than a political response because there is a need to be seen to be doing something, but there is grave doubt about the effect of that upon the perceived problem. It was noted earlier (see, for example, the approach adopted by Hogwood and Gunn, pp. 50–1) that some of those who seek to give advice to 'top' policy makers urge them to work with a clear cause/effect model, but the political need for a response may make this a vain hope. We find instead a variety of initiatives, many of which may be described as 'symbolic' (Edelman, 1971). The study of the implementation of such policies provides evidence that pours scorn upon the rational model of the policy-formulation, decision-making and implementation process (see, for example, Yanow, 1993). Yet it is reasonable to ask: Is there any point in systematic implementation studies in these circumstances? And is it reasonable to use the particular difficulties associated with responses to 'wicked problems' to condemn the study of implementation in general? In other words those who study implementation should beware of being lured into the systematic study of policies formulated without any serious attention to their actual implementation.

There is a need to beware of a particular 'dead end' here that seems attractive to the researcher eager to show that 'the Emperor has no clothes'. The latter is the case when what is involved is showing that something has not happened that no one seriously expected to happen. There are some difficult issues here about sorting out the implications of policy rhetoric. We in no way wish to condemn the study of policy rhetoric, but do want to distinguish that study from implementation research.

This leads us on, however, to a very important issue. In the chapters exploring the development of implementation theory, it was noted how the famous Pressman and Wildavsky subtitle led to a strong emphasis in much early work upon 'implementation deficit', making much implementation research what Rothstein calls 'misery research' (see Chapter 4, p. 79) and Linder and Peters call the 'horrors of war' approach to implementation (1987: 460). There has thus been a danger that implementation studies work with a taken-for-granted assumption that aspirations will not be achieved, that policies will not live up to the rhetoric of those who formulate them and that 'disasters' will occur. In the same vein there has been a tendency to work with the notion of 'perfect administration' (see note on Hood, p. 51), so that the inevitable adjustments, compromises and short-falls in the real world are used to challenge the aspirations of the policy formers or to condemn the efforts of the implementers. Throughout this book we have recognized the importance of the normative questions that these notions throw up, acknowledging that accountability and control issues are important. We will return to these in the next chapter. However, they do raise severe problems for the design of implementation research, which may often be avoided by framing questions about dependent variables in terms that do not have implicitly normative assumptions about 'success' or 'failure' built into them. This is a point that has been made cogently by Lester and Goggin:

> One of the most intractable problems in implementation research has been how to measure the concept of successful implementation. In our view, policy implementation is a **process**, a series of subnational decisions and actions directed toward putting a prior authoritative federal decision into effect. The essential characteristic of the implementation process, then, is the timely and satisfactory performance of certain necessary tasks related to carrying out the intent of the law. This means rejecting a dichotomous conceptualization of implementation as simply success or failure.(1998: 5)

DeLeon echoes this point, noting that

> 'things' do get implemented and carried out on a regular basis. ... The main problem with implementation is that the discrepancy between 'something' and 'that idealized thing' is often a matter of rose-colored expectations. ... It might be long and arduous and uncertain but implementation is a bureaucratic fact of everyday life. (1999a: 322)

Winter (1999) more prosaically emphasizes that the process emphasized by Lester and Goggin needs to be explained by its outputs.

This emphasis on 'process' and 'outputs' leads us to the last of our preliminary remarks, which is to reiterate a point made in Chapter 1 about the relationship between 'implementation' research and 'evaluation' research. Implementation studies are concerned with similar questions to evaluation studies and are certainly likely to use similar dependent variables. But, as was noted in Chapter 1, the difference is their particular emphasis upon what DeLeon calls 'what happens between policy expectations and (perceived) policy results' (1999a). In a sense implementation studies are not so much different from evaluation studies as a sub-set of them, particularly emphasizing (as of course many evaluation studies do) issues about why particular 'results' happened, and about the extent to which the answers to that question go beyond issues about the characteristics of the policy.

Quantification

There are some issues to be addressed about the extent to which systematic implementation research can involve quantification. As was the case with the arguments about causal analysis mentioned above, we similarly have no intention of getting into the methodological and philosophical arguments about the use of quantification in political research. Our stance is a pragmatic one that (a) it seems appropriate to answer questions about 'what happened' using quantitative methods wherever multiple observations can be available, and (b) that in the last analysis the argument between quantitative and qualitative methods is a sterile one since there is a case to be made that use of either (or both) depends upon the situation and on the data that are available. We will go on from those two propositions to explore their particular applicability to implementation research.

At the core of this issue are two distinctions that can initially be put side by side within a simple matrix. The study of implementation may involve multiple or single implementing organizations and it may involve multiple or single events. Hence we may set out these two as in Table 7.1.

TABLE 7.1 Categories of implementation studies

Events	Organizations	
	Single	Multiple
Single	1	3
Multiple	2	4

It does not require much imagination to see that if you have a single actor, say a government, implementing a policy that in its essence involves a single 'event', say the reorganization of a ministry or the privatization of a utility, then researchers have little scope for the carrying out of a study in which quantitative methods can be used to try to explain 'what happened'. Of course it may be objected that the examples given here are actually sequences of events – reorganization or privatization involve processes that imply linked events over a period of time. Nevertheless that does not contradict the basic proposition, that what is involved offers no basis for the making of quantifiable comparisons. There are some interesting questions to be raised here about the scope for comparison through comparative studies – for example, 'Was a utility privatization process implemented differently in different countries?' – but such studies are still likely to need to be broadly qualitative in nature because of the difficulties in securing a policy definition that holds constant across nation states.

Hence it is unlikely that studies in category 1 can involve quantitative analysis. In all the other categories quantification may be feasible; what this will involve varies from case to case.

In category 2 you have a single organization making multiple decisions. The first point to make is another obvious one: it all depends upon what 'multiple' means. We may use two contrasting examples here. One is a centralized social security agency, like the British Benefits Agency, the other a central regulatory agency, making decisions about allowable levels of pollution from large enterprises. Two considerations influence the feasibility of quantification. One of those is simply the methodology textbook issue that with a limited number of observations you have limited scope for statistical analysis of the impact of the relevant independent variables. The second is particularly pertinent to implementation studies: that is, that when you have a limited number of 'events' there are likely to be close connections between them. The numbers of separate actors within the organization are likely to be small and the decisions involved may be visible to those upon whom the policy impacts. In other words feedback and organizational learning issues are likely to be very salient. Hence, while in the social security case a large sample of separate decisions may be relatively easily assembled, in the pollution control case the combination of a smaller sample with issues about interconnections between decisions may imply that a qualitative study is more appropriate.

Where, as in the social security example used above, there are large numbers of quite separate decisions implementing a single policy within a single organization, two rather different opportunities for quantitative research open up. One is the study of the way decisions may change over time. In Chapter 6 some studies of this kind were noted. Agency characteristics may change over a period, or new external influences upon the agency may emerge (here political changes are particularly pertinent), and this may be charted through the use of appropriate statistical models, taking into account time-lag effects. One particular variation on this was noted in Chapter 6, namely the efforts by Durant (1984) and Durant and Legge (1993) to take into account a waxing and waning process as enthusiasm for a new policy first emerges and then gradually decays.

The other opportunity for quantitative research on the work of a single agency arises when there are many separate implementation decisions. Multiple decision making is likely to mean the need for multiple decision makers, and perhaps even the division of a single agency into separate sections or local offices. Such is the case within an organization like the Benefits Agency in the United Kingdom, making large numbers of separate social security decisions. Hence Walker, Huby and their colleagues were able to carry out studies of some of the influences upon discretionary decisions in social security (Walker and Lawton, 1988; Huby and Dix, 1992).[1]

Category 3 involves single events but multiple implementing organizations, for example the privatization of a local government service. Here the two qualifications mentioned in relation to category 2 are again of course relevant. The second of those points about interconnections is particularly relevant, but in this case it may be very important to explore questions about these. This is central to the 'mandates' research discussed in Chapter 6 (see pp. 125–6). The issue is that if the policy formulator seems to have a distinct agenda about how a policy should be implemented – as certainly has been the case with many central policy initiatives to be implemented by local government in the UK – then it may be particularly important to try to develop techniques to detect both how that agenda is received and how strong the alternative forces upon behaviour may be. This sort of situation calls very much for mixed methods: quantitative studies backed up by qualitative case studies.

One of the advantages of the existence of more than one separate implementing agency is that the factors that influence implementation are more likely to be in the public arena, and data assembly may be easier. We will return below to two aspects of this sort of situation that are important for the implementation research agenda and yield plenty of data for study, but which make operationalization very difficult. One of these is situations in which the legitimacy of the policy former may be challenged; the other is cases where action involves multi-agency collaboration.

On reaching category 4 there is little more to be said. Clearly in this case – where multiple organizations make multiple unrelated decisions – the scope for quantitative study is considerable and cross-agency differences may be compared with within-agency differences. Much of the work of local authorities, police agencies, health authorities, and so on, comes within this category. Whilst this is obvious territory for sophisticated implementation analysis it is pertinent to note that some scholars who specialize in quantitative studies warn about problems of 'too many variables'. Thus Kenneth Meier cautions: 'If policy implementation is as complex as contemporary theory portrays it with numerous policy instruments affected by myriad variables interacting over several levels of government and conditioned by radically different environments (or policy types), then I despair that we will ever make much progress' (1999: 6). Hence he suggests: 'Any policy implementation scholar who adds a new variable or a new interaction should be required to eliminate two existing variables' (p. 6).

Notwithstanding that reservation, Meier has both worked effectively with conventional multi-variate techniques to analyse implementation processes (see the discussion of his work in Chapter 6, p. 121 and p. 125) and joined with others to argue for the development of new techniques designed to highlight specific features of the behaviour of particular implementation actors (Keiser and Meier, 1996; Gill and Meier, 2000). One particular contribution has been the advocacy and exploration of the use of 'substantively weighted analytical techniques' (SWAT) (see in particular Meier and Gill, 2000). These techniques

> involve weighting data to reveal how certain organizations, programs or policies differ in their impact upon their target populations. It [*sic* – *there seems some doubt whether this should be described as a single technique or a group of techniques* – MH/PH] may be thought of as a form of regression diagnostics with a different twist. Rather than avoiding the unusual and seeking the safety of techniques that are highly resistant to outlying cases, SWAT encourages the analyst to seek out the unusual cases and understand the valuable information they contain. (Meier and Gill, 2000: 2)

This discussion so far has attempted to delineate the scope for quantitative studies and to explore some of the logical limits to their use. As two European authors we are impressed by how much bolder Americans have been in the use of quantitative methods for the study of implementation than have our own compatriots. There is scope for an increase in their use in European studies. Equally there is a case for qualitative studies even in situations in which there is no lack of numbers of organizations or events. Crucially that case rests upon three considerations: (a) difficulties in operationalizing and/or quantifying key phenomena; (b) the value of the exploration the way actors have understood and/or interpreted processes; and (c) the fact that it may be important to work qualitatively in order to formulate appropriate quantifiable hypotheses.

The last of those three points needs amplification, since it does not emerge naturally from the discussion above. Prior to any formal modelling there is need for the systematic accumulation of existing insights on a specified sub-theme within the field. Whilst this should be done as far as possible through deduction from existing theory, we are, as has been noted earlier in the book, dealing with a field where few solidly founded and grounded causal connections have been established. Qualitative research has therefore an important role to play bridging the gap between theory and the specification of hypotheses.

We will conclude this section by emphasizing the view expressed above that it is futile to argue the respective cases for quantitative and qualitative models, not only because this must in the end be a matter of 'horses for courses', but also because we believe that good work can combine both. Indeed, it is possible that an alternative way of looking at Meier and Gill's argument for statistical techniques for analysing outlying or 'deviant' cases is to say that effective research on implementation should be prepared to apply qualitative case-study techniques to those cases.

The dependent variable

The above discussion of quantitative research leads us naturally to a closely related issue: the specification of dependent variables. Problems about dependent variables in implementation studies arise because of a confusion between issues about ends (goals), issues about the relationship between means and ends (whether means chosen are appropriate) and issues about success in adopting means. Typical policy goals are such things as reduction of crime levels, air pollution, unemployment, teenage pregnancy or smoking. Policies to achieve these may then be respectively: increasing numbers of police on the beat; curbing the activities of specific pollution emitters; creating places on a youth training programme; making contraception more available; increasing health education. In each of these cases there are two separate questions about effectiveness, one being 'Are the specified activities established?' the other 'Do they have any effect on the problem?'

These two alternative groups of dependent variables are generally defined as 'outputs' and 'outcomes'. It was noted in Chapter 6 that some implementation studies choose the former for their dependent variables, whilst others choose the latter. In principle it seems desirable to choose the latter wherever possible, inasmuch as the objective is to judge policies in terms of what they really achieve. But there are three problems that follow from that. The first of those was discussed in Chapter 6: outcomes may be influenced by factors that have nothing to do with the policy intervention: unemployment may fall because the world economy moves out of recession; pollution may be reduced because economic activities reduce, and so on. In principle, as was suggested in Chapter 6, research models can try to factor in these 'environmental' variables. We return to this theme below.

The second problem is that a judgement about outcome may be a judgement about the appropriateness of the policy not about its implementation. The policy may be an inappropriate response to the problem. More police may have no impact on crime; curbing some emissions may increase others; training may not reduce unemployment; the availability of contraceptives may not change risk-taking behaviours by teenagers; health education may have no impact on smoking, and so on. The classic issue here concerns so-called 'symbolic policy'. When symbolic policy fails, this should not be seen as implementation failure if there is simply no realistic consideration of the relationship between means and end.

This third problem is particularly difficult in the common situation where the supposition is that system changes will lead to better outcomes. Hence, in the United Kingdom at the time of writing there is a great emphasis upon the achievement of more co-ordinated working between different professions in social services. Organizational changes are tried that are seen as leading to that end. There may then be seen to be a sort of hierarchy of potential dependent variables. It may be asked: Does the organizational change occur, or does that change lead to more effective collaboration between the relevant professionals? But the ultimate outcome question is surely about the impact of the policy change upon the members of the public served by the new arrangements.

But that leads us to a fourth problem: Can unambiguous and agreed outcome variables be established? In social policy interventions desired outcomes may be disputed. The customers of services may have expectations of services that are not shared by those who deliver them. Exceptionally services may be designed to control behaviour rather than to deliver what people want. The choice of an outcome variable may require the researcher to recognize competing policy goals, and indeed perhaps even make a choice as to 'whose side am I on'. On the other hand, in trying to evade that problem it is important not to choose variables that impose an unrealistic test of implementation, as Spence notes (1997: 212), by the choice of a dependent variable other than 'agency policy choice'. While we would not go as far as that, we agree that Spence does offer a relevant warning against unrealistic analysis. Moreover, it is important to bear in mind that if the focus of a study is upon implementation rather than evaluation (see Chapter 1, pp. 11–12) it may be quite feasible to examine what influenced an outcome or output without in any sense accepting it as desirable.

In relation to these issues about choice of dependent variables, particularly the last one, we cannot arrive at any clear recommendation. It is not a matter here of saying 'in the interests of scientific rigour' avoid 'outcome' variables. That would be to discard any attempt to address the fundamental questions about what policy really achieves. Rather what we are counselling here is the need for careful consideration of choice of dependent variable, recognizing goal ambiguity and the normative conflict there may be around this subject. Winter goes rather further than that, arguing the case for focusing upon 'implementation behavior' (essentially 'outputs') rather than 'goal achievement' (outcomes) (1999: 2). His secondary argument is that goals are difficult to operationalize, a practical point with which we certainly do not disagree. But his primary argument is that the likely contribution of any specific policy to the achievement of a goal is likely to be small. In other words the choice of such dependent variables is likely to contribute to pessimism about implementation. This is another pertinent comment on the problem of expecting 'perfect implementation' discussed above, but it should surely not drive implementation researchers away from a concern with outcomes (when that is feasible).

Handling the formation/implementation relationship in research

Chapter 1 made a case for the study of implementation in terms of the notion that it can be identified and analysed as a separate part of the policy process. But some of the difficulties about doing this were identified. The examination of the key theoretical contributions explored the controversy about this matter, and in the work of writers like Ripley and Franklin (pp. 61–3), Matland (pp. 74–7) and Rothstein (pp. 79–81) we found efforts to specify situations in which it may be more or less easy to make this separation. It was suggested in Chapter 6 (p. 124), that these efforts do not seem to result in any robust typology that would assist researchers to deal with this problem. Furthermore, in Chapter 5 it was shown that modern approaches to governance tend, on the whole, to make its solution more complicated. (We return to that theme – once again stressing the value of trying to identify stages wherever that is feasible – in Chapter 8, see pp. 182–4) What, therefore, can be said now by way of practical advice to researchers wrestling with the problem? There is a rather obvious point that what a policy is trying to do will affect its ease of implementation. We may perhaps go on to suggest that it may be necessary for researchers to say in some situations, for example when negotiating a commissioned project, that the implementation of a particular policy is unresearchable. The key issues about the policy here will be its complexity, and the extent to which it can be specified in unambiguous terms. As already noted, a rather similar point will need to be made about symbolic policies. The whole topic relates back to the issues about the dependent variable discussed in the previous section, inasmuch as it is vital to try to sort out what a policy intervention is trying to achieve before attempting to examine its implementation. That last point also takes us back to the issues about systematic methodology discussed at the beginning of the chapter. It may be that narrative and interpretative research designs are most appropriate in such circumstances.

Where policy formation is an iterative process it may be possible to recognize key points at which key reformulations occur – a common example of this is adjustment of funding. In these circumstances research designs that recognize phases and use time-series data may be able to handle these phenomena quite satisfactorily.

Another solution to this problem is, again, to see qualitative and case-study designs as likely to be more able than quantitative ones to deal with these issues. It will probably be the case that it is as important for the understanding of implementation to be studying how policy reformulation occurs as to be identifying that it occurs. Here are two examples of the use of this approach.

Glennerster et al. (1994) studied the early history of a British health policy initiative designed to enable primary health care doctors to secure hospital services for their own patients by entering into contracts without reference to health authorities. These 'general practitioner fundholders' were allocated budgets based upon the size of their lists and past referral practices. The initial setting of those budgets was very much a matter of 'trial and error'. Similarly the establishment of rules to regulate this activity – to prevent possible abuses of autonomy and to cope with unexpected problems – was an evolutionary process, involving collaboration between the health authorities, the national Department of Health and the 'fundholders' themselves.

Glennerster and his colleagues describe this as 'Lewis and Clark planning' (adapting an idea from Schultze, 1968):

> The American explorers, Lewis and Clark, were merely told to find a route to the Pacific. They did so by finding the watershed, following the rivers to the sea using their wits as they went.
> The implementation of fundholding can be seen as a Lewis and Clark adventure – but in this instance there was telephonic contact between the field explorers and the equivalent of Washington and regular flights back to discuss progress with other explorers. (1994: 30)

This is an analogy illustrative of the way the implementation of a policy initiative may involve exploratory activity. Research on such an initiative has to mirror and record that exploration.

The second example comes from a study of education policy. Here the issue was the development, under the 1988 Education Act, of a 'national curriculum' in England and Wales, setting parameters for school teaching. In this case the legislation did little more than prescribe broad subjects to be included (mathematics, English, science, and so on). Organizations and procedures were set up to determine more detailed content and to enforce compliance. Then even within the implementation process there was – not surprisingly given the complexity of the issues – considerable latitude to enable individual schools and teachers to select topics to emphasize, approaches to teaching, and so on. Bowe et al. (1992) use a concept from sociology and linguistics, 'texts' (Atkinson, 1985), to explain this process. They argue:

> Texts carry with them both possibilities and constraints, contradictions and spaces. The reality of policy in practice depends upon the compromises and accommodations to these in particular settings. ... [o]ur conception of policy

has to be set against the idea that policy is something that is simply done to people. ... (p. 15)

For Bowe and his colleagues, then, 'policy texts' are a variety of official documents, together with speeches and other commentaries designed to make sense of these. Taken as a whole these are 'not necessarily internally consistent and clear', 'fraught with the possibility of misunderstanding' and never exhaustive (p. 21). They go on to make the point that 'policy is not done and finished at the legislative moment', and embellish this by saying 'it evolves in and through the texts that represent it, texts have to be read in relation to the time and particular site of their production. They also have to be read with and against one another – intertextuality is important' (p. 21).

Thus Bowe et al. argue:

> Policies ... are textual interventions but they also carry with them material constraints and possibilities. The responses to these texts have 'real' consequences. These consequences are experienced in ... the arena of practice to which policy refers.... [p]olicy is not simply received and implemented within this arena rather it is subject to interpretation and then recreated. (pp. 21–2)

Their qualitative study therefore involved the examination of the development, elaboration and interpretation of these texts using, like Glennerster and his colleagues, systematic and carefully documented case studies.

Levels and layers in the implementation process

Issues about links and levels can be systematically brought into implementation designs. However, in Chapter 6 we also introduced the idea that the existence of separate 'layers' of government with partially separate legitimacies might be a problem here. This issue needs exploring a little further.

There is a need to be very aware of the implications of 'layers' of government and consider whether it may not be most appropriate that specific implementation studies confine their attention to single layers, treating the contributions of the other layers as providing either policy parameters or inputs into the process not dissimilar to those of other interest groups. This may involve more than just recognition of layers of government but also the possibility that the activities within, for example, specific organizations, such as schools and hospitals, can also be analysed as subordinate policy making within an externally provided set of parameters.

The alternative to handling policy-making layers in this way is provided by Pressman and Wildavsky's analysis of the handling of a policy issue in an inter-institutional context, in which layers of this kind are seen as making distortion of the original policy goals more probable. We prefer to recognize that there is likely to be what may be described as interpretative space within a complex inter-institutional framework, allowing 'agencies' to exercise discretion. We are particularly unhappy about the use of a concept like 'implementation deficit' when this alternative approach is used.

These points may be put together by suggesting that there may be distinguishable goals applicable to parts of a total system – of, for example, central government, local government, schools, and so on. Questions about the success of any one part of that system in imposing its *goals* upon other parts need to be separated from questions about the capacity of the stakeholders in any single part to secure the *implementation* of those goals.

Cline (2000) picks up this issue in a rather different way. He contrasts two theoretical contributions (examined in Chapter 4), that from Goggin and his associates and that from Stoker. Exaggerating their emphases a little, in our view, he suggests for the former vertical public administration involves communication problems between agencies, while for the latter it sets collaboration problems. In the first case the issue is about how to get the 'messages' right; in the second it is about the management of a bargaining process. While it is clearly both, and the issues about how to do it are the concern of the next chapter and not this one, the distinction Cline makes is pertinent to the issues about claims to legitimate participation in the policy-formation process. Inasmuch, then, as implementation studies focus upon these collaboration problems, they are likely to need to draw upon game theory. Then in methodological terms hypotheses may be developed about the way those games are likely to proceed. There is therefore a need, given the abstract nature of much game theory, for careful qualitative study of the way those games occur.

Horizontal inter-organizational relationships

As Chapter 5 has indicated, inter-organizational collaboration is seen as very central to modern approaches to 'governance'. It is also the case that a great deal of the 'misery' emphasis in writing on implementation has been in relation to problems where horizontal collaboration is very important (see Challis et al., 1988; Hardy et al., 1992).

On the other hand, that 'problem' focus can lead on to a discussion of ways of overcoming such problems (see Mattesich and Monsey, 1992; Hudson et al., 1999). This is also an area where sociological studies of organizations, falling on the margins of the concerns of this book, have been very important. Emphasis tends to be upon circumstances in which 'domain consensus' (J.D. Thompson, 1967) and 'resource dependency' (Benson, 1975) can be developed. A variety of ideas that are clearly susceptible to operationalization for research have been developed here – about collaborative capacity and purpose, about trust, and about ways in which collaborative roles can be engendered at street level. Powell and his colleagues (2001) conceptualize this in terms of the importance of three streams: policy streams concerning 'the extent to which local goals are shared' (p. 44); process streams concerning the 'mechanisms or instruments to achieve the goals' (p. 44); and resource streams – money of course. In this way we see issues arising about the links between earlier parts of the implementation process and later ones (a theme we return to in Chapter 8).

The section on horizontal inter-organizational relationships in Chapter 6 noted this as an issue on which qualitative work seems to be dominant. The question here is whether this dominance is inevitable. *Prima facie* it should be possible for data on some of the following to be factored into a quantitative study:

- the salience of a collaborative relationship with others where the behaviour of one (lead) agency is under scrutiny;
- the quality of collaborative relationships within an implementation system depending upon a network;
- attitudes to collaboration, and the extent of trust of other organizations; and
- the extent to which collaborative roles are developed (the classic formulation of this was Friend et al.'s notion of the importance of the presence of 'reticulists' [1974]).

Work by Meier and O'Toole (O'Toole and Meier, 1999; Meier and O'Toole, 2001) is trying to inject a more comprehensive quantitative approach into the exploration of this important subject.

Looking at part of the process

Just as it may be useful to split the examination of processes into separate parts when there are distinct layers to it, so it is also important to bear in mind that understanding of implementation may be enhanced by close attention to specific levels. We have in mind in particular here the importance of studies of street-level bureaucrat behaviour. In Chapter 2 some of the close connections between implementation studies and work on the sociology of law and on organizational behaviour were highlighted. In Chapter 3 Michael Lipsky's work on street-level bureaucracy was presented as an important contribution to implementation theory. From those starting points we went on in Chapter 6 to explore some important empirical work with a street-level bureaucracy focus.

Hence we endorse Lester and Goggin's argument that

> in order to understand more fully the strategic choices of implementors and to be able to explain and predict implementation outcomes, we also need to know what are the interests, motives, and resources of individual implementors. ... In other words, what role orientations do they ultimately adopt and whose interests are served? (1998: 5)

Causal versus manipulable variables

Careful consideration of wider factors that cannot be brought under the control of those who formulate and implement policy is very important for a satisfactory implementation study. The success or failure of implementation studies depends upon this. The pessimistic view of both policy interventions and their implementation is that their real effects are often determined by factors outside government control. This point was made above in relation to the issue of the choice of outcomes for dependent variables, where the example was given of changes in the world economic environment as the 'real' determinant of a fall in unemployment, not a government intervention. The same point may even be made of many output measures, for example (in the same context) successful placements of people in jobs.

The critique of implementation studies as taking an unnecessarily pessimistic view of policy processes rests to some extent upon the fact that researchers have had difficulty in taking into account variables outside the policy process. To continue with the employment policy example, a change in the economic environment might have made unemployment much worse and placement activities much more difficult had it not been for the policy innovation under review. In that case it may be unreasonable to interpret the fact that implementation had become more difficult as 'implementation deficit', implying ineffectiveness or culpability on the part of the implementers.

It is therefore important for implementation researchers to work with methodologies that take into account and 'control for' environmental variables. It is also important to take a broad rather than a narrow view of those variables. In that sense the label 'macro-environmental factors', used in relation to this topic in Chapter 6, may be a little misleading. Within the limitations of real-world research methodology, factors in the previous category – the impact of responses of those affected – may need to be treated as if they were 'macro-environmental factors'. For example, it may be very difficult to identify in any specific way, let alone any quantifiable way, the resistance of powerful industries to pollution control policy. Nevertheless it may be possible to build into a research design some 'controls' for the relative strength of industrial interests in different districts.

A worked example

To illustrate the issues about doing implementation research we will end this chapter with a short example, which pulls together the various problems in relation to a single policy issue. In this section the headings from the earlier discussion are referred to in italics and the key points emergent from the discussion are marked with 'bullet' points.

We have chosen a real issue, on which there are data available, that could well be the subject of an implementation study. It is an issue that would be comparatively simple to study. That obviously makes our task easier, but we make no apology for this as one of the contentions in this chapter has been that if implementation research is to progress – and avoid being labelled 'misery research' – it must focus upon issues that are susceptible to straightforward analysis.

The issue is adoption. The British government has decided that every effort should be made to see that children who come into the long-term care of the local social services authorities are resettled into stable homes, and that this should, wherever possible, involve their adoption (adoption in this case meaning the permanent establishment of them with new parents with full parental rights and obligations). This policy is not yet embodied in legislation but rather expressed in advice to local authorities, reinforced by the fact that an indicator has been included in the 'performance assessment framework' used for judging the work of local authorities. That indicator is defined, and justified, as follows:

> Definition = the number of looked after children adopted during the year ended 31st March. Purpose/rationale = to encourage the use of adoption. Action required = to make additional efforts to increase the proportion of looked after children who are adopted. (Department of Health, 1999: 52, indicator C23)

We have here a very clear policy direction, provided by central government, requiring action by local government. At the same time its implementation depends upon complex, and not easily directly controlled, local action. Children who come to be 'looked after' (that expression in the above definition is the current euphemism for being in the temporary legal care of local authorities and placed in foster homes or institutional care) are very rarely tiny babies; they are children from troubled families who often have psychological problems and disabilities. These children are not easily placed with new families, and many prospective adopters will be unprepared to take them on. 'Successful' advancement of this policy poses problems for implementers. Furthermore, the government initiative has been seen by some as pushing local authorities to move too quickly, in individual cases, from the child protection goal of restoring children to a strengthened and supported family of origin to that of establishing them in completely new families. It has been argued that

> [i]t calls into question the extent to which the State should act as an arbiter and regulator of family life, and in seeking to build permanent new families raises vital questions about the status to be accorded to original families. ... More than anything else, perhaps, adoption has reflected in microcosmic form key social issues of the times and it continues today to operate as a barometer of public attitudes to families, child care and parenting. (Ryburn, 1996: 196)

In effect this is a policy initiative that gives local social services staff a task that is not easy and in respect of which the strong emphasis upon adoption is likely to be questioned as inappropriate by some people.

The *dependent variable* in this case is completed adoption of children previously in local authority 'care'. (For clarity, it seems better to use this older expression rather than the ambiguous 'looked after'.) It is a little difficult to place this in terms of the outputs/outcomes distinction. It is clearly an outcome inasmuch as a radical, and hard to reverse, change in the lives of the children will have occurred. Yet it is in other senses an output from local authority work and there is a very difficult to identify 'real' outcome that is being aimed at: a satisfactory re-start in these young lives with real benefits for their future.

However, the existence of national statistics on these adoptions offers a broadly satisfactory dependent variable. In the discussion of this topic above (pp. 145–7), reasons were offered for talking of outputs or outcomes rather than success or failure. In this case it would be very difficult to identify an explicit success rate. What the government are looking for is a growth in numbers adopted. The Department of Health report for 1999–2000 (Department of Health, 2000) mentions an increase throughout England from 4 to 4.7 per cent of children successfully adopted. As further returns accumulate over the years the trend can be measured and attempts can be made to explain it. Ironically one of the features of this policy is that the more children adopted, the more likely the remaining unadopted will be 'harder to place'.

The feature of the Department of Health returns that really facilitates implementation analysis is the fact that they provide data for individual local authorities. Hence the interesting questions are about variation amongst the 150 English authorities. At one extreme three authorities had secured adoptions for over 10 per cent of the children for whom they were responsible and eight had secured them for 8 per cent. At the other extreme there were eleven authorities in which, according to a note on the Department of Health's published table, there was a need for 'urgent investigation'. In these under 2 per cent had been adopted. It is issues about the explanation of this variation that will be discussed here (Department of Health, 2000: Table C23).

To sum up this part, two phenomena have been identified:

- a readily quantifiable dependent variable, which is perhaps part-output/part-outcome, reminding us of the importance of considering the available alternatives in this respect; and
- scope for quantitative comparison arising from the presence of a variety of alternative implementing authorities, each with the same mandate. Where governments are collecting, using and making public monitoring data, this can provide a good foundation for such quantitative work.

As far as the analysis of the *formation/implementation relationship* is concerned, as an independent variable we have in this case a 'constant': the method used for presenting and supporting the policy and 'mandating' local authorities is broadly the same across England. Some central government advisory sources to local authorities are organized on a regional basis, but it is unlikely that they would be sending divergent messages to authorities. However, it may be possible to secure data for Scotland and Wales and explore whether there are differences in how the policy is being formulated in those countries. Also, a time-trend study rather than a single-date one might reveal differences over time in central support for the policy.

Nevertheless, a study of the policy as a whole can look at issues about how the policy is being projected: what advisory circulars are saying to local authorities about some of the complexities of this policy (for example, how to deal with issues about ethnicity), and what may be being done to ensure funds are targeted towards this objective. The funding issue is rather complex in the context of British central/local relations, and will not be analysed here, but the Department of Health is shifting towards more explicitly targeted special grants.

Issues about mandates are highlighted by this discussion, as follows:

- Whilst there is a single mandate here, other research may well raise questions about alternative mandates.
- Nothwithstanding the lack of scope for comparison, there are nevertheless important research questions about how a mandate is framed and supported.

There are some interesting questions here, relating to the issue of *levels and layers*, that could take the discussion deep into questions about British central/local government relationships – about the very explicit way the government is setting goals for local authorities in an area where many would argue local authorities should have greater autonomy. Also interesting, in relationship to our discussion of governance in Chapter 5 (see particularly p. 99), is the way control is by way of a retrospective examination of a performance indicator rather than by means of a direct initial expectation. Clearly over time one might become more like the other inasmuch as performance standards could be set, using previous output indicators.

There is also a topic for research here, where a qualitative rather than quantitative approach is needed, about what the Department of Health's comment on the need for urgent investigation means in practice, or indeed the comment on a further forty-five local authorities that they need to 'ask questions about performance'. Hence we may identify here an underlying question about layers of government. Indeed to address it would be to go beyond a simple implementation study into issues about authority legitimacy. Nevertheless that could be very important in a more contested central/local framework (particularly a federal one).

While in the earlier discussion attention was given to arguments for attention to specific *parts of the implementation process*, the relative simplicity of this case means that a study of the whole process is by no means inappropriate. In Chapter 6 some examples of studies using data on agency 'disposition' were quoted, including one on English local authorities where party-political control was an important variable. Adoption has been presented as an issue on which there are distinct divergences of opinion, but they are unlikely to be on party-political lines. It might, however, be pertinent to raise questions about religious beliefs and ethnic identities within the local authorities. But then, even if such data were readily obtainable, the problem about this variable is that it is likely to be close to 'street level', amongst the staff responsible for decision making, rather than at political or managerial levels, that these factors have an impact. Another possibility is that professional orientation is relevant. For example, and this is a very speculative hypothesis (with no grounding in any data) offered to illustrate the point, it could be that higher levels of professionalization have an impact. More professionalized staff might both hold stronger pro-family of origin attitudes and be more resistant to being told what to do by central government, or vice versa. It could be possible to collect data on levels of qualifications amongst relevant staff.

In the previous paragraph some variables on agency disposition were identified that might, assuming data collection problems could be overcome, be incorporated into a statistical explanatory model. But perhaps more important for explanation of the variations in agency response would be issues about how they organize and fund adoption services, and the priority they give these relative to other activities. Hypothetically there may be ways to quantify these – such as funding and numbers of staff used (relative to case-loads and other activities) – but there is also a great deal to be said for qualitative examination of such factors. This is where there is a strong case for methods that use quantitative techniques to identify special cases – results hard to explain, authorities with exceptional characteristics – and then move on to the case-study examination of them. It would be possible to collect a variety of other data on local authority resources and organization, but it would be unlikely to be particularly useful in this case, given the very specialized nature of the policy issue and the relative uniformity of English local authorities.

However, the investigation of an issue like adoption also calls for some close examination of what happens at the street level. This should involve not only the examination of the attitudes and behaviour of staff with crucial roles in the process but also the impact of responses from those affected. Note again the discussion in Chapter 6 of the American studies that looked at some of the factors influencing the implementation of measures to try to influence school attendance through welfare policies (see pp. 132–3). At the very core of the adoption issue are questions about how already troubled children respond to the prospect of adoption, and about the attitudes of potential parents, who might really prefer a new baby. We have here a good example of an issue meriting careful detailed study that could be developed quite separately, but that could also be embedded within an overall implementation study.

We are thus able to highlight a case for examination of implementation processes, both within and between organizational levels:

- There is likely to be considerable scope for the statistical modelling of the impact of authority characteristics and disposition.
- Notwithstanding such modelling, there is also scope for looking at the factors that influence street-level behaviour.
- Above all a mixed approach may be particularly useful, highlighting statistical variation and then explaining it more precisely.

The example chosen for this discussion is not a particularly good one for the exploration of the variables that come under the heading *horizontal inter-organizational relationships*. Other local authority social services work, for example that with adults, would have offered better scope for the exploration of this issue in the light of the importance of the social services/health interface. However, there are two respects in which inter-organizational relationships are relevant here. First, whilst social services authorities are very much the lead agencies in respect of adoption, collaboration with others – particularly community health services, education authorities and the police – is important for child protection work as a whole. Decisions about the suitability of children for adoption and about the suitability of adopters are likely to require help from these sources. Hence, while it would be difficult to quantify the impact of these links in such a way as to be able to build it into a model to compare authorities, the examination of adoption processes at the micro- or case-study level would be likely to need some examination of these relationships. Furthermore, some local authorities sub-contract all or part of adoption work to private and voluntary agencies. It should be possible to explore – quantitatively as well as qualitatively – the extent to which this has an impact upon performance.

Bearing in mind the comments earlier on the undeveloped nature of horizontal studies of inter-organizational implementation, and the limitations of this particular case example as a vehicle to bring out the issues, we nevertheless note the following:

- A full examination of even a simple case like this raises questions about relationships with other agencies.
- In the context of modern governance, with its preoccupation with tackling social problems as wholes, it is very important to develop ways to examine how organizations actually interact.

To insiders, the list of authorities with their differences in performance highlighted (in the Department of Health's [2000] Table C23) immediately starts to suggest hypotheses, which bring to attention the importance for implementation research of care about the relationship between *causal and manipulable variables*. Above all the denominator of the dependent variable needs careful attention: To what extent does having more children in the 'care' of an authority make the task of securing adoptions for them easier or more difficult? The argument may run either way. An authority with few children in its care may have a greater concentration of children who are hard to place, or conversely it may have few child protection problems overall and operate in a social context in which these are easier to solve. Data are needed on the social and economic contexts in which the authorities are operating, and of course much of this is available in the returns from local authorities and other public databases. It is certainly feasible that the issues about the low performers that so concern the Department of Health can be explained in terms of variables – affecting the characteristics both of the children and of potential adopters – that are largely out of implementer control. Without digressing unduly, it is worth perhaps alluding to a very fraught issue in this field, that is, the extent to which children and adopting parents should be 'matched' in respect of ethnic backgrounds. Clearly, if such matching is expected, some authorities will have much greater difficulties than others. A shift away from matching, on the other hand, may challenge strongly held values that affect 'street-level' practice.

Hence an examination of this case shows the following:

- There is likely to be a need for careful attention to causal variables that are not controllable by those involved in the policy process, either as policy formers or as implementers.
- A concern about 'control' for these sorts of variables is important whether the dependent variable is an output or an outcome, even though it is more obviously important in the latter case.
- Issues about what can or cannot be controlled may link back to normative questions about what kinds of activities should be attempted.

In this section we have explored some of the issues about doing implementation research by using a real example. In doing so we have aimed to bring out the following crucial general points, on which we will end this chapter:

- There is considerable scope for using an implementation research approach to highlight issues about a contested policy initiative.
- Statistical modelling for such a project will be likely to be feasible if there are data that distinguish outputs/outcomes at different points in time or in different places.
- Inasmuch as governments are collecting, using and making public monitoring data, this can provide a good foundation for such quantitative work.
- It may be important to look for ways of embedding qualitative work within quantitative work, recognizing the difficulties in exploring the mechanics of implementation processes by statistical techniques alone.
- Research techniques that 'control' for the variables that those involved in the policy process cannot control are necessary to ensure that it is really implementation processes that are being examined.

Note

1   The constraints in cases like this are likely to arise not from an absence of comparable material but from an unwillingness on the part of an agency to allow its inconsistencies to be the subject of scrutiny. This has been a longstanding problem within the culture of secrecy surrounding much British government decision making.

8

Governance and Managing Implementation

Introduction

Practitioners in public administration are working under action impera-
tives. They constantly need to answer questions about how to act. In this
chapter we want to tap some notions from the analytical knowledge presented in the previous chapters and condense them into something that
can be worthwhile for practitioners to reflect on in the concrete situations
they have to deal with. If, in doing that, we go beyond the realm of empirical evidence available from existing research, this is justified by a need
for a conceptualization that is inviting enough to reflect on. The central
question here is: Given the developments in the practice of public administration and the state of the field of implementation theory and research
as described in this and the previous chapters, what kind of advice can be
given to practitioners?

In the first half of this chapter a *description* is given of implementation in
practice and of practice-notions in implementation studies. Then the question
is asked: Which factors can be seen as guiding political-administrative

action? On the basis of the normative principles exposed there, in the second half of the chapter a *prescriptive* orientation is developed.

The next section focuses on what happens when public policies are being implemented, against the background of what appears to be a variety of national institutional environments. Then the policy recommendations formulated in the implementation literature are reviewed. After these descriptions some normative principles relevant in Western democracies are related to modes of governance. In the section that follows, the variation in contexts in which governance is practised is explored; therefore the concept of governance is differentiated. Accordingly, prescriptive perspectives on managing implementation are developed. After that, an exposition is given of what implementation means in the context of modern governance. The chapter ends with some conclusions.

The practice of managing implementation

Managing implementation in practice

Sometimes the results of a policy are judged as disappointing, or even worse (Bovens and' t Hart, 1996). Particularly in judgements expressed in daily conversations, analytical distinctions between outcomes and outputs, between content and process are not always made. Rather, such judgements have a highly 'political' character: they tell something about the way the world is observed, interpreted and evaluated. A standard reaction to policy results perceived as disappointing is to blame the implementers of that policy. The degree to which such blaming is justified, however, is an empirical question. In what kinds of circumstances do policy implementers as well as policy formers do their work? And what is the relationship between the work of both? In order to give practitioners some prescriptive notions for reflection later in this chapter, it is necessary to make some descriptive observations of their practice. On the basis of empirical evidence, we try to sketch a picture of 'policy in process' that may be recognizable for practitioners.

The world of implementation   At the very end of the line between policy intentions and policy outputs, street-level bureaucrats interact with citizens. Facing all sorts of dilemmas in those daily contacts, these public servants practise coping strategies, as Lipsky (1980) and others have pointed out. Though the relationships between bureaucrats and citizens are certainly not symmetrical, there is a mutual dependency and negotiation may even take place. Much of what police officers, teachers, social workers and other public functionaries are doing has not been laid down in a formal document. In circumstances that have never been foreseen and confronted with norms that are often vague, these public servants have to act. In such situations they see themselves as required to interpret the public policy involved in a creative but justifiable way. Being implementers, they may, in fact, sometimes practise 'formulation and decision making' additional to the policy formally at hand.

It is obvious that empirical reality varies greatly here. One of the dimensions along which implementation practices vary is the type of implementation organization involved. Not only is a general hospital an organization different from a fire station, but the way in which each of those types of organization is structured may vary as well. And while social workers clearly differ from medical practitioners, also within each of these groups the professional styles may vary. What all of these professionals in public service have in common is that they are working in direct contact with individual citizens on behalf of the 'general interest'. Because of the *public* character of their work they are confronted with the rules and regulations of the government policies that, in one way or another, they are expected to implement. At the same time, because they have a self-image of being *professionals*, these deliverers of public services consider themselves to be working in *practice*, as opposed to working in the 'civil service', as symbolized by labels like 'Washington' or 'Whitehall'. When such a label is used to refer to the locus of the formation of a certain policy, a perception of distance is expressed. This may be expressed in terms like: 'Those people there seem to know everything better; while we are doing the dirty work here.' In this way perhaps the relationship between policy implementation and policy intentions has a material side: by their 'inhabitants' the two seem to be experienced as separate worlds.

The world of policy intentions At the other end of the line between outputs and intentions, policy formers, at the ministries in that very same 'Whitehall' or 'Washington', do not always fully understand why the rules and regulations they laid down in laws and other official documents are sometimes not entirely executed in the way they intended. In the event of disappointing results these policy formers, like the lay observers referred to above, tend to blame the implementers. The former are inclined to see the objectives of the policy involved as clearly stated and the means as provided; the rest is implementation. However, the connection between these different elements in the world of implementation as pictured above may not always be seen as a straight line going from problem to solution. Official policy documents, as formulated and decided upon in the national capital, may be seen by implementers as less clear and directive than the policy formers in the ministries might think they are.

Often the formulations in such a policy document are the result of compromises, of various natures. A policy document is as much the product of bureau-political struggle as a rational answer to a political or social problem (Allison, 1971). As such it can be ambiguous in its messages to implementers. It may be the case that a specific policy instrument, for instance a subsidy, was chosen not because it was seen as the means fitting the ends, but because the struggle of governmental politics was 'won' by a ministry that used subsidies as central in its standard repertoire. In addition to that, a policy document is seldom the fruit of the pure intellectual cogitation of one single actor sitting behind his or her desk. Simon (1945) indicated the cognitive limitations that inhibit 'rational' decision making in administrative behaviour, while Lindblom (1959) showed that these limitations may be compensated to a certain extent by the social interaction in which policies are made. Such interaction takes place in the formation of a policy. The compromises resulting from there may add to the ones stemming from the ideological and party-political struggle in the agenda-setting process, the previous 'stage' of the policy cycle.

It seems no wonder, then, that implementers sometimes have difficulty in knowing not only how to implement a policy adequately but also what is to be implemented.

Inter-organizational relations   Between the formulation of the intentions of a policy, for instance to guarantee a minimum level of existence, and the delivery of related policy outputs, such as assistance benefits, in fact a process of transformation takes place (Van der Veen, 1990). This process is embedded within a range of vertical and horizontal relations between organizations involved in the making of the specific policy. In the world of implementation, horizontal relations concern the connections between the organization primarily responsible for the implementation and related organizations. In the example used here, the delivery of National Assistance benefits in the Netherlands to citizens entitled to them is a task for local government. The Municipal Social Services Department has a central position in a local network in which, for instance, the Labour Office, Social Work and the Tax Office are other actors involved.

Also in the world of policy intentions there are horizontal linkages: between political parties and other societal organizations, such as those of employers and employees; between departments; between the units of one such department, and so on. Vertically, there is the general system of inter-governmental relations within which public policies in a country are formed and implemented. In addition, there is a 'trajectory' specific to a policy. This 'policy trajectory' entails the range of organizations involved in the policy process at stake. In the case of Dutch National Assistance the formal administrative layers of the Ministry of Social Affairs and Employment and of the municipalities are particularly involved, but alongside those also, for instance, client organizations participate as stakeholders.

Two worlds, different reactions   In a stylized form the picture above sketches the variety of actors and factors that play a role in the implementation of public policy. Earlier in this book we described the notion of 'the implementation gap' as analytically somewhat difficult. In research the notion has hardly any explanatory value. Nevertheless, it seems as if in practice the perception of different 'worlds' has a relevance for action. When the results of a policy are seen as disappointing, actors involved in that specific policy process may commonly blame the 'other world'. Various consequential actions follow.

On the street level, actors directly held accountable for the delivery of policy outputs may react to perceived shortcomings by streamlining standard operating procedures, enhancing professionalism, strengthening leadership and perhaps restructuring their organization. The public servants who directly interact with citizens are familiar with the need to cope with shortcomings in as justifiable a way as possible. For them, almost by definition, resources are scarce, while nevertheless the conceptions of their occupation, practised in public service, urge them to make the best of it.

When policy formers initially responsible for a specific policy process are confronted with disappointing results, their standard reaction will be a different one: they will be inclined to take additional measures. Those actors accountable for the managing of the policy process involved will aim at a more strict control of the implementation of that policy by making more (internal) rules and regulations. Stated briefly, the outcome of disappointing policy results will be more policy. As In't Veld observes: 'The general reaction of government to successful policy and not-successful policy is identical: successful policy breeds a taste for more of the same, while not-successful policy asks for corrections in the form of new policy, naturally made by that same government' (1984: 19). In't Veld speaks here of the *accumulation of policy*. Paradoxically, the empirical consequence for implementers will be a policy discretion that, unintendedly, may be greater rather than smaller (Hupe, 1993a).

Because of the different 'logic' working in the two worlds as pictured, real-world perceptions of a 'gap' may be expected to continue. Yet recently in countries like the United Kingdom and the Netherlands the awareness of the relevance of implementation among policy formers seems to have increased. The possibility cannot be excluded that there is a relation here with the occurrence of results of some policies that were obviously perceived as disappointing but at the same time could not be waved away as entirely caused by bad implementation. After all, sometimes economic and cultural developments may have changed the function of a policy in society. (More divorces, for instance, produce more single mothers, which leads to more claims for social assistance.) And besides, it may be the exact content of a policy, as formulated in the world of policy intentions, that can make it difficult to implement. In the countries mentioned it looks as if this *discovery of implementation* has led to a greater inclination towards a self-critical look by policy formers at the very substance of the laws and policies they formulate. In the Netherlands a few years ago 'implementation checks' and 'implementation assessments' were introduced in the policy formation part of the policy process. Checklists thus force policy formers to give explicit attention to implementation aspects of a policy proposal *before* the final political decision making at cabinet level takes place.

The picture of the two worlds as given above, each with its specific logic, has revealed such a variety of factors and dimensions that in the practice and management of implementation two completely identical situations can hardly be expected. This is even more evident when the variance between institutional environments in different countries is taken into account. In Chapter 2 we looked at the issue of democratic leadership over administration, raised by Woodrow Wilson and others. There we also discussed institutional theory. In Chapter 5 we made some comparative statements about the USA, the UK and the Netherlands. Now we will take a further step in the exploration of this theme and look at the differences in national administrative arrangements and political-administrative cultures that form the context within which implementation is being managed.

Varying institutional environments

At the end of a comparative investigation of differences between nations in style of regulation, in the use of certain policy instruments preferred most, in modes of network formation and in enforcement routines, Van Waarden (1999a) asks: Does nation matter here? He goes on to argue that the national differences in handling political and administrative issues discussed in the successive chapters of the book are related to the institutional environment, particularly the political, juridical and public service institutions specific to each respective country. Van Waarden argues that there is a need to look together at policy and regulatory styles, using those terms as equivalents.[1] Part of the regulatory style is the enforcement style: the style in the stage of implementation, enforcement and sanctioning. Van Waarden reaches the following conclusions. Characteristic of the USA is activist interventionism and a rigid, legalist, formal formulation and application of rules. This legalist interventionism takes place within government–corporate business relations characterized by distance and conflicts. The German style is relatively legalist and formal, too. On the other hand, there the government–corporate business relations are more intensive, more consensual and corporatist rather than liberal-pluralist. Law is used in a less activist way than in the USA. France has an activist approach and a somewhat inflexible rule-application in common with the

TABLE 8.1 *National policy styles*

Dimensions	Country USA	UK	NL
Mode and degree of state intervention			
(a) Dominant source of regulation	Market	Market	Association
Related ideology	Liberalism	Liberalism	Corporatism
(b) Active/passive intervention	Active	Reactive	Moderately active
(c) Integration/ fragmentation	Fragmentation	Fragmentation	Planning/integration
Policy making process: mode of interaction with societal organizations			
(a) Antagonism/ consensualism	Antagonism	Consensualism	Consensualism
(b) Formalism/ informalism	Formalism	Informalism	Formalism
Implementation and enforcement			
Legalist/pragmatic	Legalist	Pragmatic	Pragmatic

Source: Simplified version of the table in Van Waarden, 1999a: 339.

USA. Government–corporate business relations, however, are more informal and more paternalist. Dutch and British officials follow a more pragmatic and consensual style, with the difference that the Dutch style is characterized by formalism and corporatism, while relations in the UK have traditionally been informal, within liberal-pluralist networks (Van Waarden, 1999a: 338). Van Waarden's analysis is summarized in Table 8.1.

In a further chapter Van Waarden (1999b) goes on to explain civil servants' behaviour from the national differences as presented above. His assumption is that this behaviour is, to a large extent, pre-structured by the macro-institutional framework within which they are working. As clusters of factors Van Waarden mentions the political, juridical and administrative institutions of the state. Also important are the separation of public and private law; the degree and nature of constitutional checks and balances on the political and administrative exercise of power; the recruitment, selection and training of civil servants; and their professional identity. In addition, civil servants' styles are related to the structure of the civil society (position of societal organizations and so on); the general political culture; and basic norms and values (for example, levels of trust in government). One of Van Waarden's findings is that the stronger the checks on the implementation activities of civil servants in a country, the greater their inclination to execute rules 'according to the book', in order to protect themselves from possible liability claims or public accountability.

For Van Waarden, American liberalism and activism, legalism and formalism are related to federalism and the fragmentation of political power. Congress is powerful, while the check on legislation by judges has enhanced a *litigious* juridical culture. Government bureaucracy has developed relatively late. In the civil service there is a high external but low internal mobility. Civil servants have limited discretion, while the policy influence of interest organizations is relatively weak. In the British case liberalism and pragmatism are connected with the *common law* tradition. Political power is centralized in Parliament; there is no strong separation of powers. A check on legislation by judges is absent. The voting system and the relatively disciplined political parties have enhanced strong majority cabinet regimes. In the civil service external mobility is low, but internal mobility – within life-time careers – is high. There is a preference for generalists to specialists and a relatively high public trust in the civil service. The latter is surrounded by a *civil society* that is particularly informally organized. According to Van Waarden, Dutch corporatism and activism, consensualism and pragmatism, as well as the tradition of planning, can to a certain extent be attributed to the tradition of Roman law. There is a separation of state functions, with a concentration on executive power. The likelihood of a check on legislation by judges is present, but in a limited form. The voting system of proportional representation and the tradition of collegial governing enhance the necessity of the formation of coalition cabinets. The internal and external mobility of civil servants is limited, while they have a reasonable status in society. The history of pillarization based on the presence of strong societal organizations, a delegation of state tasks to those organizations, and a fragmented public service goes back to the times of the Republic (Van Waarden, 1999b: 371–2).

Given this empirical reality of differences in policy styles and political-administrative cultures, what kind of advice does the existing implementation theory and research have to offer to practitioners?

Policy recommendations in implementation studies

The stages heuristic

The policy process is viewed by Anderson as a 'sequential pattern of action involving a number of functional categories of activity that can be analytically distinguished ... problem identification and agenda formation, formulation, adoption, implementation, and evaluation' (1975: 19). Others have provided a very similar image of the way public policy is made. As we indicated in Chapter 1, the essence of that image is that the policy process can be decomposed into a number of successive phases or stages. Though the terms may vary, usually these stages are designated as agenda setting, policy formation – consisting of policy formulation and decision making – implementation and evaluation. This framework – Nakamura (1987) calls it the 'textbook approach'; Sabatier (1999) speaks of the 'stages heuristic' – is used in many academic textbooks on public policy (for instance, Kuypers, 1973; Hoogerwerf, 1978). It has enhanced a certain degree of specialization within the policy sciences. Referring to some 'devastating criticisms' like the ones given by Nakamura (1987) and himself (Sabatier, 1991; Sabatier and Jenkins-Smith, 1993), Sabatier comes to the 'inescapable' conclusion that 'the stages heuristic has outlived its usefulness and needs to be replaced with better theoretical frameworks' (1999: 7). As more promising for understanding the policy process he mentions 'institutional rational choice', 'the multiple streams framework', the 'punctuated-equilibrium framework', his own 'advocacy coalition framework', the 'policy diffusion framework' and 'the funnel of causality and other frameworks in large-n comparative studies' (pp. 8–10).[2]

Knowledge and action

However, it is undesirable to write off the 'stage model' of the policy process completely – particularly if it is expressed in a dynamic variant sometimes referred to as the 'policy cycle'. There are theoretical reasons (see DeLeon, 1999b), but, as important, also empirical ones for not doing so. Though the stage model of the policy process may not provide researchers with a tool 'to grasp how the entire system works *in verifiable ...* theory' (DeLeon, 1999b: 28), it, indeed, fulfils heuristic functions in both the study and practice of public administration. In the latter world the perceived phased character of the policy process supplies actors with insight into their own positions in that process, and, related to that, provides clues about how to act. Additional to, but distinguished from, this cognitive function of the stage heuristic is the normative function that gives sense, direction and legitimation to the things actors at various positions in the policy process are expected to do.

Illustrating the way this perspective offers a point of departure to relate knowledge and action, Mazmanian and Sabatier formulate a set of six 'sufficient conditions of effective implementation':

1. The enabling legislation or other legal directive mandates policy objectives which are clear and consistent or at least provides substantive criteria for resolving goal conflicts.
2. The enabling legislation incorporates a sound theory identifying the principal factors and causal linkages affecting policy objectives and gives implementing officials sufficient jurisdiction over target groups and other points of leverage to attain, at least potentially, the desired goals.

3. The enabling legislation structures the implementation process so as to maximize the probability that implementing officials and target groups will perform as desired. This involves assignment to sympathetic agencies with adequate hierarchical integration, supportive decision rules, sufficient financial rules, and adequate access to supporters.
4. The leaders of the implementing agency possess substantial managerial and political skill and are committed to statutory goals.
5. The program is actively supported by organized constituency groups and by a few key legislators (or a chief executive) throughout the implementation process, with the courts being neutral or supportive.
6. The relative priority of statutory objectives is not undermined over time by the emergence of conflicting public policies or by changes in relevant socioeconomic conditions which weaken the statute's causal theory or political support. (1983: 41–2)

Similarly Hogwood and Gunn (1984) state that what happens at the so-called 'implementation' stage will influence the actual policy outcome. Hence they argue that the probability of a successful outcome will be increased if, at the stage of policy design, thought is given to potential problems of implementation. In their exploration of why some degree of 'failure' in the real world seems almost inevitable, Hogwood and Gunn formulate ten preconditions that would have to be satisfied if perfect implementation were to be achieved. We presented them in Chapter 3 (pp. 50–1). These preconditions range from the requisite that the circumstances external to the implementing agency do not impose crippling constraints; via the availability of adequate time and sufficient resources to the programme; to the precondition that those in authority can demand and obtain perfect compliance (Hogwood and Gunn, 1984: 199–206). As Hogwood and Gunn are aware, it is obvious that these preconditions are at the same time the reasons why in practice the phenomenon of 'perfect implementation' does not occur.

In Chapter 5 we observed that focusing on the explanation of a specific 'implementation gap' can often be connected to a 'reform' orientation. It is this orientation towards improvement that makes analysts formulate the kinds of checklists presented here. They want to formulate recommendations for policy makers, whom they see as both competent and legitimized to pursue measures by which the formation and implementation of policies can be improved. Because these policy makers are seen as in command of the vertical chain implied by the stage model, the successive stages as distinguished in that model are used as 'coat hangers' for the respective elements of advice to them. The analytical rationality of presentational logic (aiming at z means starting with a and then going to b and so on) and the normative wish to formulate advice for policy makers in a system of representative democracy strengthen each other here. This orientation of 'reform' can be observed in many of the implementation studies aiming at description and/or explanation that have been published since the beginning of the seventies. These pursue the kind of research agenda established by theorists like Pressman and Wildavsky, Van Meter and Van Horn, and Sabatier and Mazmanian (see Chapter 3).

Recommendations in detail

The next question is then what kind of concrete advice to policy makers can be found in those studies. In a survey of 300 of such publications O'Toole (1986) searched for policy recommendations for implementation. He shows, first, that most of the scanned publications, in fact, contain few detailed recommendations. He suggests that 'prescription is rarely a central focus of work in the implementation literature' (p. 191). Second, O'Toole observes that the advice offered often seems largely unsupported by the empirical research base. Third, much of the advice offered in the literature on multi-actor implementation is contradictory. O'Toole speaks of situations in which social scientific findings are sometimes used for the 'buttressing of established perspectives, as symbolic and pseudo-authoritative support for positions already staked out' (p. 196). O'Toole explains his findings in terms of the normative disagreement in the field, particularly on what constitutes 'success', and the fact that the empirical theory is not well advanced. The state of the field's development imposes 'a real constraint on the quality of advice available for those in the policy process' (p. 198). There is a 'lack of focus and cumulation'. The recommendations that can be found often take on a proverbial character. (He echoes here Simon's famous analysis of the contradictory 'proverbs' of administration, [1945].) Referring to a set of principles apparently so sensible that they can serve to guide action from the centre, aiming at maximizing the probability of implementation success, O'Toole speaks of the 'top-down perspective's conventional wisdom'. This 'conventional wisdom' implies a policy design in which the degree of required behavioural change is kept low; a structure of implementation as simple as possible in which the number of actors is minimized; the taking into consideration of the problems of implementation during the initial stages of policy formation; and attributing the responsibilities for the implementation of a specific policy to units sympathetic to that policy (O'Toole, 1986: 200).

Clearly the lists of conditions favourable for policy implementation, cited above, are part of this conventional wisdom.[3] From a 'bottom-up' perspective O'Toole adds a criticism of the elements mentioned here. He states that the kind of efforts at central control as presented direct attention to variables that, in general, are difficult or impossible to manipulate. The productive effects and necessity of conflict, negotiation and politics during implementation are ignored. Potentially important participants in the implementation process are neglected. The fact that many policy problems can only be addressed through widespread discretion, local presence and an adaptive implementation mode is overlooked. Actually, in O'Toole's view the 'conventional wisdom' concerns an attempt to perform the impossible: '[D]ecide all the important questions at the outset (thus ignoring the learning that must perforce take place as policy problems are actually tackled)' (1986: 201).

Since O'Toole's 1986 scan of the implementation literature many more implementation studies have been performed. So many that it becomes even more difficult to be fully comprehensive, as we found in carrying out our survey of recent work when preparing Chapter 6. The result of many of those implementation studies has been the adding of a few new variables to the list so long already. Rothstein (1998) states that it is not clear what to make of lists of variables and checklists like those presented above. They say nothing 'about which factors are more important than others, and under what conditions, or which types of programmes are harder to implement than others, and not much about which organizational forms are suitable for which tasks. Many of the factors seem so obvious as to be trivial' (p. 69). Besides, in many implementation studies that aim at description of the implementation of a particular policy or at the explanation of a specific implementation gap, there has been an orientation toward failure. Hence Elmore argues: 'Analysis of social policy has come to consist of explaining why things never work as intended; a high level of knowledge about social policy has come to be equated with a fluent cynicism' (1983: 213). Rothstein's criticism of this pessimism has been noted (see p. 79) and in Chapter 7 it was suggested that the concept of the implementation gap is not a helpful one for implementation research (p. 140). Pressman and Wildavsky's emphasis on the problems about multiple clearance points (see p. 44), engendered a similar pessimism. For Goggin et al. (1990) this message provided a reason to plead for research designs meant to avoid any preoccupation with what could be seen as 'exceptional failure'. Unless adequate attention to the relationship between causal and manipulable variables is guaranteed, descriptive implementation studies cannot provide any specific advice for practitioners about how to handle concrete circumstances.

New insights

Sometimes, however, real new insights are gained that may have constructive consequences for the actions practitioners can take. The chance that this will happen is enhanced by the degree to which the research design has a systematic and explicitly accumulative character. Brown et al. (1998), for instance, investigated the function of local partnerships in the implementation of a geographical information system (GIS) in the USA. They found, first, that partnerships are neither more nor less successful than single-organizational arrangements; multiactor outcomes themselves are contingent on more nuanced features of the case. Second, structurally more complex arrangements do not lead to higher spending, although such institutional settings do seem to be associated with reduced outcomes as measured in certain ways. Finally, while the number of units involved in decision making is significant and somewhat negative in relation to outcomes, the use of formal procedures and leadership that inspires motivated contributions by participants can offer distinct advantages in multiunit arrangements. (pp. 522–3).

On the basis of these findings Brown et al. formulate some clear recommendations: '[M]anagers interested in gaining the benefits of GIS [*the concerned information system* – MH/PH] should institute formal procedures, develop strong leadership and cap growth in the number of actors involved and the number of resources shared' (p. 522).

Keiser and Meier (1996) investigated child-support enforcement in the USA. A federal law requires the American states to locate absent parents, establish paternity, determine child-support obligations, enforce support obligations and collect support payments. In each state a central office establishes the rules and regulations governing child support in that state and monitors the activities of local officials. The authors remark that, because the child-support enforcement bureaucracy exists in a macro-structural arrangement with states at the apex, it is appropriate to study that bureaucracy's enforcement by examining and comparing state-level outputs. As categories within which the authors formulate central variables, the authors distinguish policy design variables (policy context, policy coherence, target population characteristics, tractability), bureaucratic variables, political forces, task requirements and economic capacity. The first broad hypothesis is that policy design plays a role in determining enforcement level. The second one argues that local implementation forces determine enforcement level. The research findings show support for the broad assumption that policy design matters. The results are consistent with the hypothesis that the policy context and tractability of the policy problem have an impact on enforcement success. In contrast, the authors observe that policy coherence and target population characteristics do not seem to play a strong role in affecting enforcement; they may be sufficient conditions but they are not necessary. Keiser and Meier point out that the findings show that

> policy context can communicate priorities to a bureaucracy if these changes fit with bureaucratic values, even if the statute does not state explicitly a change in priorities. Claims that priority specification in statutes are necessary conditions to enforcement success may be erroneous. Public managers and policy makers do not, therefore, need to be overly concerned with controlling the bureaucracy with coherent legislation. (p. 359)

Theory and practice

It may be noticed that Keiser and Meier, aiming at testing a few hypotheses while examining state-level outputs, formulate some recommendations about policy design as practised by state and federal policy makers, while Brown et al., looking at the local level, direct their advice to public managers working at that level. An example that similarly mixes top-down and bottom-up perspectives in an interesting way is Fiorino's description of a reform strategy pursued in American environmental regulation. He shows the 'backward mapping' character of that strategy and concludes that such a strategy may be appropriate 'when there is a lack of political consensus on the *need for* and the *form of* change or when mechanisms for implementing change are unreliable' (1997: 261). Having started his investigation 'at the bottom', Fiorino ends up with some suggestions for 'the top', while Brown et al. formulate recommendations for managers at that 'bottom'.

Hogwood and Gunn (1984), acknowledging that many so-called 'implementation failures' can be traced to inadequate policies, criticize 'bottom-uppers' for taking an oppositional stance to elected officials and for refraining from giving any advice to them. They do not see why the view from the top is necessarily less valid than that from other levels, and argue that the implications of a bottom-up view become less attractive when specific examples are examined. For instance, 'if a Home Secretary is committed to better relations between policemen and black youths, should we view with equanimity the persistence of "street-level" police attitudes and action which are openly racist?' Or, 'if Parliament decided to move from left-hand to right-hand drive on our roads, would we be happy to leave to "negotiation" between road-users, local authorities, and the central government such questions as when, how, and whether the change-over should take effect?' (Hogwood and Gunn, 1984: 208). Analysing the differences between the top-down and bottom-up perspectives further as far as the relationship between theory and practice issues is concerned, O'Toole (2001) notes an important underlying normative difference. Top-down analysts often express themselves in support of a representative regime and the consistent execution of choices made by political leaders. On the other hand, bottom-uppers endorse the emergence of the policy contributions of actors far from the oversight of political principals. From this major difference stem another two. Top-downers see implementation primarily as a matter of 'assembling action in support of the intentions and orders of political leaders', while bottom-uppers look at it as 'mobilizing the energies of disparate stakeholders to make sensible choices in congealing problem solving around a complex, context-specific, and dynamic policy issue'. In the former view the primary focus is on issues of compliance and monitoring; in the latter on innovation, collaboration and creativity (O'Toole, 2001: 10).

Linder and Peters (1987) suggest that the general message of bottom-up studies, though mostly implicit, seems to be that we should do what we know how to implement well. The proposition that the outcome of policy making is determined at the 'street level', is converted into a normative stance. Descriptive and prescriptive statements are thus blurred, and the empirical and the normative are not separated. Against that view, Linder and Peters argue that implementation is but one reason why policies do not succeed. Besides, they argue, 'governance is not about negotiation, it is about the use of legitimate authority' (p. 464). Rather than 'admitting defeat and turning the potential domination of implementation by lower echelons of the public bureaucracy and the environment into a virtue', it is important to design effective policies and effective implementation systems (p. 474). DeLeon (1999a), on the other hand emphasizes the need for greater clarity about the normative perspectives in both top-down and bottom-up work. They are seen to be opposed on a normative dimension similar to the one we used in Chapter 5 (p. 107) DeLeon describes the top-down view as '"more" democratic' in that policy is chosen by elected representatives while with the bottom-up perspective it is crafted by local bureaucrats. Nevertheless he opposes Matland (1995), who states that street-level bureaucrats are not particularly responsible to their constituents, calling this a peculiar contention. DeLeon pleads for a greater emphasis on a participatory-democratic orientation to implementation, 'buttressed by more of a post-positivist orientation and methodology' (p. 330).

O'Toole argues that there is a need to improve implementation theory whilst at the same time giving attention to the needs of practical decision makers. But he remains cautious: 'There have not been striking successes evident thus far in finding ways of linking theoretical efforts with practical advice' (2001: 32). This remark draws attention to the specific relation between the world of analysis and the world of practice. There sometimes is, but more often is not, a one-to-one relationship at stake in which the analyst gives direct advice to the practitioner about what to do. Scholarly attention to the relationship between knowledge and policy suggests that in general there is an 'enlightenment function' rather than an instrumental use of academic knowledge in the practice of public policy (Weiss, 1977; D.K. Cohen and Lindblom, 1979; R.A. Scott and Shore, 1979). The logic of political-administrative practice is different from the one expressed in academic knowledge. It is often driven by 'position' or 'situational logic' rather than 'knowledge'. As noted above, for the practitioner the question that constantly needs to be answered is: How to act? Moreover, that question has to be answered in a wide range of different institutional arrangements and power configurations, varying not only between practitioners but also from case to case for the same practitioner as well. When implementation scholars want to take the relationship between theory and practice seriously, they should specify contexts from the beginning to the end.

Therefore, it is the identification of these contexts that will be central to the second half of this chapter. That identification is necessary for making practice-relevant statements on managing implementation, in the final sections.

The quest for appropriate action

Description and prescription

When we aim to specify the contexts in which implementation takes place, two fundamental dimensions need to be kept in mind. First, there is the distinction between what is *general* and what is *specific*. Reform ideologies like the ones described in Chapter 5 have an almost universal character, but their application is context-bound. The moment and pace of introduction of such reform ideologies as 'meta-policies' (Dror, 1986; Hupe, 1990), and the variants and institutional settings, will differ. But there will also be differences in the political perseverance with which they are pursued. These factors will all influence the 'local' success of those 'global' reform ideologies. Second, the distinction between *what is* and what *should be* is relevant. Social trends, like the global phenomenon of cultural individualism, have objective, material consequences and on a general level are hard to control (Ester et al., 1993). For economic trends, like the merging of multi-national mass media corporations into large worldwide conglomerates, that is also true. At the same time, however, there may be reasons to pose limits to the 'natural' character of such trends and a wish to counteract their adverse consequences. In order to try to manage these developments, nation states can make treaties and other arrangements. In these cases issues about judicial competence will arise. However, it may be political will that is critical in the first place, in which case we are back in the realm of the normative. The description–prescription oppositions at stake here are set out in Table 8.2.

TABLE 8.2   *Description–prescription oppositions*

	Empirics	**Normative**
General	Reform ideologies Social and economic trends	Principles
Specific	Institutional environments	Context-bound application

In the practice of action the normative, the empirical, the general and the specific are linked together in concrete answers to the questions about what to do in practice. What is to be seen as appropriate action is in an important way related to the composite nature of the specific context of that action. As argued, reform ideologies and social and economic trends may be less manipulable than influential in the context involved. More or less the same applies for the institutional environment; this is not only to a large extent given, but also has a character that varies in time and space. In normative terms there may be reason to uphold certain general principles.

In order to be able to specify the character of those contexts, and given the remarks made above on reform ideologies, trends and institutional environments, the normative principles seen as guiding political-administrative action need further elaboration here. It is only on that explicitly normative basis that prescriptive statements can be made later in the chapter.

General principles

For people working in public administration reform ideologies, sociological trends and economic developments belong to a large degree to the realm of what is given. Opposite (in the sense set out in Table 8.2) to these is the world of the normative or the political. As the classic philosophers pointed out already, *Sein und Sollen*, what is and what should be, can never be equated with each other. Between them there is a 'logical gap' (Brecht, 1959). Though implementation researchers may be committed to changing reality, the nature of their trade makes them engaged in the quest for truth. Contrastingly, practitioners in public administration may also practise intellectual cogitation, but, primarily, they are working under an imperative to act. Two sets of general normative principles are guiding their deeds: those of the *Rechtsstaat* or the rule of law, and those of democracy (see also Chapter 2, pp. 22–3). The *Rechtsstaat* implies the existence of a separation of powers and the existence of institutions needed to maintain the rule of law in a legitimate way. In those institutions values like justice, equity and fairness are expressed. Equal treatment of equal cases is a highly valued principle here. Democracy involves the freedom of speech, the right of self-organization and other rights as laid down in the Universal Declaration of Human Rights. Specific institutions, particularly representative organs and general elections that are regularly held, are needed to provide for the guaranteed consummation of these rights. There is a third set of principles that has been more controversial: the principles embodied in what is called the welfare state. Rather than an intended and well-designed 'project', the welfare state can be seen as a set of desired but unintended by-products of collective action. When there is steady economic growth, in combination with the rule of law and a form of democracy, the possibility arises for social exchanges and the realization of a proper level of prosperity for the average citizen. A variety of types of welfare state can be observed, within which different values are expressed, like equality and solidarity, or social control and minimum benefits. These varying principles may be related to political and institutional contexts (see Esping-Andersen, 1990).

It is implementation that keeps all these institutions performing their functions in society. Therefore, implementation always matters. In the last instance, the implementation of public policy entails the maintaining of values collectively seen as important (Vickers, 1965). Finally, the *res publica* and the wellbeing of the *polis* itself are at stake.

Modes of governance

The application of the general normative principles set out here happens in contexts that may vary considerably. These variations, as has been shown above, can be observed on the macro-level of national systems and cultures, on the meso-level of inter-organizational relations, and perhaps above all within specific micro-contexts. Varying along lines of academic discipline, there have been several attempts to develop taxonomies to typify these settings. Etzioni (1961), for instance, looks at the reasons why people in organizations comply with rules. Calling power 'an actor's ability to induce or influence another actor to carry out his directives or any norms he supports' (p. 4), Etzioni states that power differs according to the means employed to make the subjects comply. These means may be physical, material or symbolic. He distinguishes coercive, remunerative and normative power. Next, Etzioni defines involvement as the 'evalua- tive orientation of an actor to an object, characterized in terms of intensity and direction' (p. 9). Etzioni distinguishes between alienative, calculative and moral involvement. The first type refers to an involvement with a negative orientation, like the one experienced by conscripted men and women in basic training. Calculative involvement designates either a negative or a positive orientation with low intensity (compare the relation- ships of merchants with continuous business contacts). Moral involvement concerns a positive orientation of high intensity, like that of a devoted member of a political party.

Etzioni combines the two groups of concepts – kinds of power and kinds of involvement – as dimensions of a typology of compliance rela- tions. He then argues that three combinations are more likely than others. These 'congruent' combinations are alienative involvement and coercive power, calculative involvement and remunerative power and moral involvement and normative power. Next, Etzioni wants to examine the relationship between compliance and goals. He therefore distinguishes between three types of organizational goals: order, economic and cultural goals. In the first type, prohibiting deviant behaviour is important. The production of commodities and services is central in organizations with economic goals, while organizations with culture goals 'institutionalize conditions needed for the creation and preservation of symbolic objects, their application, and the creation or reinforcement of commitments to such objects' (p. 73). Etzioni expects that organizations serving order goals will tend to have a coercive compliance structure; those serving economic goals will tend to have a utilitarian compliance structure; and organizations serving culture goals will tend to have a normative compliance structure. His general argument is that effective organizations show a balanced mix: the levels of coercion and alienation are low, while those of remuneration and calculation as well as those of normative and moral involvement are high.

In his book *Politics and Markets* (1977) Lindblom depicts some elementary mechanisms of 'social control': authority, exchange and persuasion (p. 12). He defines authority as existing 'whenever one, several or many people explicitly or tacitly permit someone else to make decisions for them for some category of acts' (pp. 17–18). Following the legitimate exercise of authority is the basis of the membership of formal organizations like churches, clubs, corporations and unions. A government is a formal organization *par excellence*: '[C]onsequently, the authority relationship is the bedrock on which government is erected. Authority is as fundamental to government as exchange is to the market system' (p. 13). Persuasion is an 'ubiquitous form of social control' appearing in three variants: propaganda, commercial advertising and 'mutual persuasion'. With the latter variant Lindblom refers to the '"free competition of ideas" [as] fundamental to liberal democracy' (p. 13).

Since Etzioni and Lindblom developed their typologies, similar threefold frameworks have been used frequently and with wider applications. Boulding (1990), an economist, for instance, speaks of 'three faces of power'. He distinguishes the following dimensions along which variants of power can be identified: the nature of its consequences, characteristic behaviour and the sort of institutions by which power is exercised. On the first dimension Boulding distinguishes destructive power, productive power, and integrative power. Corresponding to these three categories is the tripartition of characteristic behaviour: threat, exchange and love. As related institutions, Boulding mentions those of, respectively, political and military power (such as tax, army); economic power (firms, households); and social power (family, churches, non-profit organizations). He acknowledges that all of these categories are 'fuzzy sets' (p. 24), which means, for example, that integrative power also has a destructive and productive aspect. Nevertheless, Boulding sees these classifications as a necessary way of dealing with complex reality.

Thompson et al. (1991) speak of hierarchies, markets and networks as three general models of social coordination. Ouchi (1991) distinguishes between bureaucracies, markets and clans. Bradach and Eccles (1991) refer to authority, price and trust. Colebatch and Larmour (1993) focus on the process of organizing. Following certain 'patterns of action' people draw on existing models. They may organize by 'following rules defined by hierarchic authority' (bureaucracy); through 'individual exchanges which serve their interests' (market); or by 'acting in ways which are appropriate for some group of which they are a part' (community) (p. 104). In the 'bureaucratic' model of organization, authority and rules are organizing principles; in the 'market' model, incentives and prices are central; while in the 'community' model, norms, values and networks are key factors (p. 17).

Referring to Colebatch and Larmour, Parsons observes that in the empirics of public service delivery there are almost always mixes (1995: 492). As Colebatch and Larmour state: 'The task is to identify the nature of the mix, not to place the organization into one box or another' (1993: 80). Parsons distinguishes four sorts of such mixes: a governmental mix, regarding layers of government; a sectoral mix, concerning public–private relationships; an enforcement mix, regarding modes of enforcement; and a value mix, referring to underlying values (1995: 492). For the enforcement or compliance mix, particularly relevant here, Parsons makes a distinction between two dimensions. The organizational settings of the enforcement mix obviously will vary, and because of that, so will the modes of enforcement. Parsons states that when the mode of organization is hierarchy, enforcement requires 'effective methods of command and the use of coercion or threat to ensure compliance with authoritative rules'. In the market mode of organization the problem of gaining compliance will be perceived as one 'rooted in self-interested behaviour'. Network or 'community' organizational forms 'will rely on the operation of custom, tradition, common moral codes, values and beliefs, love, a sense of belonging to a "clan" (see Ouchi, 1991), reciprocity, solidarity and trust' (Parsons, 1995: 518–19).

The two dimensions referred to are used by Parsons to position the classifications made by some authors as shown in Table 8.3.

TABLE 8.3 *Modes of Enforcement and Modes of Organization*

Modes of organization	Modes of enforcement/compliance			
	Rigby	Etzioni	Boulding	Bradach and Eccles
	(1964/1990)	(1961)	(1990)	(1991)
Market	Contract	Remunerative	Exchange	Price
Hierarchy/ bureaucracy	Command	Coercive	Threat	Authority
Network/ community	Custom	Moral	Love	Trust

Source: Parsons, 1995: 518

The range of variants following on the conceptualizations developed by Etzioni and Lindblom suggest their general and comprehensive character. Their function is that they include both 'conditions for ordered rules' and 'governing mechanisms', therefore enabling the description and analysis of any related empirical phenomenon on the level of separate organizations as well as on system level. The terms quoted in the previous sentence stem from Milward and Provan's definition of governance adopted in this book (1999: 3). In fact, all the distinctions mentioned here refer to what, on the basis of our exposition of this concept in Chapter 1, can be called *modes of governance*.

Pierre and Peters (2000) describe contemporary governance as having a 'multi-level' character where international, national and sub-national processes of governance are interlinked in a negotiated fashion. They see an emerging role of international organizations, taking over specific tasks of nation states. Seen from the level of the latter, Pierre and Peters speak of tasks 'moving up'; where greater importance is achieved by regions, localities and communities, they describe tasks as 'moving down'; while an increasing relevance of phenomena like privatization is called the 'moving out' of government tasks. Under the heading of 'models of governance' Pierre and Peters sketch three 'scenarios': towards 'reasserting control'; 'letting other regimes rule'; and towards 'communitarism, deliberation, and direct democracy'. In doing so, they use the concept of governance and its distinctive modes in an effort to generalize about historical trends. In Chapter 5 of this book, in fact, something similar was done in describing the successive paradigms. Given the broad definition of the concept as adopted from Milward and Provan (1999), the actual governance paradigm entails not a singular but several 'modes of governance', each with equal analytical relevance. Given the normative action imperative implied by the principles of the *Rechtsstaat* and democracy, and to a certain extent by those of the welfare state, the answer to the question 'How to act?' for practitioners in public administration differs from context to context. Therefore, it may be helpful if the descriptive paradigms as developed by Pierre and Peters and in Chapter 5 of this book are then analytically transformed into prescriptive models. Making the link with Lindblom's terminology, the distinction can thus be made between three modes of governance: by *authority*, by *transaction* and by *persuasion*.

Towards governance as prescription

In the authority mode of governance the central subject of government action is regulation and imposition and the delivery of products and services is seen as having an exclusive ('public good') character, like flood control or assistance benefits. There are both constitutional bases and democratic mandates that justify the government's monopoly position here. Government constitutes and 'steers on' structure, content and process and is involved in all parts of what can be called the 'governance cycle'. Making directive decisions and seeing that they are managed accordingly are in the core focuses of the political and administrative functionaries involved. The government role can be labelled as that of a *Chief Executive Officer* (CEO) (for an elaboration see Hupe and Klaassen, 2000).

Governance by transaction implies a stress on the creation of frameworks in which other actors can perform, while at the same time there is a task to evaluate and ensure that these frameworks keep functioning well. These tasks are founded in a corresponding constitutional basis and democratic mandate. Government 'steers' mainly on structure, involved as it is in the beginning and end of the governance cycle. Legislation is important, as well as institutional design, especially the institutionalization of oversight. The role of government is one of a regulator and *Inspector*.

In the third mode, governance by persuasion, giving direction and inviting others to participate are central. The constitutional basis and democratic mandate regard end-situations as what are to be aimed at. Government determines content. Objectives are aimed for in joint efforts between government and other actors in society. The beginning (initiative) and middle part of the governance cycle are important, but – though the general direction is given – the explicit end is open. Vision and the development of a basis of consensus are essential. Government has a role as *Chairperson* here.

Though the normative substance of these modes of governance differs, from an analytic and prescriptive point of view they are equal. Given the normative principles of the rule of law and democracy as points of departure, the appropriateness of each of the three modes of governance depends on the character of the circumstances involved. Just as the contexts adequate for application vary, so do the prescriptive consequences of each separate mode of governance. How to manage implementation in context and case by case depends to a large extent on the specific configuration of factors, including political will. This is why simple rules for implementation, generalizable across all contexts, are inapplicable. We shall investigate the preconditions for application of the respective modes of governance, and from there develop context-bound answers to the question 'How to act?' Therefore we first move on to explore the dimensions along which these contexts can vary.

Governance in context

A framework for contextualization

The need to specify contexts has been acknowledged by some implementation researchers. Rothstein (1998; see Chapter 4 of this book), for instance, relates types of government measures to 'operative conditions'. In the epilogue of an interesting volume on the empirical study of governance, Ellwood (2000) pleads for a specification of jurisdictions, policy types and government problems. Faced with the very different situation in Hungary, O'Toole (1994) stresses the necessity to include the multi-level character of institutional contexts in the research design of implementation studies. In a later paper, O'Toole (2001) makes a distinction between 'core circumstances' and 'external circumstances'. With the former, O'Toole refers to the objectives, information and power of those involved in the implementation process. External circumstances he conceives as working through, and thus perhaps modifying, the core circumstances. 'An implementation manager, equipped with the basic logic, can consider a particular circumstance and identify which, if any, external circumstances might potentially alter the value of one of the central variables' (p. 32). In addition, O'Toole also indicates the need to specify the identity of the 'practitioners' who are dealing with implementation. Elsewhere, O'Toole (1993) warned against a too mechanistic view on ways to link 'problems' and 'structures', as is argued for in the so-called 'contingency approach' (Scharpf, 1986).

In the following section we develop an analytical framework that can be helpful for practitioners to make an assessment of the context in which they are expected to act. Recognizing the specific character of that context is important, as well as acknowledging the consequences of certain ways of acting. In between, of course, there is normative judgement and political will.

Beyond the stages heuristic: the three levels of governance

In Chapters 6 and 7 we distinguished the following categories of independent variables: policy characteristics; policy formation; vertical relations (layers); agency characteristics and front-line staff behaviour; horizontal inter-organizational relationships; responses from those affected; and wider macro-environmental factors. When locating these variables in the political-administrative system as a whole, it is possible to compress them into three major 'loci' in that system to which they, respectively, can be related: the locus of macro-relations between government and society (macro-environmental factors – though perhaps partly, policy characteristics and policy formation); the locus of intermediary institutional relationships (vertical layers and horizontal inter-organizational relationships); and the locus of the 'street level' on which contacts between individuals take place (agency characteristics, front line staff behaviour, responses from those affected by the policy).[4] In a 'meta-theoretical synthesis of institutional approaches' Kiser and Ostrom (1982) make a distinction between three levels of analysis: the level of constitutional choice, that of collective choice and the operational level. They speak of

TABLE 8.4 *Analytical framework: The three Levels of Governance*

| Locus in political-societal relations | Level of action | | |
	Constitutional	**Directive**	**Operational**
Political-administrative system	Designing political and administrative institutions	Formulation and decision (designing legislation and policy statutories)	Managing policy processes
	System design (e.g. inter-governmental relations)	Creating policy frameworks (e.g. institutionalizing oversight)	
Institutional relations	Systems maintenance	Designing and maintaining implementation trajectories	Managing inter-organizational relations
'Street level'	Designing local institutions	Designing local 'implementation policies'	Managing external and internal contacts

three 'worlds of action'. In our view this variety of action can be seen as three types of activities, each of which can be observed in any of the distinct loci. What we propose, therefore, is to speak of constitutional, directive and operational 'levels of action' and to link these with the 'loci' in political-societal relations. These loci can be designated as, respectively, policy setting, institutional setting and micro-setting. In each locus different kinds of action can then be observed. Thus, we adapt the stages heuristic described above into a systematic 'map' in which political-societal relations can be located and the variety of activities headed under the label of governance can be systematized (see Table 8.4).

The institutional environments, socio-cultural and economic developments, and reform ideologies as described above have consequences in the various loci of political-societal relations. They should be seen as 'causal' rather than 'manipulable' variables, however. In relation to the table presented here, focusing on *activities* of governance as it does, those variables can be located outside that table: in a 'meta-'locus. The configuration and relative importance of the variables that can be manipulated, in each of the distinct loci, will vary as to time and place. Coherent ways of structuring such 'manipulation' can be provided by the three modes of governance we distinguished. In their varying consequences for managing implementation as governance on the operational level, the authority, transaction and persuasion modes of governance will be elaborated below.

When we want to specify which of these ways can be seen as appropriate *action* in what kind of circumstances in which implementation is managed, focusing on the relevant column in Table 8.4, it is necessary to specify those *circumstances* first. In doing that, we are not trying to build a new theory of implementation here, but presenting an analytical framework that enables a structured view of the subject. In the following paragraphs for each of the three loci the dimensions are explored within which the respective variety can be captured. We specify the kinds of factors that characterize, respectively, the policy setting, the institutional setting and the micro-setting.

Policy settings

The locus in political-societal relations that we called the 'political-administrative system' refers to the spots where there is legitimate attention to and responsibility for the whole. In practical terms, this means the layer of national government and the 'high institutions of state' around it. Many implementation theorists, like Hogwood and Gunn (1984), have stressed the importance of what is designed there, in terms of 'public policies', for the implementation of those policies. As indicated in Chapter 4 (p. 75–6), Matland (1995) sees policy ambiguity and policy conflict as central variables. Policy ambiguity refers to the degree of 'clarity' of a formulated policy. Policy conflict is an indication of the degree of struggle that can be observed in the policy formation stage and thus can be expected to continue in the implementation stage. With these two dimensions Matland distinguishes four types of implementation: administrative, political, experimental and symbolic. We agree with Matland that how policy outcomes are specified is important. Is the product of policy formation the specification of the expected outcomes, or of outputs? Or is the result a general description of the expected outcomes? Rothstein (1998) seems to refer to a characteristic of a policy similar to Matland's policy conflict, the degree of consensus about it, when he looks at the 'value choices' involved. What may be seen as a separate factor here is the degree to which there are alternative power sources, for example those of the traditional professions. In addition, the character of the constitutional and legislative basis for the government action involved can play a role, as can the availability of alternative required technical competence and the degree of political interest. It may be asked: Are we talking about a policy of strategic value for political survival or not?

It is variables of this kind that provide the dimensions necessary to characterize the specific policy setting involved. Summarizing the exposition of this category with an eye on the aim to make prescriptive statements on managing implementation later in this chapter, we highlight the question: With what label for the policy-formation process can the policy setting involved be characterized? Is there a distinct policy-formation process that is meant to guide implementation in a clear and controlled way? Or is there a policy-formation process mainly supplying a framework in which various actors in separate roles are supposed to deliver specified shares? Or is the policy formation open-ended and supposed to continue during implementation?

Institutional settings

The locus of intermediary institutional relations entails the vertical and horizontal relations between organizations. First, the structure of the inter-governmental system involved is important: How many layers are there, what is the character of their legitimate authority (both general and in the case of a specific policy), and how do they relate to each other? This, in fact, entails the 'action aspect' of the federalism/layers issue identified as a methodological problem in Chapter 6. What is decisive for the institutional setting is the character of the inter-organizational relationship involved. Is there a system of command, the supply and demand relationship of the marketplace, or something that can be called a network?

Micro-settings

For the locus of the 'street level' the variety of implementing organizations has to be mapped first.[5] Distinguishing between dimensions regarding the character of outputs and outcomes, James Q. Wilson (1989) speaks of production organizations, procedural organizations, craft organizations and coping organizations (see also Gregory, 1995a, 1995b). Considine and Lewis (1999) investigated the impact of system changes on front-line staff in Australia. They specified four distinctive images of bureaucratic work: procedural bureaucracy, corporate bureaucracy, market bureaucracy and network bureaucracy. These images each have different foci on the use of goals, relationships with clients, approaches to supervision, disciplinary strategies, and relations with other organizations. What Considine and Lewis found in practice was only three distinct images: 'Practitioners appeared to follow three common repertoires, but these were not determined by the type of organization they worked in' (p. 467). The distinct market and corporate orientations seemed to have merged into a single one.

Aiming at parsimony and summarizing the insights from various disciplines, in which the classifications of organizations are numerous, we propose to characterize implementation organizations as task-oriented, market-oriented or professional organizations. Though in most instances a specific kind of organization is first responsible for the implementation of a specific public policy on the street level, often the co-operation of a variety of locally operating organizations is required – if not formally, then certainly in a material sense (compare Hjern and Porter's concept of 'implementation structures' [1981]). The 'regimes' under which these different organizations work may vary (C. Stone, 1989; Stoker, 1991), as can the responses from target groups: business corporations or citizens. The degree of that variation may influence implementation. The behaviour of front-line staff has been analysed by scholars like Kagan (1978) and other sociologists of law, as well as by organizational sociologists (see Chapter 2 of this book). Some of the former distinguish styles of rule application (Knegt, 1986). In their coherence, the resources, norms and schemes of interpretation used constitute what Terpstra and Havinga (1999) call 'implementation styles'. As a summarizing characteristic for micro-settings the nature of the prevailing orientation can be used. Is that orientation one of rule application, service, or one directed towards consultation and consensus?

Summarizing settings

As can be observed, in each locus of political-societal relations there is a substantial variety of factors that together constitute the specific context of action in which implementation is to be managed. Aiming at achieving parsimony, for all the three settings we distinguished a number of dimensions that seem to be among the most relevant. For each setting we distinguished a summarizing variable. In their (vertically) congruent relations these variables or dimensions 'add up to' what can be seen as the three earlier identified ideal-typical modes of governance (see Table 8.5).

What arises now are loosely coupled logical constructions for each of the modes of governance that have been distinguished. Table 8.5 needs to be read as follows:

TABLE 8.5   *Summarizing characterizations of settings*

Policy settings			
Character of policy formation	Distinct policy formation	Framework policy formation	Ongoing policy formation
Institutional settings			
Character of inter-organizational relations	System of command	Marketplace	Network
Micro-settings			
Orientation	Rule application	Service	Consultation and consensus
Fitting label for mode of governance	Authority	Transaction	Persuasion

If one looks at the implementation of policy P

(a)   and observes in the micro-setting a service orientation

(b) while the inter-organizational relations can be characterized as having a market character
(c) and the formation of that policy has a framework character,

then the mode of governance observed here can be called the transaction mode.

Starting not from the implementation of a policy but from the official document in which it has been laid down, the order of the observations from (a) to (c) could as well be reversed. What is important here, however, is the vertical *congruency* shown within each of the columns. It is obvious that in practice conflict and ambiguity (Matland, 1995) as much as this ideal-typical congruence can be expected. Janet Newman, in a study of governance in Britain under 'new Labour', argues that governance is 'always likely to be characterized by multiple and conflicting models' (2001: 39).[6]

Because, nevertheless, practitioners always have to act, we shall deal with the implications of incongruencies later in this chapter. The constructions presented here supply the demand for structure that authors like Matland have, justifiably, required.[7] Let us therefore first see if we can cut the cake further in an ideal-typical way by connecting a 'substantive' action perspective to the 'neutral' analytical constructions presented in the three columns. Or, to be more precise, to see if we can develop different prescriptive perspectives on managing implementation that can be logically connected with the three modes of governance indicated above.

Managing implementation

Preconditions and modes of governance

What was set out above are analytical dimensions; to answer questions about appropriate action more is needed. For a practitioner in public administration it is important to be aware of the situation on all relevant dimensions of the multi-loci framework in which he or she is functioning. At the same time, this practitioner will have to act from a specific position, in a particular locus. Let us take the position of a group of policy formers at a ministry then, working on the directive level of governance, in the locus of the political-administrative system as a whole. Let us assume that these civil servants want to give advice to their minister on how to act in a systematic way, regarding a specific major issue. What do they need to look at? Given the normative principles of the rule of law and democracy, on the one hand, and the empirical situation on the various dimensions of the settings we have distinguished, on the other, basically there are two preconditions of fundamental importance for a judgement on the appropriateness of a specific mode of governance. These preconditions concern the *level of steering ambitions* and the *degree of independence* of the government actor involved, as observed on the directive level of governance, particularly in the policy setting. In the case of a specific public task like national defence, the level of steering ambitions will be high, while government has the competence necessary to fulfil this task 'in-house'. Then the authority mode of governance can be seen as appropriate. When the level of steering ambitions is high, but dependency on other actors is also high, the government actor is in a position in which it may be important to invite the latter to contribute to the public goals. There is reason to adopt the persuasion mode of governance. In relation to specific tasks there may be a specified role for government, while other societal actors are seen as explicitly competent here. Then, in a transaction mode of governance, government may create a framework in which those actors can do their specific job, while it checks the aggregated results of their performance.

Thus the appropriateness of a specific mode of governance depends on the degree to which, on the directive level of governance, particularly in the policy setting, the preconditions are met as expressed in the combination of political will and administrative competence; of 'willing' and 'being able'.[8]

Prescriptive perspectives

Ideal-typically, the fitting of the label of a certain mode of governance implies that the forms taken by the dimensions of the policy setting, the institutional setting and the micro-setting show congruence. Since the structural dimensions of the three kinds of setting for the distinct modes of governance were indicated (see Table 8.5), we were able to discuss in the previous section the considerations for advice about the appropriate mode of governance that might be given by civil servants at a ministry. We can now go further and give attention to the modes of action corresponding to other positions and loci in the analytical framework of governance we presented above. In particular, what must be the consequences for the managing of implementation? As we argued, managing implementation takes place in three different loci in political-societal relations. There it takes the form of, respectively, managing policy processes, managing inter-organizational relations and managing external and internal contacts.[9] What do the prescriptive perspectives that in an ideal-typical and heuristic way can be related to the three modes of governance, look like?

For the governance-by-authority mode, the congruent action perspective is the *enforcement perspective* on managing implementation. Within this perspective management via inputs is central. Managing policy processes implies the assignment of an explicit responsibility to fulfil such a task when and where the specific policy is applied. At the same time this requires adequate attention, in the formulation of policy and in decision making on laws and policy programmes, to the clear assignment of responsibilities. For the management of inter-organizational relations, clarity about tasks and spheres of competence is essential. On the street level, managing external and internal contacts or interaction means taking care of standard operating procedures and ensuring compliance to them, demonstrating leadership, enhancing motivation and internalization, and providing training on the job.

The perspective on managing implementation congruent with governance by transaction can be called the *performance perspective*. Here management on outputs takes place. In the managing of policy processes creating 'interfaces' is important. On the directive level – 'prior' to the operational level of action – appropriate policy frameworks need to be provided. Enhancing contract compliance is a key activity in the daily process of managing inter-organizational relations. On the street level, managing interaction is all about enhancing and maintaining a service orientation. Compliance with output targets is important.

For governance via persuasion the compatible perspective is the *co-production* perspective on managing implementation. The focus is managing outcomes as shared results (Whitaker, 1980; Parks et al., 1981). Managing of policy processes here means leaving discretion to other actors and inviting them to participate. For the managing of inter-organizational relations this implies, for instance, realizing 'implementation partnerships' (Hupe, 1993a). Micro-management involves enhancing professionalization and institutionalizing client participation. Peer assessment is important, as well as establishing complaint procedures. Externally the realization of a co-ordinated supply of local public services is relevant. Internally, organizing 'account management' ('one-stop shops') contributes to effective functioning.

Coherent implementation demands appropriate vertical connections. In the ideal-typical congruence of governance by authority with an enforcement perspective on implementation there is a vertical chain-like link between the micro-setting, the institutional setting and the policy setting, particularly the ambition/competence assessment expressed there on the directive level. In the alternative ideal-typical situation of governance by transaction, connected with a performance perspective on implementation, the couplings (contracts) are looser, though still vertical. As opposed to the chain metaphor it is appropriate to speak of a vertical rope. With the loose couplings and a more co-ordinated character of the relationships among actors, in the case of governance by persuasion with a co-production perspective on implementation, the metaphor (if any) of a woven thread may be used.

TABLE 8.6 *Prescriptive perspectives on managing implementation*

| | **Prescriptive perspective management via** | | |
	Enforcement (Inputs)	**Performance Management via (Outputs)**	**Co-production (Outcomes as shared results)**
Operational activities			
Managing policy processes	Making responsibilities explicit	Creating 'interfaces'	Making discretion explicit
Managing inter-organizational relations	Creating clarity on tasks and competence Taking care of sufficient resources	Enhancing contract compliance	Realizing partnerships
Managing external and internal contacts	Enhancing motivation and internalization	Enhancing and maintaining service orientation	Enhancing professionalization
	Realizing compliance to standard operating procedures	Rewarding target compliance	Institutionalizing client participation
	Leadership		Enhancing co-ordinated service delivery
	Training on the job		Account management

Illustration

The argument developed here may be illustrated with the use of the example of protection against fire. Representative organs will provide the executive with a clear mandate to design an effective fire-protection policy. In such a policy the outcomes are specified: fires must be prevented and, when they occur, must immediately be extinguished. Though there always will be normal bureaucratic politics, during the formulation of and decision making on this policy no major conflicts are to be expected. Depending on the specific macro-institutional environment, fire protection may be seen as a legitimate government monopoly. Then there will hardly be any alternative power sources, while the required technical competence will be 'in-house'. Because the consequences of fires can be fatal, the stake of the responsible political functionaries is high. In a policy setting that shows such a combination of high ambitions and a large degree of independence, such a mix of political will and material competence, from a normative-prescriptive point of view the *governance-by-authority* mode of governance can be seen as appropriate.

If the implementation of the fire-protection policy takes place in a unitary system of inter-governmental relations, then the character of the authority of the political-administrative layer most proximate to the operational fire brigades clearly is an executive one. Consistently, the vertical relation will be one of subordination. There may be a local or regional network in which the fire brigade is one public utility department among others, but competence and responsibilities are unambiguously formulated and exclusively assigned. On the street level the variety of regimes is relatively low: as far as extinguishing fires is concerned, the fire brigade is the dominant organization. It is a task-oriented organization with a specific *esprit de corps*. While the firefighters are highly trained, they work within a strict system of rules. The implementation style in their organization may be not 'administrative' in the desk-bound sense, but it certainly is far from commercial. In general, people affected by a fire comply with the orders given to them by the members of the fire brigade.

Ambiguous reality

The analytical constructions presented here may fulfil heuristic functions. At the same time reality is often different. First, it may show a greater variety of phenomena than captured in these constructions. For instance, within the implementation of one policy different implementation strategies may be used. In an analysis of multi-organization partnerships that uses a model very like that outlined here, Lowndes and Skelcher (1998) speak of a 'partnership life cycle'. Within this, 'pre-partnership collaboration is characterized by a network mode of governance'; 'partnership creation and collaboration' involves the use of hierarchy to establish formalized procedures; 'partnership programme delivery' is by market 'mechanisms of tendering and contract'; and in 'partnership termination' there is 'a re-assertion of a network governance mode' (1998: 320). While we may be dubious about this attempt to generalize on the basis of studies of urban regeneration partnerships in England, the important point here is the idea of variation of practices over what may be seen as a single implementation process.

Second, some phenomena can be seen as problematic. Looking at what we call the 'street level', Terpstra and Havinga (1999) give an inventory of the intrinsic problems that can be expected there. Problematic aspects of rule-led bureaucracies are – also thought of in an analytical construction – red tape; legalism and formalism; insufficient tailor-made case treatment; and lack of an orientation towards effectiveness. For corporate or market-oriented implementation organizations the authors mention as negative aspects the fact that moral, political and professional values are made subordinate to cost control and efficiency; and these may enhance the chance of arbitrariness. Problematic aspects of professional implementation organizations concern their uncontrollability (in terms of costs, deviation from formal rules). Democratic 'steering' of these organizations is difficult. Because substantive considerations prevail there is a chance of unequal treatment of equal cases (Terpstra and Havinga, 1999: 51).

There is no reason to assume that in the other two loci of political-societal relations we distinguished, institutional settings and policy settings, everything will always be just fine. In institutional settings new policies may be introduced from the system locus that require an adaptation of the given institutional arrangements, for instance in relation to the character of authority given to a specific public-administrative layer (competence and allocation of resources). One can imagine, however, that such an adaptation does not take place. It is also possible that the trajectory for an existing policy, the vertical connections, has become obsolete and needs attention. These deficiencies concerning the structural dimensions of institutional settings may have consequences for the managing of inter-organizational relations. In the macro-locus of the political-administrative system, for instance, conflicts may have become visible in the policy-formation process, on the directive level, that work through in the implementation stage, the operational level. It may even be the case that the constitutional basis for a policy is controversial. Authors like Wittrock and DeLeon (1986) and Ferman (1990) observe that implementers of such a policy may function then as an extra check in the system of government.

What especially may be problematic is when, in the vertical connections, structural discrepancies have grown between what is actually happening on the street level and what can be seen as appropriate, given the combination of the degree of steering ambitions and the perception on competence, as displayed on the level of direction in the locus of the political-administrative system as a whole. In particular this may be the case when on the street level, in a situation of relative autonomy, a specific *implementation culture* has developed. Especially in such circumstances, more or less different from the situations and connections as ideal-typically supposed, it is important to make an assessment of both the configuration of factors concerning the two major preconditions mentioned above and the feasibility of changing that given configuration. Apart from other relevant factors, in a democratic *Rechtsstaat* the answer to questions on steering ambitions and perceived government competence given on the directive level is of guiding importance for implementing action. According to the character of the system of inter-governmental relations concerned, the locus of that guiding directive level may vary. Generally, in the last resort, what is wanted in the locus of the political-administrative system as a whole will provide the guiding clues here.

Dealing with non-congruent mixes

The general action imperative implies that implementation action is required whatever the mix of settings: in congruent as well as non-congruent ones. Non-congruent here refers to a 'multi-mode of governance' mix of the settings as summarized in Table 8.5. Such a mix is present when for a certain policy, for example, on the street level a service orientation is being asked for (Transaction mode of governance), while the inter-organizational relations (still) have a 'command' character (Authority mode). Non-congruency may also imply the connection between the practised implementation perspective and the character of the given mix of settings. Stressing at random the specific and binding character of central governmental authority and responsibilities in managing a certain policy process (Enforcement perspective), for instance, may create tensions in a network-like institutional setting (Persusasion mode of governance).

These kinds of non-congruent configurations of contextual factors form the reality practitioners are used to dealing with, and often have to accept. As far as they provide more room to manoeuvre, non-congruent mixes, both of settings and of mode of governance/managing implementation perspective combinations, can even be functional for the tasks at hand. However, the more seriously certain situations of implementation are being judged as structurally dysfunctional, or the more frequently this happens, the greater the likelihood that relevant actors on the constitutional and directive levels of governance will see the need to enhance congruence between the composite elements of those mixes. Negotiation, for instance, can be functional in a process of co-production between residents, associations and local government in a network configuration aiming at consensus about the exact location of a youth centre in a neighbourhood. Similarly, however, negotiation between the same actors in that neighbourhood would be seen as entirely dysfunctional if practised in the process of policy formation and implementation concerning the infrastructure for the local supply of drinking water.

The constructions made above are designed to be helpful in a cognitive and analytical way, and may provide a heuristic that assists with the diagnosis of the specific context a practitioner has to deal with. In their pure form the presented constructions will rarely be observed. Instead, in many cases mixed ('hybrid') forms will occur. Knowing when to accept non- or incongruent configurations of contextual factors and make the best of them, or when to change them, cannot be prescribed by any checklist. It is clear that determining the relevance and relative weight of the dimensions mentioned here, in concrete action situations, is a matter of judgement, and, finally, a 'political' matter.

Implementation as operational governance

Now, at the end of this chapter, we can reposition implementation in terms of the need, which we have stressed, to relate it to the concept of governance. Given the three levels of governance we distinguished, what we called *directive governance* is at the heart of all the activities mentioned. This level of governance action – or just 'governance', but then in the narrow meaning – entails legitimate, directive formulation and decision making on public tasks. Roughly speaking, we are dealing here with what we defined in Chapter 1 as policy formation. Kiser and Ostrom (1982) have pointed to the importance of another level, that of constitutional design. In our view, the level of *constitutional governance* is relevant in other loci of political–societal relations, such as the street level, as well. There, too, designing institutions is an important public task. Implementation, then, refers to that part of governance that involves activities in relation to public tasks that follow the legitimate, directive decisions on those tasks. In the beginning of the third millennium 'implementation of public policy' takes various forms, but they all can be approached as concerned with the operational part of governance. In short, implementation can be seen as *operational governance*.

Identifying, specifying and compressing distinct clusters of variables, we structured the multiplicity of environments and circumstances practitioners have to deal with as contexts of action. We did so in a threefold way. Behind each of the combinations of modes of governance and prescriptive perspectives, a specific image of implementation is understood. In the authority/enforcement image public policy is implemented – or, better now: governance is practised – in relationships with tight vertical couplings. Though implementers often work in teams, their work is driven by high standards related to the public task at hand. These standards make them internalize the imposed formal authority. The implementers are being held accountable only vertically: by executive powers embodying that formal authority. It makes the implementers bureaucratic subordinates, in a relationship in which accountability is managed by rules. In this perspective, implementation is generally a matter of following standards. What perhaps is lacking in terms of material autonomy is gained at the level of ideals and the acceptance of public responsibilities.

In the transaction/performance image the couplings, often with a contract character, are looser, though still vertical: the 'agents' being contractually accountable to the 'principals'. What drives implementers is meeting the targets they are committed to. It is not the formal but the material power, in terms of incentives or sanctions, that influences implementers whilst they perform their jobs. In this perspective implementation is a matter of achievement.

In the persuasion/co-production image the relative autonomy of the implementers is acknowledged, as well as the joint framework within which they are fulfilling their tasks. Trust, among other things in their professionalism and expert judgement, is a driving force. Accountability is multiple, implementers are treated as partners, in relationships that are both vertical and horizontal. Accountability is co-produced in interaction. In this perspective, implementation is a matter of co-producing shared results.

GOVERNANCE AND MANAGING IMPLEMENTATION 195

Conclusions

From an analytical point of view all of the three ideal-typical modes of governance and related perspectives on managing implementation developed in this chapter are of equal value. Given the general normative principles referred to, the appropriate application of these mode of governance/mode of action combinations depends on the specific configuration of factors in the multiple contexts in which practitioners of public administration have to act.

This being so, it is obvious that real-world policy processes run across the columns of the presented analytical constructions in a variety of ways. Then, whilst congruent and non-congruent alternatives will be evident, incongruity will come in many forms and will, from case to case, cause greater or lesser problems. Choices, inasmuch as they are available, will be about minimizing incongruities rather than about mapping out an ideal implementation process that simply imitates top-down prescriptions regardless of context. Essentially, the plea for contextualization made here implies recognizing alternative modes of governance.

Notes

1 Van Waarden (1999a: 306) makes a comparison following three main dimensions, each of them subdivided. (1) To what extent is there government intervention in a country (state/association/market; active–intensive/passive–reactive; planned integration/fragmentation)? (2) How are societal organizations approached, especially in the stages of policy making and regulation (antagonist/paternalist/consensual; formalization/openness/exclusivity)? (3) How does the process of implementation, enforcement and sanctioning develop (legalism/pragmatism)?

2 In his volume on theories of the policy process, Sabatier, for reasons that he explains, has omitted some other frameworks. He mentions 'cultural theory' ('too incomplete and unclear'), 'constructivist frameworks' (ideas left 'unconnected to socioeconomic conditions or institutions and ... to specific individuals and thus largely nonfalsifiable') and the 'policy domain framework' as 'difficult to understand' (1999: 11).

3 In a summary of the 'top-down perspective's conventional wisdom', O'Toole (1986) refers to Mazmanian and Sabatier (1981) and Pressman and Wildavsky (1984). At the same time he mentions O'Toole and Montjoy (1984) as well.

4   For the distinction between locus and focus see Chapter 1.
5   It is hard to give a term a specific definition when this term with a different meaning is used in daily practice. At the same time it seems even less useful to reformulate a term like 'street level' – in our conceptualization a 'locus' rather than a 'level' – when it is so commonly used in the implementation literature as it is.
6   Newman describes that conflict in terms of two dimensions: involving tension between continuity and innovation, on one dimension, and between centralization and differentiation, on the other. From those dimensions Newman distils four models of governance: the self-governance model, towards devolution based on citizen or community power; the open-system model, towards flexibility, based on the flow of power within networks; the hierarchy model, towards control, based on formal authority; and the rational goal model, towards output maximization, based on managerial power (Newman, 2001: 38). The 'pragmatism in the new millennium' we described in Chapter 5 involves the playing out of the tensions between these models.
7   See Matland's observation as quoted in Chapter 4 (p. 74) of this book concerning the need for *structure* instead of more variables.
8   Pierre and Peters (2000) speak of a 'state-centered' conception of governance. They give both empirical and normative reasons for such a stance. It is interesting that they do not hesitate to use the term 'steering' in this context. We share the considerations given by these authors in the following sense. Given the context at hand, in practice it may be appropriate if certain public tasks in the public domain are performed by so-called 'private' actors, that is to say, business corporations or non-profit organizations. Normatively, in our view the decision to have such tasks fulfilled this way, being a 'value choice' (Rothstein, 1998) with a *public* character, needs an explicit legitimation. The decision on the 'appropriateness' can be seen as a result of an analytically supported political assessment 'on the spot'. In that assessment the specific combination of available ambition and competence is leading.
9   Berman (1978) makes a distinction between 'macro-implementation' and 'micro-implementation'.

9

Conclusions

We started from the position, set out in Chapter 1, that within political science and public administration a sub-discipline concerned with policy implementation seems to have been established. After our introductory remarks, including explanations about the terminology we use in the book, in Chapter 1, we reviewed the literature about implementation, in Chapters 2 to 4. There we observed that it was a development from a longstanding concern to explain, and probably try to reduce, the 'gap' between initial policy formulation and policy output.

We showed that the 'mainstream' implementation literature, broadly speaking originating from Pressman and Wildavsky's influential book *Implementation* (1973), to some extent supplemented, and to some extent bypassed, other relevant literature on politics, public law and public organizations. Within the specific implementation literature a lively debate developed, dominated by arguments about whether 'top-down' or 'bottom up' views of implementation were more appropriate. Whilst that argument was partly about methodology, it was perhaps primarily driven by concerns about accountability. The top-down preoccupation with the elimination of the 'gap' between formulation and output contrasted with the bottom-up view that this phenomenon was a product of the inevitable, and perhaps desirable, participation of other actors in later stages of the policy process.

Then, as is the way with debates of this kind, gradually the literature moved away from a simple confrontation between the top-down and bottom-up perspectives. Writers became critical of the 'misery' perspective that led top-downers to be preoccupied with a process of policy modification. From a methodological point of view it became recognized that it is much more fruitful to seek to explain and understand the implementation process than to be preoccupied by a need to explain an inevitable 'gap'. From a normative point of view it became recognized (a) that there are alternative views about the accountability of public policy that cannot be resolved by an academic literature, and (b) that in many situations the exploration of the way alternative 'accountabilities' can fuse together is a more fruitful way forward for those anxious to control implementation than a preoccupation with domination by any single party.

Chapter 5 then added to that review the perspective that the evolution of the debate needs to be seen not simply in terms of a developing academic argument but also in its relationship to a changing perspective on the role of government in the policy process. The latter has involved what we, alongside many other contemporary writers, see as an evolution from *government* to *governance*. Central to this development was, first, the exploration of public policy delivery through private organizations using market mechanisms and public–private partnerships, followed by a recognition of the importance of networks for policy delivery. At the time of writing these appear to be being moulded together, so that it seems necessary to develop an approach to the policy process that suggests that different issues in different institutional contexts require implementation in different ways. Whilst this is often described as 'the third way', between traditional public bureaucracies and market systems, it seems to us more appropriate to see this as a developing pragmatism in respect of the arguments about the 'best' way.

Chapter 5 then asked: What is the implication of the new world of *governance* for the old issues about the implementation process? It was noted that there are writers who see in these new developments the 'death' of the study of implementation. We agree that governance makes the top-down/bottom-up debate seem rather dated, and the top-down control emphasis in the work of some of the top-down writers particularly irrelevant. Implementation theory has evolved away from that debate to take on board complexity in respect both of the process and of the related issues of control. Nevertheless it seems wrong to see the implementation perspective as no longer appropriate. On the contrary, in our view it is the very complexity of the issues facing modern governance that makes it important to give attention to implementation. One of the virtues of the work of the early top-down theorists was that they emphasized issues about purposive action and control over policy processes. Those issues remain important regardless of the stance one takes on who should be in control. While we recognize that there has been a tendency in some postmodernist writing on public administration to see the policy process as having a shapeless, 'garbage can', character, we share the more widespread concern about the need to raise questions concerning how policy processes may be influenced.

Chapter 5 thus led on to the later part of the book, which bifurcated into two separate discussions, one about researching the implementation process (Chapters 6 and 7) and the other about influencing that process (Chapter 8). We separated these two concerns, notwithstanding the fact that we recognize that many researchers want to influence implementation and that actors in the policy process need research to help them understand it. Throughout the implementation literature we have identified these dual concerns about how to *study* and how to *control* the phenomenon of implementation.

In Chapter 6 we reported on the state of the art of implementation studies at the begining of the twenty-first century. We started accumulating the material for that chapter in the belief that we could assemble a comprehensive database of implementation studies carried out during the 1990s. This belief proved to be mistaken; given the diversity of the subject we soon discovered that it was an impossible task. Studies claiming to be about implementation had been carried out without reference to the mainstream theoretical literature, whilst excellent insights relevant to the theoretical debate had been provided by studies apparently indifferent to that mainstream. However, our examination of the state of the art enabled us to give some shape to the range of empirical questions that need to be addressed if the implementation process is to be understood. We did this using a framework that highlighted some of the key issues about ways to segment or separate the empirical analysis of implementation, and ways to frame hypotheses. It originated from a 'top-down' literature, and listed the independent variables in a way that corresponds to a 'stagist' and perhaps top-down perspective. However, whilst (as was recognized) the choice of the dependent variable may be influenced by perspectives on the old top-down/bottom-up argument, the location of policy definition at the top of the political-administrative system implies a normative choice. A great deal of the more innovatory literature sets out to deal with questions about the role of staff at or near the bottom of the system or about how they receive and transform the efforts of others to 'mandate'. In other words, there is always a 'top' in the analytical sense that somewhere is formulated and decided what has to be implemented, but the location of that 'top' may vary: it may be even 'at the bottom'.

We also showed, in Chapter 6, how a range of approaches to research – both quantitative and qualitative, and deriving from various concerns in both the study of political science and public administration and other disciplines – contribute to the understanding of implementation. Chapter 6 therefore leads on in Chapter 7 to observations on the way forward for implementation studies. Our stance is that the systematic development of insights into the implementation process is possible using traditional social science methods influenced by the positivist tradition. We do not accept the postmodernist perspective that is totally dismissive of that tradition. At the same time we do not think that it is necessary for work to be bound into the more narrow tenets of some exponents of that tradition that dismiss efforts to advance interpretation and qualitative understanding in favour of rigid quantitative models. Since this is not a text on methodology or the philosophy of science, we go no further other than to state our position on these issues. We note, however, that practitioners are still asking researchers to answer questions on 'what works' and 'how implementation may be influenced'. Chapter 7 is a contribution to helping people to deal with these questions, by setting out ways of organizing research work – segmenting parts of the policy process, highlighting key questions and looking at ways quantitative and qualitative methods may be combined. In the last analysis it is important to try to develop the systematic study of implementation, separating theoretical and methodo-logical questions from the normative ones about control over the policy process.

However, we noted at the beginning of Chapter 8 that practitioners in public administration 'constantly need to answer questions about how to act'. We therefore set out to address those questions. In Chapter 3 we had noted theorists addressing answers to notional questions likely to be asked by specific practitioners, at the top or bottom. Appropriate answers in the new world of governance have to be framed without that clear pri-vileging of specific actors. In Chapter 4 we had observed theorists strug-gling with ways to situate action advice with reference to policy issues or policy contexts. The problem with these is the difficulty of achieving generalizations that hold across varying cultural and institutional contexts.

Hence, our approach to both these issues is to make use of an approach to specifying policy contexts that owes a great deal both to Etzioni's typo-logy of organizations and to efforts by Lindblom and others to handle the variations in the forms of governance (hierarchies, markets and net-works). From there we arrived at a trilogy we called 'authority, trans-action and persuasion'. To these we added a recognition that – if the stages heuristic in policy process studies is used with caution – these modes of governance both can be seen in different *loci* and imply different *levels of action*. The result is not a single set of propositions about how to structure implementation, such as offered by some of the top-down theorists. Nor it is a threefold recipe on modes of implementation arguing that in this situation hierarchy is best, in that markets are best and in the other networks are best. Rather we offer an approach to sensitizing actors about the opportunities, constraints and problems that they may face in differ-ent situations where a combination of factors – deriving from the issues at stake, the interests involved, the institutional arrangements and answers to key normative questions about what is desired – are put together.

The message of Chapters 7 and 8 is that implementation is a complex matter. This recognition came to scholars as they moved away from the early arguments about the subject, at just the same time as the complexi-ties of *governance* as opposed to government were being recognized. As such it is neither easy to research nor easy to influence. In the face of such recognition one way forward is the pessimistic route of saying it is all too difficult; researchers therefore can only describe what happens and policy actors can only operate intuitively. The alternative is to recognize processes that can be understood by research and influenced by policy actors, in a context in which there is much that is both intriguing to under-stand and worthwhile to control. This is the alternative we advocate.

Appendix

Notes on the Survey of Empirical Articles

Methodological account

In order to examine how implementation research was being operationalized during the 1990s we assembled a database of articles. These were collected from the political science and public administration journals in the
United States, Canada, Australia, the United Kingdom, the Netherlands
and elsewhere in Europe. A complete list of the journals concerned is
shown in Table 1. We recognize that we could have gone outside political
science, looking at organization studies and sociology and at journals concerned with substantive policy areas (social policy, health policy, environment policy, and so on). But that would have enlarged our task too much,
and vastly increased the number of articles that would have to be scruti-
nized but would not be relevant.

We chose publications in English and Dutch. When social scientists
publish for an international audience, it is usually in English. Since one of
the authors of this book is Dutch, and knows Dutch public administration
well, Dutch journals were included. Two French articles in the journal
Canadian Public Administration have also been analysed.

The database of articles was assembled from the years 1990 up to and
including 1998, so nine years in total. Articles were selected using the
following key words (in their titles or synopses): implementation, policy
learning, discretion, policy evaluation, policy outputs.[1] The search was
done for most journals in the electronic database Social Sciences Citation
Index (SSCI). Two journals could only be found in the database International Political Science Abstracts (IPSA). The Dutch journals and the
Journal of Public Administration Research and Theory had to be scanned
manually because they were not in any available electronic database.
Concerning the *Journal of Public Administration Research and Theory*, issues
1 and 3 of volume 1 (1991), issue 4 of volume 2 (1992) and issue 2 of
volume 8 (1998) were not available. However, from the index of titles of
these volumes (in the other issues), it became clear no relevant articles for
the research were in these missing issues. Table 1 shows all journals
scanned, the source used for the scan and the amount of articles it yielded.

TABLE 1 *Journals*

	Journal	Source	Number of Articles
	British		
1	British Journal of Political Science	SSCI	0
2	Journal of Public Policy	IPSA	5
3	Policy and Politics	SSCI	7
4	Political Studies	SSCI	0
5	Public Administration	SSCI	6
	American		
6	Administration and Society	SSCI	4
7	Administrative Science Quarterly	SSCI	1
8	American Journal of Political Science	SSCI	9
9	American Political Science Review	SSCI	3
10	American Politics Quarterly	SSCI	2
11	American Review of Public Administration	SSCI	7
12	Comparative Political Studies	SSCI	1
13	Governance	SSCI	3
14	International Review of Administrative Sciences	SSCI	2
15	Journal of Policy Analysis and Management	SSCI	7
16	Journal of Public Administration Research and Theory	Manually	13
17	Policy Sciences	SSCI	6
18	Policy Studies Journal	SSCI	13
19	Political Research Quarterly	SSCI	1
20	Public Administration Review	SSCI	12
21	Publius	SSCI	10
	Dutch		
22	Acta Politica	Manually	0
23	Beleid en Maatschappij	Manually	5
24	Beleidsanalyse	Manually	5
25	Beleidswetenschap	Manually	9
26	Bestuurskunde	Manually	7
27	Bestuurswetenschappen	Manually	1
	Other European		
28	European Journal of Political Research	SSCI	1
29	Journal of European Public Policy	SSCI	3
30	Scandinavian Political Studies	SSCI	2
31	West European Politics	IPSA	5
	Other countries		
32	Australian Journal of Public Administration	SSCI	9
33	Canadian Public Administration – Administration Publique du Canada	SSCI	6
			165

A total of 165 possible articles were collected from 33 journals published between 1990 and 1998. These were all copied and then examined to determine whether they were really relevant for the intended analysis. To be included in the analysis an article had to have some discussion of findings from empirical research, even if only to support a theoretical discussion. We did not include articles that were purely theoretical or purely prescriptive, though it will be noted from the discussion below that some were included that had prescription or theory building as their primary purpose. Secondly, an article had either to draw explicitly upon implementation theory (by which we mean some discussion of it, not just the odd footnote) or to be formulated in such a way that it could be seen as implicitly a discussion of implementation. For the purposes of the latter identification we took this to involve some form of concern about explaining the presence or absence of an implementation 'gap', however defined. Excluding those that on closer scrutiny were found not to be about implementation, not to report empirical studies or were about implementation of policy from a supra-national body (e.g. the EU) we arrived at a final database of 88.

A scan was also made of books on policy implementation from the databases of the British Library, the Library of Congress and the Dutch Central Catalogue (*Nederlandse Centrale Catalogus*, NCC). From this scan, it became clear that there are very few books reporting on empirical studies of implementation. The largest part of reports on full-fledged empirical studies is reported on in articles or in 'grey' literature not easily accessed via databases. The important books about implementation are primarily theoretical.

Some data from the sample of articles

Of the 88 articles only 39 both drew upon implementation theory *and* were concerned to analyse or explain 'implementation gaps'. A further 6 drew upon theory but did not discuss 'gaps'. A large group – 33 – was concerned with gaps but did not explicitly refer to implementation theory. In this category were many articles that were framed theoretically in terms of the longstanding concerns about the extent to which politicians have an impact upon bureaucracies. Finally there were 10 articles that neither discussed implementation theory nor explored issues about implementation gaps, which we kept in the sample as borderline cases.

Sixty-four of the authors were from the USA, 6 from the Netherlands, 4 from Canada, 3 from the UK, 3 from Australia and 2 from Israel. Other (e.g. China) countries were represented only by single figures. In all but a small number of cases the authors' studies were based in their own country.

The policy areas covered were very diverse. A rough classification of policy areas to convey the diversity of the cases covered is given in Table 2.

It is worth noting how salient environmental regulation is amongst the sample of studies. Regulatory acts, and sometimes their outputs, provide widespread comparable data. These are three areas where we might perhaps have expected to find more studies: urban renewal and employment (as key concerns of many of the early implementation studies)

TABLE 2 *Policy areas*

Environmental regulation	21
Meta-policy change	20
Social policy (inc. health and education)	18
Economic regulation	7
Employment policy, economic development	3
Urban renewal	3
Police/criminal justice policy	4
Equal opportunities policy	2
Others (inc. hard to classify)	10

TABLE 3 *Research areas*

Description	27
Causal explanation	37
Theory building	20
Prescription	2
Other	2

and police and equal opportunities policy (where there are some very obvious – and quantifiable – implementation issues on the agenda).

Forty-two articles involved quantification, and all but five of these went on to carry out some form of statistical analysis. Thirteen of the 42 articles involved the use of time-series data. The research goals of the authors were as shown in Table 3.

Note

1 In Dutch translated as *(beleids)implementatie, (beleids)uitvoering, beleidsleren, leren in het openbaar bestuur, beleidsvrijheid, discretionaire ruimte, (beleids)evaluatie, (beleids)outputs, beleidsprestaties.*

References

Note

Following standard Dutch practice names containing the forms 'van', 'in't', 't,' 'ter', do not appear here in the alphabetical order indicated by the prefix. Thus, for example, H.R. van Gunsteren comes in the place appropriate to Gunsteren. The exception to this rule is two American authors – Van Meter and Van Horn – who are normally indexed under the letter 'v' in English publications.

Aalders, M.V.C. (1987) *Regeltoepassing in de ambtelijke praktijk van Hinderwet en Bouwtoezichtafdeling*. Groningen: Wolters-Noordhoff.

Aberbach, J.D., Putnam, R.D. and Rockman, B.A. (1981) *Bureaucrats and Politicians in Western Democracies*. Cambridge, Mass.: Harvard University Press.

Abma, T. (1999) 'Introduction: narrative perspectives on program evaluation' pp. 1–27 in T. Abma (ed.) (1999) *Telling Tales: On Evaluation and Narrative. Advances in Program Evaluation, Volume 6*. Greenwich, Conn.: JAI Press.

Abma, T. (ed.) (1999) *Telling Tales: On Evaluation and Narrative. Advances in Program Evaluation, Volume 6*. Greenwich, Conn.: JAI Press.

Aldrich, H.E. (1976) 'Resource dependence and inter-organizational relations: Local employment service offices and social services sector organizations', *Administration and Society*, 7 (4): 419–54.

Alford, R.R. (1975) *Health Care Politics: Ideological and Interest Group Barriers to Reform*. Chicago: University of Chicago Press.

Algemene Rekenkamer (1987) *Privatisering Staatsvissershavenbedrijf*. The Hague: Staatsuitgeverij.

Algemene Rekenkamer (1998) *Privatisering van het ABP*. The Hague: Sdu Uitgevers.

Allison, G.T. (1971) *Essence of Decision: Explaining the Cuban Missile Crisis*. Boston: Little, Brown and Company.

Anderson, J.E. (1975) *Public Policy-Making*, New York: Praeger.

Argyris, C. (1964) *Integrating the Individual and the Organization*. New York: Wiley.

Atkinson, P. (1985) *Language, Structure and Reproduction: An Introduction to the Sociology of Basil Bernstein*. London: Methuen.

Axelrod, R. (1984) *The Evolution of Cooperation*. New York: Basic Books.

Axelrod, R. and Keohane, R. (1985) 'Achieving cooperation under anarchy: Strategies and institutions', *World Politics*, 39 (1): 226–54.

Bailey, S.K. and Mosher, E.K. (1968) *ESEA: The Office of Education Administers a Law*. Syracuse, NY: Syracuse University Press.

Baldwin, R. (1995) *Rules and Government*. Oxford: Clarendon Press.

Bardach, E. (1977) *The Implementation Game: What Happens after a Bill Becomes a Law*. Cambridge, Mass.: MIT Press.

Bardach, E. (1998) *Getting Agencies to Work Together: The Practice and Theory of Managerial Craftsmanship*. Washington, DC: Brookings Institution Press.

Bardach, E. and Lesser, C. (1996) 'Accountability in human services collaboratives – For what? And to whom?', *Journal of Public Administration Research and Theory*, 6 (2): 197–224.

Barrett, S.M. and Fudge, C. (1981a) 'Examining the policy-action relationship', in S.M. Barrett and C. Fudge (eds), *Policy and Action: Essays on the Implementation of Public Policy*. London: Methuen. pp. 3–34.

Barrett, S.M. and Fudge, C. (1981b) 'Reconstructing the field of analysis', in S.M. Barrett and C. Fudge (eds), *Policy and Action: Essays on the Implementation of Public Policy*. London: Methuen. pp. 249–78.

Barrett, S.M. and Fudge, C. (eds) (1981c) *Policy and Action: Essays on the Implementation of Public Policy*. London: Methuen.

Barrett, S.M. and Hill, M.J. (1981) 'Report to the SSRC Central–Local Government Relations Panel on the "core" or theoretical component of the research on implementation', unpublished.

Baudrillard, J. (1973) *Le miroir de la production ou l'illusion critique du matérialisme historique*. Tournai: Casterman.

Baudrillard, J. (1981) *Simulacres et simulation*. Paris: Galilée.

Bellamy, C. and Taylor, J. (1992) 'Informatisation and new public management: An alternative agenda for public administration', *Public Policy and Administration*, 7 (3): 29–41.

Benson, J.K. (1975) 'The inter-organizational network as a political economy', *Administrative Science Quarterly*, 20 (2): 229–49.

Benson, J.K. (1977) 'Organizations: A dialectical view', *Administrative Science Quarterly*, 22 (1): 1–21.

Benson, J.K. (1982) 'A framework for policy analysis', in D.L. Rogers and D.A. Whetten (eds), *Interorganizational Coordination: Theory, Research and Implementation*. Ames: Iowa State University Press. pp. 137–76.

Bentley, A.F. (1967) *The Process of Government*. Cambridge, Mass.: The Belknap Press.

Berke, J.S., Kirst, M.W., Bailey, S.K. and Britell, J.K. (1972) *Federal Aid to Education: Who Benefits? Who Governs?* Lexington, KY: Heath.

Berman, P. (1978) 'The study of macro- and micro-implementation', *Public Policy*, 26 (2): 157–84.

Bevir, M. and Rhodes, R.A.W. (2000) 'Analysing networks: From typologies of institutions to narratives of beliefs', paper presented by Rod Rhodes on 24 January at a staff seminar of the Department of Public Administration, Erasmus University, Rotterdam.

Blau, P.M. (1955) *The Dynamics of Bureaucracy: A Study of Interpersonal Relations in Two Government Agencies*. Chicago: University of Chicago Press.

Blowers, A. (1983) 'Master of fate or victim of circumstance: The exercise of corporate power in environmental policy-making', *Policy and Politics*, 11 (4): 393–415.

Blowers, A. (1984) *Something in the Air: Corporate Power and the Environment*. London: Harper & Row.

Boaden, N. (1971) *Urban Policy-Making: Influences on County Boroughs in England and Wales*. Cambridge: Cambridge University Press.

Boulding, K.E. (1990) *Three Faces of Power*. Newbury Park, Calif.: Sage.

Bovens, M.A.P. and 't Hart, P. (1996) *Understanding Policy Fiascoes*. New Brunswick, NJ: Transaction Publishers.

Bovens, M.A.P., Derksen, W., Witteveen, W.J., Kalma, P. and Becker, F. (1995) *De verplaatsing van de politiek*. Amsterdam: Wiardi Beckman Stichting.

Bowe, R., Ball, S.J. and Gold, A. (1992) *Reforming Education and Changing Schools: Case Studies in Policy Sociology*. London: Routledge.

Bowen, E.R. (1982) 'The Pressman–Wildavsky paradox', *Journal of Public Policy*, 2 (1): 1–21.

Bozeman, B. (1987) *All Organizations are Public: Bridging Public and Private Organizational Theories*. San Francisco: Jossey-Bass.

Braak, M. ter (1931) *Afscheid van domineesland*. Brussel: Stols.

Bradach, J.L. and Eccles, R.G. (1991) 'Price, authority and trust: From ideal types to plural forms', in G. Thompson, J. Frances, R. Levacic and J. Mitchell (eds), *Markets, Hierarchies and Networks: The Coordination of Social Life*. London: Sage. pp. 277–92.

Braybrooke, D. and Lindblom, C.E. (1963) *A Strategy of Decision: Policy Evaluation as a Social Process*. New York: Free Press of Glencoe.

Brecht, A. (1959) *Political Theory: The Foundations of Twentieth-Century Political Thought*. Princeton: Princeton University Press.

Bressers, J.T.A. and Ringeling, A.B. (1989) 'Beleidsinstrumenten in drie arena's: Beleidsvorming, uitvoering en doorwerking', *Beleidswetenschap*, 3 (1): 3–24.

Brooks, D. (2000) *Bobos in Paradise: The New Upper Class and How They Got There*. New York: Simon & Schuster.

Brown, M.M., O'Toole, L.J., Jr, and Brudney, J.L. (1998) 'Implementing information technology in government: An empirical assessment of the role of local partnerships', *Journal of Public Administration Research and Theory*, 8 (4): 499–525.

Burns, T.R. and Stalker, G.M. (1961) *The Management of Innovation*. London: Tavistock Publications.

Campbell, E. (2001) 'Prosecution and diversion: Implementing a policy initiative'. PhD thesis, University of Newcastle upon Tyne.

Castellani, P.J. (1992) 'Closing institutions in New York state: Implementation and management lessons', *Journal of Policy Analysis and Management*, 11 (4): 593–611.

Castells, M. (1996) *The Rise of the Network Society*. Cambridge, Mass.: Blackwell.

Cater, D. (1964) *Power in Washington: A Critical Look at Today's Struggle to Govern in the Nation's Capital*. New York: Random House.

Challis, L., Fuller, S., Henwood, M., Klein, R., Plowden, W., Webb, A., Whittingham, P. and Wistow, G. (1988) *Joint Approaches to Social Policy: Rationality and Practice*. Cambridge: Cambridge University Press.

Chan, H.S., Wong, K.-K., Cheung, K.C. and Lo, J.M.-K. (1995) 'The implementation gap in environmental management in China: The case of Guangzhou, Zhengzhou, and Nanjing', *Public Administration Review*, 55 (4): 333–40.

Chaney, C.K. and Saltzstein, G.H. (1998) 'Democratic control and bureaucratic responsiveness: The police and domestic violence', *American Journal of Political Science*, 42 (3): 745–68.

Chapman, R.A. (1970) *The Higher Civil Service in Britain*. London: Constable.

Choi, Y.-C. (1999) *The Dynamics of Public Service Contracting: The British Experience*. Bristol: Policy Press.

Cimitile, C.J., Kennedy, V.S., Lambright, W.H., O'Leary, R. and Weiland, P. (1997) 'Balancing risk and finance: The challenge of implementing unfunded environmental mandates', *Public Administration Review*, 57 (1): 63–74.

Clark, M.J. (1997) 'Implementation of aged care policy in the Australian federal system', *Australian Journal of Public Administration*, 56 (3): 53–64.

Clarke, J. and Newman, J. (1997) *The Managerial State: Power, Politics and Ideology in the Remaking of Social Welfare*. London: Sage.

Clegg, S.R. (1990) *Modern Organizations: Organization Studies in the Postmodern World*. London: Sage.

Cline, K.D. (2000) 'Defining the implementation problem: Organizational management versus cooperation', *Journal of Public Administration Research and Theory*, 10 (3): 551–71.

Coase, R.H. (1937) 'The nature of the firm', *Economica*, 4: 386–405.

Cohen, D.K. and Lindblom, C.E. (1979) 'Solving problems of bureaucracy', *American Behavioral Scientist*, 22 (5): 547–60.

Cohen, M.D., March, J.G. and Olsen, J.P. (1972) 'A garbage can model of organizational choice', *Administrative Science Quarterly*, 17 (1): 1–25.

Colebatch, H.K. and Larmour, P. (1993) *Market, Bureaucracy and Community: A Student's Guide to Organisation*. London: Pluto Press.

Considine, M. and Lewis, J.M. (1999) 'Governance at ground level: The frontline bureaucrat in the age of markets and networks', *Public Administration Review*, 59 (6): 467–80.

Cox, R.H. (1989) *Corporation and Social Policy: The development of the Modern Dutch Welfare State*. PhD dissertation, Indiana University, Bloomington.

Creveld, M. van (1996) 'The fate of the state', *Parameters*, 26 (1): 4–19.

Cronin, T.E. (1980) *The State of the Presidency*. 2nd edn. Boston: Little, Brown and Company.

Crozier, M. (1964) *The Bureaucratic Phenomenon*. Chicago: University of Chicago Press.

Crozier, M. and Friedberg, E. (1980) *Actors and Systems: The Politics of Collective Action*. Chicago: University of Chicago Press.

Daalder, H. (1966) 'The Netherlands: Opposition in a segmented society', in R.A. Dahl (ed.), *Political Opposition in Western Democracies*. New Haven: Yale University Press. pp. 188–236.

Daemen, H. and Schaap, L. (eds) (2000) *Citizen and City: Developments in Fifteen Local Democracies in Europe*. Delft: Eburon.

Dahl, R. (1961) *Who Governs? Democracy and Power in an American City*. New Haven: Yale University Press.

Danziger, J.N. (1978) *Making Budgets: Public Resource Allocation*. Beverly Hills: Sage.

Davis, G., Wikeley, N.J. and Young, R. (1998) *Child Support in Action*. Oxford: Hart.

Davis, K.C. (1969) *Discretionary Justice: A Preliminary Inquiry*. Baton Rouge: Louisiana State University Press.

Dekker, P. (1998) 'Nonprofit sector, civil society and volunteering: Some evidence and questions from the Netherlands and the rest of Western Europe', *Third Sector Review*, 4 (2): 125–43.

DeLeon, P. (1999a) 'The missing link revisited: Contemporary implementation research', *Policy Studies Review*, 16 (3/4): 311–38.

DeLeon, P. (1999b) 'The stages approach to the policy process: What has it done? Where is it going?', in P.A. Sabatier (ed.), *Theories of the Policy Process*. Boulder, Colo.: Westview Press. pp. 19–32.

Denis, J.-L., Champagne, F., Constandriopoulos, A.-P., Cazale, L. and Barbir, C. (1993) 'Les contraintes à l'efficience allocative dans le système de santé', *Canadian Public Administration*, 36 (3): 429–41.

Department of the Environment, Transport and the Regions (1998) *Modern Government in Touch with the People*. Cm 4014. London: HMSO.

Department of Health (1999) *The Personal Social Services Performance Assessment Framework: Local Authority Circular*. London: Department of Health.

Department of Health (2000) *Social Services Performance in 1999–2000*. London: Department of Health.

Derrida, J. (1993) *Spectres de Marx: L'état de la dette, le travail du deuil et la nouvelle Internationale*. Paris: Galilée.

Derthick, M. (1970) *The Impact of Federal Grants: Public Assistance in Massachusetts*. Cambridge, Mass.: Harvard University Press.

Derthick, M. (1972) *New Towns In-Town: Why a Federal Program Failed*. Washington, DC: Urban Institute.

Dewey, J. (1927) *The Public and its Problems*. New York: Holt.

Dewey, J. (1935) *Liberalism and Social Action*. New York: Capricorn Books.

Dicey, A.V. (1905) *Lectures on the Relations between Law and Public Opinion in England during the Nineteenth Century*. London: Macmillan.

DiMaggio, P.J. and Powell, W.W. (1983) 'The iron cage revisited: Institutional isomorphism and collective rationality in organizational fields', *American Sociological Review*, 48 (1): 147–60.

Dolbeare, K.M. and Hammond, P.E. (1971) *The School Prayer Decisions: From Court Police to Local Practice*. Chicago: University of Chicago Press.

Douglas, M.T. (1982) *In the Active Voice*. London: Routledge and Kegan Paul.

Dror, Y. (1986) *Policymaking Under Adversity*. New Brunswick, NJ: Transaction Publishers.

Dror, Y. (1989) *Public Policymaking Reexamined*. 2nd edn. New Brunswick, NJ: Transaction Publishers.

Drucker, P.F. (1995) 'The network society', *The Wall Street Journal Europe*, 30 March.

Dryzek, J.S. (1990) *Discursive Democracy: Politics, Policy, and Political Science*. Cambridge: Cambridge University Press.

Dunleavy, P. (1991) *Democracy, Bureaucracy and Public Choice: Economic Explanations in Political Science*. New York: Prentice Hall.

Dunn, W.N. (1981) *Public Policy Analysis: An Introduction*. Englewood Cliffs, NJ: Prentice Hall.

Dunsire, A. (1978a) *The Execution Process, Volume 1: Implementation in a Bureaucracy*. Oxford: Martin Robertson.

Dunsire, A. (1978b) *The Execution Process, Volume, 2: Control in a Bureaucracy*. Oxford: Martin Robertson.

Dunsire, A. (1995) 'Administrative theory in the 1980s: A viewpoint', *Public Administration*, 73 (1): 17–40.

Durant, R.F. (1984) 'EPA, TVA and pollution control: Implications for a theory of regulatory policy implementation', *Public Administration Review*, 44 (4): 305–15.

Durant, R.F. (1985) *When Government Regulates Itself: EPA, TVA, and Pollution Control in the 1970s*. Knoxville: University of Tennessee Press.

Durant, R.F. (1993) 'Hazardous waste, regulatory reform, and the Reagan revolution: The ironies of an activist approach to deactivating bureaucracy', *Public Administration Review*, 53 (6): 550–60.

Durant, R.F. and Legge, J.S., Jr (1993) 'Policy design, social regulation, and theory building: Lessons from the traffic safety policy arena', *Political Research Quarterly*, 46 (3): 641–56.

Dworkin, R.M. (1977) *Taking Rights Seriously*. London: Duckworth.

Easton, D. (1965) *A Framework for Political Analysis,* Englewood Cliffs, N.J.: Prentice Hall.

Easton, D. (1953) *The Political System.* New York: Alfred A. Knopf.

Edelenbos, J. (2000) *Proces in vorm: Procesbegeleiding van interactieve beleidsvorming over lokale ruimtelijke projecten.* Utrecht: Lemma.

Edelenbos, J. and Monnikhof, R.A.H. (eds) (2001) *Lokale interactieve beleidsvorming: Een vergelijkend onderzoek naar de consequenties van interactieve beleidsvorming voor het functioneren van de lokale democratie.* Utrecht: Lemma.

Edelman, M.J. (1971) *Politics as Symbolic Action: Mass Arousal and Quiescence.* New York: Academic Press.

Eisinger, P.K. (1988) *The Rise of the Entrepreneurial State: State and Local Economic Development Policy in the United States.* Madison: University of Wisconsin Press.

Ellison, B.A. (1998) 'The advocacy coalition framework and implementation of the Endangered Species Act: A case study in western water politics', *Policy Studies Journal,* 26 (1): 11–29.

Ellwood, J.W. (2000) 'Prospects for the study of the governance of public organizations and policies', in C.J. Heinrich and L.E. Lynn, Jr (eds), *Governance and Performance: New Perspectives.* Washington, DC: Georgetown University Press. pp. 319–35.

Elmore, R.F. (1978) 'Organizational models of social program implementation', *Public Policy,* 26 (2): 185–228.

Elmore, R.F. (1980) 'Backward mapping: Implementation research and policy decisions', *Political Science Quarterly,* 94 (4): 601–16.

Elmore, R.F. (1981) 'Backward mapping and youth employment', unpublished paper prepared for the third meeting of the International Working Group on Policy Implementation.

Elmore, R.F. (1983) 'Social policymaking as strategic intervention', in E. Seidman (ed.), *Handbook of Social Intervention.* Beverly Hills: Sage. pp. 212–36.

Elmore, R.F. (1985) 'Forward and backward mapping: Reversible logic in the analysis of public policy', in K. Hanf and T.A.J. Toonen (eds), *Policy Implementation in Federal and Unitary Systems: Questions of Analysis and Design.* Dordrecht: Nijhoff. pp. 33–70.

Elster, J. (1998) *Deliberative Democracy.* Cambridge: Cambridge University Press.

Esping-Andersen, G. (1990) *The Three Worlds of Welfare Capitalism.* Cambridge: Polity.

Ester, P., Halman, L.C.J.M. and Moor, R.A. de (eds) (1993) *The Individualizing Society: Value Change in Europe and North America.* Tilburg: Tilburg University Press.

Ethridge, M.E. and Percy, S.L. (1993) 'A new kind of public policy encounters disappointing results: Implementing learnfare in Wisconsin', *Public Administration Review,* 53 (4): 340–7.

Etzioni, A. (1961) *A Comparative Analysis of Complex Organizations: On Power, Involvement, and Their Correlates.* New York: Free Press.

Ferman, B. (1990) 'When failure is success: Implementation and Madisonian government', in D.J. Palumbo and D.J. Calista (eds), *Implementation and the Policy Process: Opening Up the Black Box.* New York: Greenwood Press. pp. 39–50.

Fielding, N. and Fielding, J. (1991) 'Police attitudes to crime and punishment', *British Journal of Criminology,* 31 (1): 568–90.

Fimister, G. and Hill, M. (1993) 'Delegating implementation problems: Social security, housing and community care in Britain', in M. Hill (ed.), *New Agendas in the Study of the Policy Process.* Hemel Hempstead: Harvester Wheatsheaf. pp. 110–29.

Fiorino, D.J. (1997) 'Strategies for regulatory reform: Forward compared to backward mapping', *Policy Studies Journal*, 25 (2): 249–65.

Fischer, F. (1980) *Politics, Values, and Public Policy: The Problem of Methodology*. Boulder, Colo: Westview Press.

Fischer, F. (1995) *Evaluating Public Policy*. Chicago: Nelson-Hall.

Fix, M. and Kenyon, D. (eds) (1990) *Coping with Mandates*. Washington, DC: Urban Institute Press.

Flynn, N. (1993) *Public Sector Management*. 2nd edn. New York: Harvester Wheatsheaf.

Flynn, R., Williams, G. and Pickard, S. (1996) *Markets and Networks: Contracting in Community Health Services*. Buckingham: Open University Press.

Fox, C.J. (1990) 'Implementation research: Why and how to transcend positivist methodologies', in D.J. Palumbo and D.J. Calista (eds), *Implementation and the Policy Process: Opening Up the Black Box*. New York: Greenwood Press. pp. 199–212.

Fox, C.J. and Miller, H.T. (1995) *Postmodern Public Administration: Toward Discourse*. Thousand Oaks, Calif.: Sage.

Frederickson, G. (1999) 'The repositioning of American public administration', John Gaus Lecture at the annual meeting of the American Political Science Association, Atlanta.

Freidson, E. (1970) *Professional Dominance: The Social Structure of Medical Care*. New York: Atherton Press.

Friend, J.K., Power, J.M. and Yewlett, C.J.L. (1974) *Public Planning: The Inter-Corporate Dimension*. London: Tavistock Publications.

Frissen, P.H.A. (1999) *Politics, Governance and Technology: A Postmodern Narrative on the Virtual State*. Cheltenham: Edward Elgar.

Fry, G.K. (1984) 'The development of the Thatcher government's "Grand Strategy" for the civil service: A public policy perspective', *Public Administration*, 62 (3): 322–36.

Fulton Committee (1968) *Report of the Committee on the Civil Service*, Cmnd 3638. London: HMSO.

Gains, F. (1999) 'Implementing privatization policies in "Next Steps" agencies', *Public Administration*, 77 (4): 713–30.

Galligan, D.J. (1986) *Discretionary Powers: A Legal Study of Official Discretion*. Oxford: Clarendon Press.

Gerth, H.H. and Mills, C.W. (eds) (1947) *From Max Weber: Essays in Sociology*. London: Kegan Paul, Trench, Trubner.

Giddens, A. (1984) *The Constitution of Society: Outline of the Theory of Structuration*. Berkeley: University of California Press.

Giddens, A. (1998) *The Third Way: The Renewal of Social Democracy*. Cambridge: Polity.

Gill, J. and Meier, K.J. (2000) 'Public administration research and practice: A methodological manifesto', *Journal of Public Administration Research and Theory*, 10 (1): 157–99.

Glennerster, H., Matsaganis, M., Owens, P. with Hancock, S. (1994) *Implementing GP Fundholding: Wild Card or Winning Hand?* Buckingham: Open University Press.

Goggin, M.L., Bowman, A.O'M., Lester, J.P. and O'Toole, L.J., Jr (1990) *Implementation Theory and Practice: Toward a Third Generation*. Glenview Ill.: Scott Foresman/Little, Brown and Company.

Goodrick, E. and Salancik, G.R. (1996) 'Organizational discretion in responding to institutional practices: Hospitals and cesarean births', *Administrative Science Quarterly*, 41 (1): 1–28.

Gormley, W.T., Jr (1996) 'Regulatory privatization: A case study', *Journal of Public Administration Research and Theory*, 6 (2): 243–60.

Gouldner, A.W. (1954) *Patterns of Industrial Bureaucracy.* New York: Free Press of Glencoe.

Graaf, H. van de and Hoppe, R. (1989) *Beleid en politiek.* Bussum: Coutinho.

Gray, A. and Jenkins, B. (1995) 'From public administration to public management: Reassessing a revolution?', *Public Administration*, 73 (Spring): 75–99.

Greca, R. (2000) 'Institutional co-governance as a mode of co-operation between various social service carriers and providers', *Public Management*, 2 (3): 379–95.

Greenwood, R., Hinings, C.R. and Ranson, S. (1975) 'Contingency theory and the organization of local authorities. Part I: Differentiation and integration', *Public Administration*, 53 (1): 1–23.

Gregory, R. (1995a) 'Consolidating the reforms: Can the production model be counter-productive?', *Public Sector*, 17 (2): 18–21.

Gregory, R. (1995b) 'The peculiar tasks of public management: Toward conceptual discrimination', *Australian Journal of Public Administration*, 54 (2): 171–83.

Grimshaw, R. and Jefferson, T. (1987) *Interpreting Policework: Policy and Practice in Forms of Beat Policing.* London: Allen & Unwin.

Guba, E.G. and Lincoln, Y.S. (1987) 'The countenances of fourth-generation evaluation: Description, judgment and negotiation', in D.J. Palumbo (ed.), *The Politics of Program Evaluation.* Newbury Park, Calif.: Sage. pp. 202–34.

Guéhenno, J.-M. (1993) *La fin de la démocratie.* Paris: Flammarion.

Gunn, L. (1978) 'Why is implementation so difficult?', *Management Services in Government*, 33 (4): 169–76.

Gunsteren, H.R. van (1976) *The Quest for Control,* London: John Wiley and Sons.

Gunsteren, H.R. van (1998) *A Theory of Citizenship: Organizing Plurality in Contemporary Democracies.* Boulder, Colo.: Westview Press.

Halberstam, D. (1972) *The Best and the Brightest.* London: Barrie & Jenkins.

Hall, P.A. (1986) *Governing the Economy: The Politics of State Intervention in Britain and France.* Cambridge: Polity.

Ham, C. (1992) *Health Policy in Britain: The Politics and Organisation of the National Health Service.* 3rd edn. London: Macmillan.

Ham, C. and Hill, M.J. (1984) *The Policy Process in the Modern Capitalist State.* New York: St. Martins Press.

Hammond, K.R. and Adelman, L. (1978) 'Science, values and human judgment', in K.R. Hammond (ed.), *Judgment and Decision in Public Policy Formation.* Boulder, Colo.: Westview Press. pp. 119–41.

Hanf, K.I. (1993) 'Enforcing environmental laws: The social regulation of co-production', in M. Hill (ed.), *New Agendas in the Study of the Policy Process.* Hemel Hempstead: Harvester Wheatsheaf. pp. 88–109.

Hanf, K.I. and Scharpf, F.W. (eds) (1978) *Interorganizational Policy Making: Limits to Coordination and Central Control.* London: Sage.

Harbin, G., Gallagher, J.J., Lillie, T. and Eckland, J. (1992) 'Factors influencing state progress in the implementation of Public Law 99–457, Part H', *Policy Sciences*, 25 (2): 103–15.

Harden, I. (1992) *The Contracting State.* Buckingham: Open University Press.

Hardy, B., Turrell, A. and Wistow, G. (1992) *Innovations in Community Care Management*. Aldershot: Avebury.

Hargrove, E.C. (1975) *The Missing Link: The Study of the Implementation of Social Policy*. Washington, DC: Urban Institute.

Hargrove, E.C. (1983) 'The search for implementation theory', in R.J. Zeckhauser and D. Leebaert (eds), *What Role for Government? Lessons from Policy Research*. Durham, NC: Duke University Press. pp. 280–94.

Hawkins, K. (1984) *Environment and Enforcement: Regulation and the Social Definition of Pollution*. Oxford: Clarendon Press.

Heclo, H.H. (1972) 'Review article: Policy analysis', *British Journal of Political Science*, 2 (1): 83–108.

Heinemann, R.A., Bluhm, W.T., Peterson, S.A. and Kearny, E.N. (1990) *The World of the Policy Analyst: Rationality, Values and Politics*. Chatham, NJ: Chatham House Publishers.

Hendriks, F. and Toonen, T. (eds) (1998) *Schikken en plooien: De stroperige staat bij nader inzien*. Assen: Van Gorcum.

Hennessy, P. (1989) *Whitehall*. London: Secker and Warburg.

Herzberg, F. (1966) *Work and the Nature of Man*. New York: World Publishing Times Mirror.

Hickson, D.J., Hinings, C.R., Lee, C.A., Schneck, R.E. and Pennings, J.M. (1971) 'A strategic contingencies' theory of intraorganizational power', *Administrative Science Quarterly*, 16 (2): 216–29.

Hill, M. (1972) *The Sociology of Public Administration*. London: Weidenfeld and Nicolson.

Hill, M. (1997a) *The Policy Process in the Modern State*. Hemel Hempstead: Prentice Hall/Harvester Wheatsheaf.

Hill, M. (1997b) 'Implementation theory: Yesterday's issue?', *Policy and Politics*, 25 (4): 375–85.

Hill, M. and Bramley, G. (1986) *Analysing Social Policy*. Oxford: Blackwell.

Hirsch, W.Z. (1995) 'Factors important in local governments' privatization decisions', *Urban Affairs Review*, 31 (2): 226–43.

Hjern, B. (1982) 'Implementation research: The link gone missing', *Journal of Public Policy*, 2 (3): 301–8.

Hjern, B. and Hull, C. (1982) 'Implementation research as empirical constitutionalism', in B. Hjern and C. Hull (eds), *Implementation Beyond Hierarchy*. Amsterdam: Elsevier (special issue of *European Journal of Political Research*). pp. 105–15.

Hjern, B. and Porter, D.O. (1981) 'Implementation structures: A new unit of administrative analysis', *Organization Studies*, 2 (3): 211–27.

HMSO (1991) *Raising the Standard: The Citizen's Charter*. Cm 1599. London: HMSO.

Hogwood, B.W. (1995) 'Public policy', *Public Administration*, 73 (Spring): 59–73.

Hogwood, B.W. and Gunn, L. (1984) *Policy Analysis for the Real World*. Oxford: Oxford University Press.

Holdaway, S. (1983) *Inside the British Police: A Force at Work*. Oxford: Blackwell.

Hollifield, J.F. (1990) 'Immigration and the French state: Problems of policy implementation', *Comparative Political Studies*, 23 (1): 56–79.

Hood, C.C. (1976) *The Limits of Administration*. London: John Wiley.

Hood, C.C. (1998) *The Art of the State: Culture, Rhetoric, and Public Management*. Oxford: Clarendon Press.

Hood, C.C. and Jackson, M. (1991) *Administrative Argument*. Aldershot: Dartmouth.

Hoogerwerf, A. (ed.) (1978) *Overheidsbeleid: Een inleiding in de beleidswetenschap*. Alphen aan den Rijn: Samsom.

Hoppe, R., Graaf, H. van de and Dijk, A. van (1987) 'Implementation research and policy design', *International Review of Administrative Sciences*, 53 (4): 581–604.

Huby, M. and Dix, G. (1992) *Evaluating the Social Fund*. London: HMSO.

Hudson, B. (1987) 'Collaboration in social welfare: A framework for analysis', *Policy and Politics*, 15 (3): 175–82.

Hudson, B., Hardy, B., Henwood, M. and Wistow, G. (1997) *Inter-Agency Collaboration*. Leeds: Nuffield Institute of Health.

Hudson, B., Hardy, B., Henwood, M. and Wistow, G. (1999) 'In pursuit of inter-agency collaboration in the public sector: What is the contribution of theory and research?', *Public Management*, 1 (2): 235–60.

Hufen, J.A.M. and Ringeling, A.B. (eds) (1990) *Beleidsnetwerken: Overheids–semi-overheids- en particuliere organisaties in wisselwerking*. The Hague: VUGA.

Hupe, P.L. (1990) 'Implementing a meta-policy: The case of decentralisation in the Netherlands', *Policy and Politics*, 18 (3): 181–91.

Hupe, P.L. (1993a) 'The politics of implementation: Individual, organisational and political co-production in social services delivery', in M. Hill (ed.), *New Agendas in the Study of the Policy Process*. Hemel Hempstead: Harvester Wheatsheaf. pp. 130–51.

Hupe, P.L. (1993b) 'Beyond Pillarization: The (post-)welfare state in the Netherlands', *European Journal of Political Research*, 23 (4): 359–86.

Hupe, P.L. (1994) 'Het betwiste primaat van de politiek', in P. de Jong, A.F.A. Korsten, A.J. Modderkolk and I.M.A.M. Pröpper (eds), *Verantwoordelijkheid en verantwoording in het openbaar bestuur: Congrespublikatie 1994*. The Hague: VUGA. pp. 61–70.

Hupe, P.L. (1996) 'Uitvoering als partnership', in DIVOSA (ed) *Kantelende werelden: Veranderingen in de beleids- en uitvoeringspraktijk van sociale diensten*, congrespublicatie Divosa.

Hupe, P.L. (2000) 'De paradox van interactief bestuur', in P.B. Lehning (ed.), *De beleidsagenda 2000: Strijdpunten op het breukvlak van twee eeuwen*. Bussum: Coutinho. pp. 129–45.

Hupe, P.L. and Klaassen, H.L. (2000) 'De Zichtbare Staat: Over sturingsconcepties en onderhandelen', in P.L. Hupe, M.A. Beukenholdt-ter Mors and H.L. Klaassen (eds), *Publiek onderhandelen: Een vorm van eigentijds besturen*. Alphen aan den Rijn: Samsom. pp. 257–85.

Hupe, P.L. and Klaassen, H.L. (2001) 'De Zichtbare Staat: Modellen van overheidsbeleidsvoering', *Openbaar Bestuur*, 11 (6/7) 2–6.

Hupe, P.L. and Meijs, L.C.P.M. (2000) *Hybrid Governance: The Impact of the Nonprofit Sector in the Netherlands*. The Hague/Rotterdam/Baltimore: Social and Cultural Planning Office/Erasmus University/Johns Hopkins University.

Hurrell, A. and Kingsbury, B. (eds) (1992) *The International Politics of the Environment*. Oxford: Clarendon Press.

Huxham, C. (2000) 'The challenge of collaborative governance', *Public Management*, 2 (3): 337–57.

Immergut, E.M. (1992) 'The rules of the game: The logic of health policy-making in France, Switzerland and Sweden', in S. Steinmo, K. Thelen and F. Longstreth (eds), *Structuring Politics: Historical Institutionalism in Comparative Analysis*. Cambridge: Cambridge University Press. pp. 57–89.

Ingraham, P.W. (1987) 'Toward more systematic consideration of policy design', *Policy Studies Journal*, 15 (Winter): 611–28.

Ingram, H. and Schneider, A. (1990) 'Improving implementation through framing smarter statutes', *Journal of Public Policy*, 10 (1): 67–88.

Israel, J.I. (1995) *The Dutch Republic: Its Rise, Greatness, and Fall, 1477–1806*. Oxford: Clarendon Press.

Jachtenfuchs, M. (1995) 'Theoretical perspectives on European governance', *European Law Journal*, 1 (2): 115–33.

Jacob, H. and Lipsky, M. (1968) 'Outputs, structures, and power: An assessment of changes in the study of state and local politics', *The Journal of Politics*, 30 (2): 510–38.

Jenkins, W.I. (1978) *Policy Analysis: A Political and Organisational Perspective*. London: Martin Robertson.

Jenkins-Smith, H. (1991) 'Alternative theories of the policy process: Reflections on research strategy for the study of nuclear waste policy', *Political Science and Politics*, June: 157–66.

John, P. (1998) *Analysing Public Policy*. London: Pinter.

Jordan, A.G. and Richardson, J.J. (1987) *British Politics and the Policy Process: An Arena Approach*. London: Allen & Unwin.

Jowell, J. (1973) 'The legal control of administrative discretion', *Public Law*, 18: 178–220.

Kagan, R.A. (1978) *Regulatory Justice: Implementing a Wage–Price Freeze*. New York: Russell Sage Foundation.

Kaufman, H. (1960) *The Forest Ranger: A Study in Administrative Behavior*. Baltimore: Johns Hopkins University Press.

Keiser, L.R. and Meier, K.J. (1996) 'Policy design, bureaucratic incentives, and public management: The case of child support enforcement', *Journal of Public Administration Research and Theory*, 6 (3): 337–64.

Keiser, L.R. and Soss, J. (1998) 'With good cause: Bureaucratic discretion and the politics of child support enforcement', *American Journal of Political Science*, 42 (4): 1133–56.

Kellow, A. (1997) '"Problems in international environmental governance" or "A policy analyst looks at the world … this being a tale of how the hopes of mice and men in Geneva are dashed in Canberra"', *Australian Journal of Public Administration*, 56 (1): 54–64.

Kelly, M. (1994) 'Theories of justice and street-level discretion', *Journal of Public Administation Research and Theory*, 4 (2): 119–40.

Kettl, D.F. (2000) 'Public administration at the millennium: The state of the field', *Journal of Public Administration Research and Theory*, 10 (1): 7–34.

Khademian, A.M. (1995) 'When missions matter: Professional priorities and the "stepchild" of supervisory programs', *Governance*, 8 (1): 26–57.

Kickert, W.J.M. (1996) 'Bestuurskunde in de Verenigde Staten: Ontwikkelingen in historisch-maatschappelijke context', *Bestuurskunde*, 5 (3): 122–133.

Kickert, W.J.M. (1997) 'Public governance in the Netherlands: An alternative to Anglo-American "managerialism"', *Public Administration*, 75 (4): 731–52.

Kickert, W.J.M. (1998) *Aansturing van verzelfstandigde overheidsdiensten: Over publiek management van hybride organisaties*. Alphen aan den Rijn: Samsom.

Kickert, W.J.M. and van Vught, F.A. (eds) (1995) *Public Policy and Administration Sciences in the Netherlands*. Hemel Hempstead: Prentice Hall/Harvester Wheatsheaf.

216   IMPLEMENTING PUBLIC POLICY

Kickert, W.J.M., Klijn, E.H. and Koppenjan, J.F.M. (eds) (1997) *Managing Complex Networks: Strategies for the Public Sector*. London: Sage.

Kingdon, J.D. (1984) *Agendas, Alternatives and Public Policies*. Boston: Little, Brown and Company.

Kingsley, J.D. (1944) *Representative Bureaucracy: An Interpretation of the British Civil Service*. Yellow Springs, Ohio: Antioch Press.

Kiser, L.L. (1984) 'Towards an institutional theory of citizen co-production', *Urban Affairs Quarterly*, 19 (4): 485–510.

Kiser, L.L. and Ostrom, E. (1982) 'The three worlds of action: A metatheoretical synthesis of institutional approaches', in E. Ostrom (ed.), *Strategies of Political Inquiry*. Beverly Hills: Sage. pp. 179–222.

Klijn, E.H. (1996) 'Analysing and managing policy processes in complex networks: A theoretical examination of the concept policy network and its problems', *Administration and Society*, 28 (1): 90–119.

Klijn, E.H. (1997) 'Policy networks: An overview', in W.J.M. Kickert, E.H. Klijn and J.F.M. Koppenjan (eds), *Managing Complex Networks: Strategies for the Public Sector*. London: Sage. pp. 14–34.

Klijn, E.H. and Koppenjan, J.F.M. (2000) 'Public management and policy networks: Foundations of a network approach to governance', *Public Management*, 2 (2): 135–58.

Klijn, E.H. and Teisman, G.R. (1991) 'Effective policy making in a multi-actor setting: Networks and steering', in R.J. in 't Veld, L. Schaap, C.J.A.M. Termeer and M.J.W. van Twist (eds), *Autopoiesis and Configuration Theory: New Approaches to Societal Steering*. Dordrecht: Kluwer Academic Publishers, pp. 99–111.

Knegt, R. (1986) *Regels en redelijkheid in de bijstandsverlening: Participerende observatie bij een Sociale Dienst*. Groningen: Wolters-Noordhoff.

Knill, C. and Lenschow, A. (1998) 'Coping with Europe: The impact of British and German administrations on the implementation of EU environmental policy', *Journal of European Public Policy*, 5 (4): 595–614.

Knoepfel, P. and Kissling-Näf, I. (1998) 'Public policy in Switzerland: Social learning in policy networks', *Policy and Politics*, 26 (3): 343–68.

Knoke, D. (1990) *Policy Networks: The Structural Perspective*. Cambridge: Cambridge University Press.

Kooiman, J. (ed.) (1993) *Modern Governance: New Government–Society Interactions*. London: Sage.

Kooiman, J. (1999) 'Social-political governance: Overview, reflections and design', *Public Management*, 1 (1): 67–92.

Kooiman, J. and van Vliet, M. (2000) 'Self-governance as a mode of societal governance', *Public Management*, 2 (3): 359–77.

Koppenjan, J.F.M. (1991) 'Falen en leren rond de paspoortaffaire: De hardleersheid van een ministerie geanalyseerd', *Beleid & Maatschappij*, 18 (1): 20–30.

Krause, G.A. (1996) 'The institutional dynamics of policy administration: Bureaucratic influence over securities regulation', *American Journal of Political Science*, 40 (4): 1083–121.

Kuhn, T.S. (1970) *The Structure of Scientific Revolutions*. 2nd edn. Chicago: University of Chicago Press.

Kuypers, G. (1973) *Grondbegrippen van politiek*. Utrecht: Het Spectrum.

Kuypers, G. (1980) *Beginselen van beleidsontwikkeling* (2 volumes). Muiderberg: Coutinho.

Lampinen, R. and Uusikylä, P. (1998) 'Implementation deficit – Why member states do not comply with EU directives?', *Scandinavian Political Studies*, 21 (3): 231–51.

Lane, J.-E. (1983) *Creating the University of Norrland: Goals, Structures and Outcomes*. Umea: University of Umea.

Lane, J.-E. (1987) 'Implementation, accountability and trust', *European Journal of Political Research*, 15 (5): 527–46.

Lane, J.-E. and Ersson, S.O. (2000) *The New Institutional Politics: Performance and Outcomes*. London: Routledge.

Lash, S. (1988) 'Postmodernism as a regime of signification', *Theory, Culture and Society*, 5 (2/3): 311–36.

Lasswell, H.D. (1956) *The Decision Process: Seven Categories of Functional Analysis*. College Park: University of Maryland.

Lasswell, H.D. (1970) 'The emerging conception of the policy sciences', *Policy Sciences*, 1 (1): 3–14.

Laumann, E.O. and Knoke, D. (1987) *The Organizational State: Social Choice in National Policy Domains*. Madison: University of Wisconsin Press.

Lawson, T.R. (2000) 'A structural model of socio-political governance with an example of application in the United States', *Public Management*, 2 (3): 417–34.

Lerner, D. and Lasswell, H.D. (eds) (1951) *The Policy Sciences*. Stanford: Stanford University Press.

Lester, J.P. and Goggin, M.L. (1998) 'Back to the future: The rediscovery of implementation studies', *Policy Currents*, 8 (3): 1–9.

Lester, J.P., Bowman, A.O'M., Goggin, M.L. and O'Toole, L.J., Jr (1987) 'Public policy implementation: Evolution of the field and agenda for future research', *Policy Studies Review*, 7 (1): 200–16.

Leuchtenburg, W.E. (1963) *Franklin D. Roosevelt and the New Deal, 1932–1940*. New York: Harper & Row.

Lijphart, A. (1975) *The Politics of Accommodation: Pluralism and Democracy in the Netherlands*. Berkeley: University of California Press.

Lindblom, C.E. (1959) 'The science of muddling through', *Public Administration Review*, 19 (2): 79–88.

Lindblom, C.E. (1965) *The Intelligence of Democracy: Decision Making through Mutual Adjustment*. New York: Free Press.

Lindblom, C.E. (1977) *Politics and Markets: The World's Political-Economic Systems*. New York: Basic Books.

Lindblom, C.E. and Woodhouse, E.J. (1993) *The Policy-Making Process*. 3rd edn. Englewood Cliffs, NJ: Prentice Hall.

Linder, S.H. and Peters, B.G. (1987) 'A design perspective on policy implementation: The fallacies of misplaced prescription', *Policy Studies Review*, 6 (3): 459–75.

Lipsky, M. (1971) 'Street-level bureaucracy and the analysis of urban reform', *Urban Affairs Quarterly*, 6: 391–409.

Lipsky, M. (1980) *Street-Level Bureaucracy: Dilemmas of the Individual in Public Services*. New York: Russell Sage Foundation.

Lowi, T.J. (1972) 'Four systems of policy, politics, and choice', *Public Administration Review*, 32 (4): 298–310.

Lowndes, V. and Skelcher, C. (1998) 'The dynamics of multi-organizational partnerships: An analysis of changing modes of governance', *Public Administration*, 76 (Summer): 313–33.

Lukes, S. (1974) *Power: A Radical View*. London: Macmillan.

Lynn, L.E., Jr (1996a) *Public Management as Art, Science, and Profession*. Chatham, NJ: Chatham House.

Lynn, L.E., Jr (1996b) 'Assume a network: Reforming mental health services in Illinois', *Journal of Public Administration Research and Theory*, 6 (2): 297–314.

Lynn, L.E., Jr, Heinrich, C. and Hill, C. (1999) 'The empirical study of governance: Theories, models, methods', paper presented at the Workshop on Models and Methods for the Empirical Study of Governance, University of Arizona, Tucson.

Lynn, L.E. Jr, Heinrich, C.J. and Hill, C.J. (2000) 'Studying governance and public management: Challenges and prospects', *Journal of Public Administration Research and Theory*, 10 (2): 233–261.

Lyotard, J.-F. (1979) *La condition postmoderne: Rapport sur le savoir*. Paris: Les Editions de Minuit.

McGregor, D. (1960) *The Human Side of Enterprise*. New York: McGraw-Hill.

McGregor, E.B. Jr (1993) 'Toward a theory of public management success', in B. Bozeman (ed.), *Public Management: The State of the Art*. San Francisco: Jossey-Bass. pp. 173–85.

Mack, R. (1971) *Planning and Uncertainty*. New York: John Wiley.

March, J.G. and Olsen, J.P. (1984) 'The new institutionalism: Organizational factors in political life', *The American Political Science Review*, 78 (3): 734–49.

March, J.G. and Olsen, J.P. (1989) *Rediscovering Institutions: The Organizational Basis of Politics*. New York: Free Press.

March, J.G. and Olsen, J.P. (1996) 'Institutional perspectives on political institutions', *Governance*, 9 (3): 248–64.

Marsh, D. and Rhodes, R.A.W. (eds) (1992) *Implementing Thatcherite Policies: Audit of an Era*. Buckingham: Open University Press.

Mashaw, J.L. (1983) *Bureaucratic Justice: Managing Social Security Disability Claims*. New Haven: Yale University Press.

Matland, R.E. (1995) 'Synthesizing the implementation literature: The ambiguity-conflict model of policy implementation', *Journal of Public Administration Research and Theory*, 5 (2): 145–74.

Mattesich, P. and Monsey, B. (1992) *Collaboration: What Makes it Work?* St Paul, Minn.: Amherst H. Wilder Foundation.

Maupin, J.R. (1993) 'Control, efficiency, and the street-level bureaucrat', *Journal of Public Administration Research and Theory*, 3 (3): 335–57.

May, P.J. (1993) 'Mandate design and implementation: Enhancing implementation efforts and shaping regulatory styles', *Journal of Policy Analysis and Management*, 12 (4): 634–63.

May, P.J. (1994) 'Analyzing mandate design: State mandates governing hazard-prone areas', *Publius*, 24 (2): 1–16.

May, P.J. (1995) 'Can cooperation be mandated? Implementing intergovernmental environmental management in New South Wales and New Zealand', *Publius*, 25 (1): 89–113.

May, P.J. and Burby, R.J. (1996) 'Coercive versus cooperative policies: Comparing intergovernmental mandate performance', *Journal of Policy Analysis and Management*, 15 (2): 171–201.

Maynard-Moody, S. and Musheno, M. (2000) 'State agent or citizen agent: Two narratives of discretion', *Journal of Public Administration Research and Theory*, 10 (2): 329–58.

Maynard-Moody, S., Musheno, M.C. and Palumbo, D.J. (1990) 'Street-wise social policy: Resolving the dilemma of street-level influence and successful implementation', *The Western Political Quarterly*, 43 (4): 833–48.

Mayo, E. (1933) *The Human Problems of an Industrial Civilisation*. Cambridge, Mass.: Harvard University Press.

Mazmanian, D.A. and Sabatier, P.A. (eds) (1981) *Effective Policy Implementation*. Lexington, Ky: Lexington Books.

Mazmanian, D.A. and Sabatier, P.A. (1983) *Implementation and Public Policy*. Glenview, Ill.: Scott, Foresman.

Meer, F.M. van der and Roborgh, L.J. (1993) *Ambtenaren in Nederland: Omvang, bureaucratisering en representativiteit van het ambtelijk apparaat*. Alphen aan den Rijn: Samsom Tjeenk Willink.

Meier, K.J. (1999) 'Are we sure Lasswell did it this way? Lester, Goggin and implementation research', *Policy Currents*, 9 (1): 5–8.

Meier, K.J. and Gill, J. (2000) *What Works: A New Approach to Program and Policy Analysis*. Boulder, Colo.: Westview Press.

Meier, K.J. and McFarlane, D.R. (1995) 'Statutory coherence and policy implementation: The case of family planning', *Journal of Public Policy*, 15 (3): 281–98.

Meier, K.J. and O'Toole, L.J., Jr (2001) 'Managerial strategies and behavior in networks: A model with evidence from U.S. public education', *Journal of Public Administration Research and Theory*, 11 (3): 271–93.

Meier, K.J., Stewart, J., Jr and England, R.E. (1991) 'The politics of bureaucratic discretion: Educational access as an urban service', *American Journal of Political Science*, 35 (1): 155–77.

Meier, K.J., Wrinkle, R.D. and Polinard, J.L. (1995) 'Politics, bureaucracy, and agricultural policy: An alternative view of political control', *American Politics Quarterly*, 23 (4): 427–60.

Merton, R.K. (1957) *Social Theory and Social Structure*. Glencoe, Ill.: Free Press.

Metcalf, D. (1982) *Alternatives to Unemployment: Special Employment Measures in Britain*. London: Policy Studies Institute.

Meyer, J.W. and Rowan, B. (1977) 'Institutionalized organizations: Formal structure as myth and ceremony', *American Journal of Sociology*, 83 (1): 340–63.

Meyers, M.K., Glaser, B. and MacDonald, K. (1998) 'On the front lines of welfare delivery: Are workers implementing policy reforms?', *Journal of Policy Analysis and Management*, 17 (1): 1–22.

Milward, H.B. (1996) 'Introduction to the Symposium on the Hollow State: Capacity, control, and performance in interorganizational settings', *Journal of Public Administration Research and Theory*, 6 (2): 193–5.

Milward, H.B. and Provan, K.G. (1999) 'How networks are governed', unpublished paper.

Milward, H.B. and Snyder, L.O. (1996) 'Electronic government: Linking citizens to public organizations through technology', *Journal of Public Administration Research and Theory*, 6 (2): 261–75.

Milward, H.B., Provan, G. and Else, B.A. (1993) 'What does the "Hollow State" look like?', in B. Bozeman (ed.), *Public Management: The State of the Art*. San Francisco: Jossey-Bass. pp. 309–32.

Mitchell, D. (1991) *Income Transfers in Ten Welfare States*. Aldershot: Avebury.

Moe, R.C. (1994) 'The "Reinventing Government" exercise: Misinterpreting the problem, misjudging the consequences', *Public Administration Review*, 54 (2): 111–22.

Moe, T.M. (1982) 'Regulatory performance and presidential administration', *American Journal of Political Science*, 26 (2): 197–224.

Montfort, A.J.G.M. van (1991) *De regels van het huis: Ambtelijke regeltoepassing bij de gemeentelijke woonruimteverdeling*. Groningen: Wolters-Noordhoff.

Montjoy, R.S. and O'Toole, L.J., Jr (1979) 'Toward a theory of policy implementation: An organizational perspective', *Public Administration Review*, 40 (5): 465–76.

Moran, M. and Wood, B. (1993) *States, Regulation and the Medical Profession*. Buckingham: Open University Press.

Morgan, G. (1986) *Images of Organization*. Beverly Hills: Sage.

Morgan, G. (1993) *Imaginization: The Art of Creative Management*. Newbury Park, Calif.: Sage.

Nakamura, R.T. (1987) 'The textbook policy process and implementation research', *Policy Studies Review*, 7 (1): 142–54.

Nathan, R.P. (1983) *The Administrative Presidency*. New York: John Wiley.

Newman, J. (2001) *Modernising Governance*. London: Sage.

Newton, K. and Sharpe, L.J. (1977) 'Local output research: Some reflections and proposals', *Policy and Politics*, 5 (1): 61–82.

Ohmae, K. (1995) *The End of the Nation State: The Rise of Regional Economies*. London: HarperCollins.

Osborne, D.E. and Gaebler, T.A. (1992) *Reinventing Government: How the Entrepreneurial Spirit is Transforming the Public Sector*. Reading, Mass.: Addison-Wesley.

O'Toole, L.J., Jr (1986) 'Policy recommendations for multi-actor implementation: An assessment of the field', *Journal of Public Policy*, 6 (2): 181–210.

O'Toole, L.J., Jr (1988) 'Strategies for intergovernmental management: Implementing programs in interorganisational networks', *Journal of Public Administration*, 25 (1): 43–57.

O'Toole, L.J., Jr (1989a) 'Alternative mechanisms for multiorganizational implementation: The case of wastewater management', *Administration and Society*, 21 (3): 313–39.

O'Toole, L.J., Jr (1989b) 'Goal multiplicity in the implementation setting: Subtle impacts and the case of wastewater treatment privatization', *Policy Studies Journal*, 18 (1): 1–20.

O'Toole, L.J., Jr (1993) 'Interorganizational policy studies: Lessons drawn from implementation research', *Journal of Public Administration Research and Theory*, 3 (2): 232–51.

O'Toole, L.J., Jr (1994) 'Economic transition, constitutional choice, and public administration: Implementing privatization in Hungary', *Journal of Public Administration Research and Theory*, 4 (4): 493–519.

O'Toole, L.J., Jr (1995) 'Rational choice and policy implementation', *American Review of Public Administration*, 25 (1): 43–57.

O'Toole, L.J., Jr (1996) 'Hollowing the infrastructure: Revolving loan programs and network dynamics in the American states', *Journal of Public Administration Research and Theory*, 6 (2): 225–42.

O'Toole, L.J., Jr (1997) 'Networking requirements, institutional capacity, and implementation gaps in transitional regimes: The case of acidification policy in Hungary', *Journal of European Public Policy*, 4 (1): 1–17.

O'Toole, L.J., Jr (2000a) 'Research on policy implementation: Assessment and prospects', *Journal of Public Administration Research and Theory*, 10 (2): 263–88.

O'Toole, L.J., Jr (2000b) 'Different public managements? Implications of structural context in hierarchies and networks', in J.L. Brudney, L.J. O'Toole, Jr, and H.G. Rainey (eds), *Advancing Public Management: New Developments in Theory, Methods, and Practice*. Washington, DC: Georgetown University Press. pp. 19–32.

O'Toole, L.J., Jr (2001) 'The theory–practice issue in policy implementation research', paper presented at the Economic and Social Research Council Seminar Series, seminar three, University of Cambridge.

O'Toole, L.J., Jr, and Meier, K.J. (1999) 'Modeling the impact of public management: Implications of structural context', *Journal of Public Administration Research and Theory*, 9 (4): 505–26.

O'Toole, L.J., Jr, and Montjoy, R.S. (1984) 'Interorganizational policy implementation: A theoretical perspective', *Public Administration Review*, 44 (6): 491–503.

Ouchi, W.G. (1991) 'Markets, bureaucracies and clans', in G. Thompson, J. Frances, R. Levačic and J. Mitchell (eds) *Markets, Hierarchies and Networks: The Coordination of Social Life*. London: Sage. pp. 246–55.

Oye, K. (1985) 'Explaining cooperation under anarchy: Hypotheses and strategies', *World Politics*, 39 (1): 1–24.

Page, E.C. (1985) *Political Authority and Bureaucratic Power: A Comparative Analysis*. Brighton: Wheatsheaf Books.

Palumbo, D.J. (ed.) (1987) *The Politics of Program Evaluation*. Newbury Park, Calif.: Sage.

Palumbo, D.J. and Calista, D.J. (1990a) 'Introduction: The relation of implementation research to policy outcomes', in D.J. Palumbo and D.J. Calista (eds), *Implementation and the Policy Process: Opening Up the Black Box*. New York: Greenwood Press. pp. xi–xviii.

Palumbo, D.J. and Calista, D.J. (1990b) 'Opening up the black box: Implementation and the policy process', in D.J. Palumbo and D.J. Calista (eds), *Implementation and the Policy Process: Opening Up the Black Box*. New York: Greenwood Press. pp. 3–18.

Palumbo, D.J. and Calista, D.J. (eds) (1990c) *Implementation and the Policy Process: Opening Up the Black Box*. New York: Greenwood Press.

Parks, R.B., Baker, P.C., Kiser, L., Oakerson, R., Ostrom, E., Ostrom, V., Percy, S.L., Vandivort, M.B., Whitaker, G.P. and Wilson, R. (1981) 'Consumers as coproducers of public services: Some economic and institutional considerations', *Policy Studies Journal*, 9 (Summer): 1001–11.

Parsons, W. (1995) *Public Policy*. Aldershot: Edward Elgar.

Patton, M.Q. (1978) *Utilization-Focused Evaluation*. Newbury Park, Calif.: Sage.

Peters, B.G. and Pierre, J. (2001) 'Developments in intergovernmental relations: Towards multi-level governance', *Policy and Politics*, 29 (2): 131–5.

Peters, T.J. (1990) 'Part one: Get innovative or get dead', *California Management Review*, 33 (1): 9–26.

Pettigrew, A., Ferlie, E. and McKee, L. (1992) *Shaping Strategic Change: Making Change in Large Organizations: The Case of the National Health Service*. London: Sage.

Pierre, J. and Peters, B.G. (2000) *Governance, Politics and the State*. New York: St Martin's Press.

Pollitt, C. (1990) *Managerialism and the Public Services: The Anglo-American Experience*. Oxford: Blackwell.

Pollitt, C. and Bouckaert, G. (2000) *Public Management Reform: A Comparative Analysis*. Oxford: Oxford University Press.

Popper, K.R. (1959) *The Logic of Scientific Discovery*. London: Hutchinson.

Powell, M., Exworthy, M. and Berney, L. (2001) 'Playing the game of partnership', in R. Sykes, C. Bochel and N. Ellison (eds), *Social Policy Review 13: Developments and Debates: 2000–2001*. Bristol: Policy Press. pp. 39–62.

Pressman, J.L. and Wildavsky, A. (1984) *Implementation*: 3rd edn. Berkeley: University of California Press. (1st edn, 1973; 2nd edn, 1979).

Pröpper, I.M.A.M. and Steenbeek, D.A. (1999) *De aanpak van interactief beleid: Elke situatie is anders*. Bussum: Coutinho.

Provan, K.G. and Milward, H.B. (1991) 'Institutional-level norms and organizational involvement in a service-implementation network', *Journal of Public Administration Research and Theory*, 1 (4): 391–417.

Pusey, M. (1991) *Economic Rationalism in Canberra: A Nation-Building State Changes its Mind*. Cambridge: Cambridge University Press.

Rae, D. and Taylor, M. (1971) 'Decision rules and policy outcomes', *British Journal of Political Science*, 1 (1): 71–90.

Ranade, W. (1995) 'The theory and practice of managed competition in the National Health Service', *Public Administration*, 73 (2): 241–62.

Reichard, G.W. (1988) *Politics as Usual: The Age of Truman and Eisenhower*. Arlington Heights, Ill.: Harlan Davidson.

Reiner, R. (1992) *The Politics of the Police*. 2nd edn. New York: Harvester Wheatsheaf.

Rhodes, R.A.W. (1981) *Control and Power in Central-Local Government Relations*. Farnborough: Gower.

Rhodes, R.A.W. (1988) *Beyond Westminster and Whitehall: The Sub-central Governments of Britain*. London: Unwin Hyman.

Rhodes, R.A.W. (1992) 'Beyond Whitehall: Researching local governance', *Social Sciences*, 13: 2.

Rhodes, R.A.W. (1996a) 'The new governance: Governing without government', *Political Studies*, 44 (4): 652–67.

Rhodes, R.A.W. (1996b) 'From institutions to dogma: Tradition, eclecticism, and ideology in the study of British public administration', *Public Administration Review*, 56 (6): 507–16.

Rhodes, R.A.W. (1997) *Understanding Governance: Policy Networks, Governance, Reflexivity and Accountability*. Buckingham: Open University Press.

Richards, S. (1992) 'Changing patterns of legitimation in public management', *Public Policy and Administration*, 7 (3): 15–28.

Richardson, G., Ogus, A.I. and Burrows, P. (1982) *Policing Pollution: A Study of Regulation and Enforcement*. Oxford: Clarendon Press.

Rigby, T.H. (1964) 'Tradition, market and organizational societies and the USSR', *World Politics*, 16 (4): 539–57.

Rigby, T.H. (1990) *The Changing Soviet System: Mono-organizational Socialism from its Origins to Gorbachev's Restructuring*, Aldershot: Edward Elgar.

Ringeling, A.B. (1978) *Beleidsvrijheid van ambtenaren: Het spijtoptantenprobleem als illustratie van de activiteiten van ambtenaren bij de uitvoering van beleid*. Alphen aan den Rijn: Samsom.

Ringeling, A.B. (1993) *Het imago van de overheid: De beoordeling van prestaties van de publieke sector*. The Hague: VUGA.

Ripley, R.B. and Franklin, G.A. (1982) *Bureaucracy and Policy Implementation*. Homewood, Ill.: Dorsey Press.

Rist, R.C. (ed.) (1995) *Policy Evaluation: Linking Theory to Practice*. Aldershot: Edward Elgar.

Roe, E.M. (1994) *Narrative Policy Analysis: Theory and Practice*. Durham, NC: Duke University Press.

Rose, R. (1973) 'Comparing public policy: An overview', *European Journal of Political Research*, 1 (1): 67–94.

Rosecrance, R.N. (1999) *The Rise of the Virtual State: Wealth and Power in the Coming Century*. New York: Basic Books.

Rossi, P.H. and Freeman, H. (1979) *Evaluation: A Systematic Approach*. Newbury Park, Calif.: Sage.

Rothstein, B. (1992) 'Labour-market institutions and working-class strength', in S. Steinmo, K. Thelen and F. Longstreth (eds), *Structuring Politics: Historical Institutionalism in Comparative Analysis*. Cambridge: Cambridge University Press. pp. 33–56.

Rothstein, B. (1998) *Just Institutions Matter: The Moral and Political Logic of the Universal Welfare State*. Cambridge: Cambridge University Press.

Ryan, N. (1995a) 'Unravelling conceptual developments in implementation analysis', *Australian Journal of Public Administration*, 54 (1): 65–80.

Ryan, N. (1995b) 'The competitive delivery of social services: Implications for program implementation', *Australian Journal of Public Administration*, 54 (3): 353–63.

Ryan, N. (1996) 'Some advantages of an integrated approach to implementation analysis: A study of Australian industry policy', *Public Administration*, 74 (4): 737–53.

Ryburn, M. (1996) 'Child welfare services: Developments in law, policy, practice and research', in J. Aldgate and M. Hill (eds), *Child Welfare Services: Developments in Law, Policy, Practice and Research*. London: Jessica Kingsley. pp. 196–212.

Sabatier, P.A. (1986) 'Top-down and bottom-up approaches to implementation research: A critical analysis and suggested synthesis', *Journal of Public Policy*, 6 (1): 21–48.

Sabatier, P.A. (1991) 'Toward better theories of the policy process', *Political Science and Politics*, 24 (June): 147–56.

Sabatier, P.A. (1999) 'The need for better theories', in P.A. Sabatier (ed.), *Theories of the Policy Process*. Boulder, Colo.: Westview Press. pp. 3–17.

Sabatier, P.A. and Jenkins-Smith, H. (1993) *Policy Change and Learning: An Advocacy Coalition Approach*. Boulder, Colo.: Westview Press.

Sabatier, P.A. and Mazmanian, D.A. (1979) 'The conditions of effective implementation: A guide to accomplishing policy objectives', *Policy Analysis*, 5 (4): 481–504.

Sabatier, P.A. and Mazmanian, D.A. (1980) 'The implementation of public policy: A framework of analysis', *Policy Studies Journal*, 8 (special issue): 538–60.

Satyamurti, C. (1981) *Occupational Survival: The Case of the Local Authority Social Worker*. Oxford: Blackwell.

Saward, M. (1997) 'In search of the hollow crown', in P.M. Weller, H. Bakvis and R.A.W. Rhodes (eds), *The Hollow Crown: Countervailing Trends in Core Executives*. Basingstoke: Macmillan. pp. 16–36.

Schama, S. (1987) *The Embarrassment of Riches: An Interpretation of Dutch Culture in the Golden Age*. New York: Knopf.

Scharpf, F.W. (1978) 'Interorganizational policy studies: Issues, concepts and perspectives', in K.I. Hanf and F.W. Scharpf (eds), *Interorganizational Policy Making: Limits to Coordination and Central Control*. London: Sage. pp. 345–70.

Scharpf, F.W. (1986) 'Policy failure and institutional reform: Why should form follow function?', *International Social Science Journal*, 38 (2): 179–91.

Scharpf, F.W. (1997a) *Games Real Actors Play: Actor-Centered Institutionalism in Policy Research*. Boulder, Colo.: Westview Press.

Scharpf, F.W. (1997b) 'Introduction: The problem-solving capacity of multi-level governance', *Journal of European Public Policy*, 4 (4): 520–38.

Schlesinger, A.M., Jr (1960) *The Politics of Upheaval*. Boston: Houghton Mifflin.

Scholz, J.T., Twombly, J. and Headrick, B. (1991) 'Street-level political controls over federal bureaucracy', *American Political Science Review*, 85 (3): 829–50.

Schultze, C.L. (1968) *The Politics and Economics of Public Spending*. Washington, DC: Brookings Institution.

Schuyt, K. and Taverne, E. (2000) *1950: Welvaart in zwart-wit*. The Hague: Sdu Uitgevers.

Schwarz, M. and Thompson, M. (1990) *Divided We Stand: Redefining Politics,Technology, and Social Choice*. New York: Harvester Wheatsheaf.

Scott, R.A. and Shore, A.R. (1979) *Why Sociology Does Not Apply: A Study of the Use of Sociology in Public Policy*. New York: Elsevier.

Scott, W.R. (1995) *Institutions and Organizations*. Thousand Oaks, Calif.: Sage.

Selden, S.C. (1997) 'Representative bureaucracy: Examining the linkage between passive and active representation in the farmers' home administration', *American Review of Public Administration*, 27 (1): 22–42.

Selznick, P. (1949) *TVA and the Grass Roots: A Study in the Sociology of Formal Organization*. Berkeley: University of California Press.

Selznick, P. (1957) *Leadership in Administration: A Sociological Interpretation*. New York: Row, Peterson.

Simon, H.A. (1945) *Administrative Behavior*. New York: Free Press.

Skocpol, T. (1995) *Social Policy in the United States: Future Possibilities in Historical Perspective*. Princeton: Princeton University Press.

Skocpol, T. and Finegold, K. (1982) 'State capacity and economic intervention in the early New Deal', *Political Science Quarterly*, 97 (2): 255–78.

Smith, A. (1997) 'Comparative and international administration: Studying multi-level governance. Examples from French translations of the structural funds', *Public Administration*, 75 (4): 711–29.

Smith, M.J. (1993) *Pressure, Power and Policy: State Autonomy and Policy Networks in Britain and the United States*. New York: Harvester Wheatsheaf.

Smith, S.R. and Smyth, J. (1996) 'Contracting for services in a decentralized system', *Journal of Public Administration Research and Theory*, 6 (2): 277–96.

Smith, T. (1994) 'Post-modern politics and the case for constitutional renewal', *The Political Quarterly*, 65 (2): 128–37.

Spence, D.B. (1997) 'Agency policy making and political control: Modeling away the delegation problem', *Journal of Public Administration Research and Theory*, 7 (2): 199–219.

Stivers, C. (1994) 'The listening bureaucrat: Responsiveness in public administration', *Public Administration Review*, 54 (4): 364–9.

Stoker, R.P. (1991) *Reluctant Partners: Implementing Federal Policy*. Pittsburgh: University of Pittsburgh Press.

Stoker, R.P. and Wilson, L.A. (1998) 'Verifying compliance: Social regulation and welfare reform', *Public Administration Review*, 58 (5): 395–405.

Stone, C. (1989) *Regime Politics: Governing Atlanta 1946–1988*. Lawrence: University Press of Kansas.

Stone, D.A. (1989) 'Causal stories and the formation of policy agendas', *Political Science Quarterly*, 104 (2): 281–300.

Strauss, A.L. (1978) *Negotiations: Varieties, Contexts, Processes, and Social Order.* San Francisco: Jossey-Bass.

Taylor, F.W. (1911) *The Principles of Scientific Management.* New York: Harper.

Teisman, G.R. (1995) *Complexe besluitvorming: Een pluricentrisch perspectief op besluitvorming over ruimtelijke investeringen.* 2nd edn. The Hague: VUGA.

Terpstra, J. and Havinga, T. (1999) 'Uitvoering tussen traditie en management: Structuratie en stijlen van beleidsuitvoering', in W. Bakker and F. van Waarden (eds), *Ruimte rond regels: Stijlen van regulering en beleidsuitvoering vergeleken.* Amsterdam: Boom. pp. 40–67.

Thomas, H. (ed.) (1968) *Crisis in the Civil Service.* London: Blond.

Thompson, F. (1997) 'Defining the new public management', in L.R. Jones, K. Schedler and S.W. Wade (eds), *Advances in International Comparative Management.* Greenwich, Conn.: JAI Press. pp. 1–14.

Thompson, G., Frances, J., Levačić, R. and Mitchell, J. (eds) (1991) *Markets, Hierarchies and Networks: The Coordination of Social Life.* London: Sage.

Thompson, J.D. (1967) *Organizations in Action: Social Science Bases of Administrative Theory.* New York: McGraw-Hill.

Thompson, J.R. and Jones, V.D. (1995) 'Reinventing the federal government: The role of theory in reform implementation', *American Review of Public Administration*, 25 (2): 183–99.

Thompson, M., Ellis, R.J. and Wildavsky, A.B. (1990) *Cultural Theory.* Boulder, Colo.: Westview Press.

Toonen, T.A.J. (1990) 'The unitary state as a system of co-governance: The case of the Netherlands', *Public Administration*, 68 (Autumn): 281–96.

Tops, P.E.W.M. (1999) 'Co-productie als bestuursstijl: Ervaringen en vuistregels', *Bestuurswetenschappen*, 53 (3): 201–25.

Torenvlied, R. (1996a) *Besluiten in uitvoering: Theorieën over beleidsuitvoering modelmatig getoetst op sociale vernieuwing in drie gemeenten.* Amsterdam: Thesis Publishers.

Torenvlied, R. (1996b) 'Political control of implementation agencies', *Rationality and Society*, 8 (1): 25–56.

Torre, E.J. van der (1999) *Politiewerk: Politiestijlen, community policing, professionalisme.* Alphen aan den Rijn: Samsom.

Truman, D. (1958) *The Governmental Process: Political Interests and Public Opinion.* New York: Knopf.

Twist, M.J.W. van (1994) *Verbale vernieuwing: Aantekeningen over de kunst van bestuurskunde.* The Hague: VUGA.

Valente, C.F. and Manchester, L.D. (1984) *Rethinking Local Services: Examining Alternative Delivery Approaches.* Washington, DC: International City Management Association.

Van Meter, D. and Van Horn, C.E. (1975) 'The policy implementation process: A conceptual framework', *Administration and Society*, 6 (4): 445–88.

Veen, R.J. van der (1990) *De sociale grenzen van beleid: Een onderzoek naar de uitvoering en effecten van het stelsel van sociale zekerheid.* Leiden: Stenfert Kroese.

Veld, R.J. in 't (1984) *De vlucht naar Isfahan? Over bestuur, planning en de toekomst van het hoger onderwijs.* The Hague: VUGA Uitgeverij.

Vickers, G. (1965) *The Art of Judgment: A Study of Policy Making.* London: Chapman & Hall.

Visser, J. and Hemerijck, A.C. (1997) 'A Dutch Miracle': Job Growth, Welfare Reform, and Corporatism in the Netherlands. Amsterdam: Amsterdam University Press.

Vliet, M. van (1993) 'Environmental regulation of business: Options and constraints for communicative governance', in J. Kooiman (ed.), Modern Governance: New Government–Society Interactions. London: Sage. pp. 105–18.

Waarden, F. van (1999a) 'Ieder land zijn eigen trant?', in W. Bakker and F. van Waarden (eds), Ruimte rond regels: Stijlen van regulering en beleidsuitvoering vergeleken. Amsterdam: Boom. pp. 303–39.

Waarden, F. van (1999b) 'De institutionele grondslag van ambtelijke gewoonten', in W. Bakker and F. van Waarden (eds), Ruimte rond regels: Stijlen van regulering en beleidsuitvoering vergeleken. Amsterdam: Boom. pp. 340–74.

Wade, H.W.R. (1982) Administration Law. 5th edn. Oxford: Oxford University Press.

Waldo, C.D. (1948) The Administrative State: A Study of the Political Theory of American Public Administration. New York: The Ronald Press Company.

Walker, R. and Lawton, D. (1988) 'Social assistance and territorial justice: The example of single payments', Journal of Social Policy, 17 (4): 437–76.

Wamsley, G.L. (1990a) 'Preface', in G.L. Wamsley, R.N. Bacher, C.T. Goodsell, P.S. Kronenberg, J.A. Rohr, C.M. Stivers, O.F. White and J.F. Wolf, Refounding Public Administration. Newbury Park, Calif.: Sage. pp. 19–29.

Wamsley, G.L. (1990b) 'The agency perspective: Public administrators as agential leaders', in G.L. Wamsley, R.N. Bacher, C.T. Goodsell, P.S. Kronenberg, J.A. Rohr, C.M. Stivers, O.F. White and J.F. Wolf, Refounding Public Administration. Newbury Park, Calif.: Sage. pp. 114–62.

Weber, M. (1947) The Theory of Social and Economic Organization. Glencoe, Ill.: Free Press.

Weimer, D.L. (1993) 'The current state of design craft: Borrowing, tinkering, and problem solving', Public Administration Review, 53 (2): 110–20.

Weir, M., Orloff, A.S. and Skocpol, T. (1988) The Politics of Social Policy in the United States. Princeton: Princeton University Press.

Weiss, C.H. (ed.) (1977) Using Social Research in Public Policy Making. Lexington, Ky: Heath.

Weissert, C.S. (1994) 'Beyond the organization: The influence of community and personal values on street-level bureaucrats' responsiveness', Journal of Public Administration Research and Theory, 4 (2): 225–54.

Whitaker, G.P. (1980) 'Coproduction: Citizen participation in service delivery', Public Administration Review, 40 (3): 240–6.

Wildavsky, A.B. (1979) Speaking Truth to Power: The Art and Craft of Policy Analysis. Boston: Little, Brown and Company.

Williams, W. (1971) Social Policy Research and Analysis: The Experience in American Federal Social Agencies. New York: American Elsevier.

Williams, W. (1980) The Implementation Perspective: A Guide for Managing Social Service Delivery Programs. Berkeley: University of California Press.

Williamson, O.E. (1975) Markets and Hierarchies: Analysis and Antitrust Implications: A Study in the Economics of Internal Organization. New York: Free Press.

Wilson, J.Q. (1968) Varieties of Police Behavior: The Management of Law and Order in Eight Communities. Cambridge, Mass.: Harvard University Press.

Wilson, J.Q. (1989) Bureaucracy: What Government Agencies Do and Why They Do It. New York: Basic Books.

Wilson, W. (1887) 'The study of administration', Political Science Quarterly, 2: 197–222.

Winter S. (1990) 'Integrating Implementation Research', p. 19–38 in Palumbo, D.J. and Calista, D.J. (eds), *Implementation and the Policy Process: Opening Up the Black Box*. New York: Greenwood Press.

Winter, S. (1999) 'New directions for implementation research', *Policy Currents*, 8 (4): 1–5.

Wistow, G., Knapp, M., Hardy, B. and Allen, C. (1992) 'From providing to enabling: Local authorities and the mixed economy of social care', *Public Administration*, 70 (1): 25–45.

Wistow, G., Knapp, M., Hardy, B. and Allen, C. (1994) *Social Care in a Mixed Economy*. Buckingham: Open University Press.

Wistrich, E. (1992) 'Restructuring government New Zealand style', *Public Administration*, 70 (1): 119–35.

Wittfogel, K.A. (1963) *Oriental Despotism: A Comparative Study of Total Power*. New Haven: Yale University Press.

Wittrock, B. (1983) 'Governance in crisis and withering of the Welfare State: The legacy of the policy sciences', *Policy Sciences*, 15 (3): 195–203.

Wittrock, B. and DeLeon, P. (1986) 'Policy as a moving target: A call for conceptual realism', *Policy Studies Review*, 6 (1): 44–60.

Woll, P. (ed.) (1966) *Public Administration and Policy: Selected Cases*. New York: Harper & Row.

Wood, B.D. (1988) 'Principals, bureaucrats, and responsiveness in clean air enforcement', *American Political Science Review*, 82 (1): 213–34.

Wood, B.D. (1991) 'Federalism and policy responsiveness: The clean air case', *Journal of Politics*, 53 (3): 851–9.

Wood, B.D. (1992) 'Modeling federal implementation as a system: The clean air case', *American Journal of Political Science*, 36 (1): 40–67.

Wood, B.D. and Waterman, R.W. (1991) 'The dynamics of political control of the bureaucracy', *American Political Science Review*, 85 (3): 801–28.

Woodward, J. (1965) *Industrial Organization: Theory and Practice*. London: Oxford University Press.

Yanow, D. (1990) 'Tackling the Implementation Problem: Epistemological Issues in Implementation Research', p. 213–228 in Palumbo, D.J. and Calista, D.J. (eds), *Implementation and the Policy Process: Opening Up the Black Box*. New York: Greenwood Press.

Yanow, D. (1993) 'The communication of policy meanings: Implementation as interpretation and text', *Policy Sciences*, 26 (1): 41–61.

Yanow, D. (1996) *How Does a Policy Mean? Interpreting Policy and Organizational Actions*. Washington, DC: Georgetown University Press.

Young, H. (1989) *One of Us: A Biography of Margaret Thatcher*. London: Macmillan.

Zarefsky, D. (1986) *President Johnson's War on Poverty: Rhetoric and History*. Alabama: University of Alabama Press.

Zuurmond, A. (1994) *De infocratie: Een theoretische en empirische heroriëntatie op Weber's ideaaltype in het informatietijdperk*. The Hague: Phaedrus.

Index